The
Dream
of the
Earth

To Joanie
Tom Berry
Feb. 1992.

The Dream of the Earth

THOMAS BERRY

Sierra Club Books
San Francisco

The Sierra Club, founded in 1892 by John Muir, has devoted
itself to the study and protection of the earth's scenic
and ecological resources—mountains, wetlands, woodlands,
wild shores and rivers, deserts and plains. The publishing program
of the Sierra Club offers books to the public as a nonprofit
educational service in the hope that they may enlarge
the public's understanding of the Club's basic concerns.
The point of view expressed in each book, however, does not
necessarily represent that of the Club. The Sierra Club has
some sixty chapters coast to coast, in Canada, Hawaii, and Alaska.
For information about how you may participate in its programs
to preserve wilderness and the quality of life, please address
inquiries to Sierra Club, 730 Polk Street, San Francisco, CA 94109.

Copyright © 1988 by Thomas Berry
Sierra Club Books paperback edition: 1990

Library of Congress Cataloging–in–Publication Data
Berry, Thomas
The dream of the earth.
Bibliography: p.224
Includes index.
1. Human ecology—Religious aspects. 2. Nature—
Religious aspects. 3. Human ecology—Philosophy.
I. Title.
GF80.B47 1988   215'.74   88–42548
ISBN 0–87156–622–2

Cover design by Bonnie Smetts
Book design by Wolfgang Lederer
Production by Felicity Luebke

SIERRA CLUB NATURE AND NATURAL PHILOSOPHY LIBRARY
Barbara Dean, Series Editor

Printed in the United States of America on recycled acid-free paper
10 9 8 7 6 5

Contents

Foreword
by Brian Swimme

I am trying to answer a question from an imaginary reader who picks up this book and asks, perhaps in confusion, perhaps in delight: "What is this?"

Not that I know, but I have studied the thought of Thomas Berry for years. Perhaps I can offer an image that will help introduce his thinking.

In fact, the only figure I can use is that of the Earth, since so much of Berry's work is concerned with our planet's well-being. However, the image I want is not contemporary Earth, but Earth in an earlier time, some six hundred million years ago, when the seas were rich with life, and the continents, after eons as storm-swept granite, now grew mossy and green.

Around this time, the eye comes into Earth's life. Up until then life had developed, even over billions of years, without eyesight. We contemporary humans identify so strongly with our visual elements of consciousness that we have some initial difficulty conceiving of a time when life proceeded without any eyes at all, but so it did. And there were great struggles, magnificent strategies, and soaring feelings, all within a blind world. And nowhere was there a vision of waterfalls, nowhere the experience of the blue sky, or the desert colors awakening in their first rain.

These essays of Thomas Berry are like the invention of the eye with which to see the Earth. They are the remodelling of the ear with which to hear the Earth. Of course, in an obvious sense we have eyes and ears and we can regard the Earth. We have photographs, geophysical surveys, historical studies, and cultural ethnographic reports, and certainly these map out something of the Earth. Our common assumption though is that such studies completely display the planet before us. We've made the measurements; we've graphed the results; we know the territory. But the vision of Earth Thomas Berry points to is something more. The subtext of much of his work is, "We cannot see or hear what is right before us." If we did, we would not carry out this assault on the Earth. To the question, "Why do we act so foolishly?" he answers, "Because we are blind and deaf." The full reality of the Earth and Universe has escaped the narrow spectrum of sensitivity in our industrial eyes and ears. These essays are the antidote; once assimilated, they begin to rework one's visual, aural, intellectual, imaginative, emotional, and spiritual orientation in the world. They are the genetic-cultural materials with which to create a new eye and ear.

To put Thomas Berry's work in its proper context, we must point to the fundamental truth of contemporary science: the universe is a developing reality. This means that the evolution of the entire universe is ongoing. And the evolution of the planet Earth is ongoing. We need to note in particular that the evolution of the eye itself is ongoing. Over all the hundreds of millions of years of its existence, the eye has been evolving continuously. And not only the eye, but the ear, the mind, the sense of touch, and sensitivity considered as a whole—all have been continuously developing. These essays mark a contemporary and vital advance in this long development.

Until fifty thousand years ago, evolutionary development anchored itself primarily by a shaping of the genetic architecture. But with the emergence of human culture, a significant dimension of our further evolution has been tied into our symbolic constructions. Thus, to understand the eye today, one certainly needs to study physiology and neurology and anatomy; but one needs to study as well the Upanishads, the art of India, the Sutras, the Bible, the Greek philosophers, the history of Rome and Russia, the Paleolithic bands, the French *Philosophes,* the Marxists, the Neo-Confucians and all significant human cultural activity generally. Our "perception" of the Earth, which we so easily regard as "neutral" or "biologically set," is in reality the end result of a long sequence of formative evolutionary events which include primate history as well as human history.

Thomas Berry is that rare being who devotes an entire lifetime pursuing a universal knowledge of our condition. In his studies of modern and medieval Europe, in his encounter with the Asian cultural tradition of India, Japan, and China, in his reflections on the biological sciences, on astronomy and physics, and especially ecology, in his study of the native traditions, in particular those of North America, in his analysis of the institutions of the modern world, the corporation, the economic systems, the technological process, the legal traditions, the educational venture, he has acquainted himself in a comprehensive way with the shaping realities of humanity. Only out of a prolonged engagement with just these powers could the further evolution of the eye and mind have been carried out.

These essays are what Thomas Berry speaks after decades of reflection on our state of existence. It must have been tempting at times to become completely taken with the intricacies of the knowledge. He would have returned then as the scholar with an impressive stack of monographs appropriate for any university archive. Instead he comes back to the culture in the ancient tradition of the shamanic personality—after long contemplation on the ultimate issues, he returns with a healing vision for the people. He comes back and speaks of the simplest things—the sky, the rivers, the soil, the human smile, the living community. He speaks of the Earth, he speaks of a vision he finds everywhere, even in the distant past, even in the unborn future.

In reading these essays, a certain amount of disorientation is to be expected. And a certain degree of confusion is perhaps unavoidable. We might keep in mind what it must have been like for the first animal to experience the shocking joy of eyesight. That is an earlier version of our new experience in the Earth through the eyes Thomas Berry offers. Colors reveal unsuspected hues, and not all of them are soothing; sounds swell with new meanings, but not all of them are comforting; human actions bespeak hitherto unimaginable significance, but not all of it is complimentary. But in both the pleasure and the pain, the Earth folds back more intimately on itself through this vision. In the magic of these words, we capture a glimpse of an unseen and unsuspected Earth beauty. We find ourselves seized by the conviction that we have made our way to a creative wellspring of the Earth adventure.

TO
the Great Red Oak,
beneath whose
sheltering branches
this book was written

Introduction

One of the more remarkable achievements of the twentieth century is our ability to tell the story of the universe from empirical observation and with amazing insight into the sequence of transformations that has brought into being the earth, the living world, and the human community. There seems, however, to be little realization of just what this story means in terms of the larger interpretation of the human venture.

For peoples, generally, their story of the universe and the human role in the universe is their primary source of intelligibility and value. Only through this story of how the universe came to be in the beginning and how it came to be as it is does a person come to appreciate the meaning of life or to derive the psychic energy needed to deal effectively with those crisis moments that occur in the life of the individual and in the life of the society. Such a story is the basis of ritual initiations throughout the world. It communicates the most sacred of mysteries. So in our Western Christian tradition the story of creation and the sequence of historical events leading from that moment to the existing human situation is recounted in the Easter Vigil ceremonies, the central moment in the yearly religious ritual.

The deepest crises experienced by any society are those moments of change when the story becomes inadequate for meeting the survival demands of a present situation. Such, it seems to me, is the situation we must deal with in this late twentieth century. We are confused at present because our historical situation has changed so profoundly. Our story, too, has changed. We no longer know its meaning or how to benefit from its guidance. Yet more than most societies, our Western society is dependent upon its story, its pattern of historical interpretation. Our story not only interprets the past, it also guides and inspires our shaping of the future. The study of our major historians reveals the visions of the future that have determined not only their interpretation of the past, but also their guidance into the future.

By profession a historian of cultures, I have written these essays in that larger tradition of Western historical interpretations that begins with the great historical vision of Saint Augustine in *The City of God*. That work, written in response to the burning of Rome by the Goths in the year A.D. 410, provided much of the guidance and the energy for bringing forth the medieval civilization and, in that manner, for creating the Western world as we know it, both in its grandeur and in its disturbing qualities.

After Augustine, this tradition of historical interpretation was taken up by Joachim of Flores in the twelfth century, with his message of the emerging age of the Holy Spirit succeeding the ages of the Father and the Son. Even in those early medieval times it was already clear that a rising money economy was diverting the human community from its more authentic destiny. It was the prophetic passages in this new spiritual vision of history that enabled the medieval world to respond so powerfully to the appearance of Saint Francis of Assisi in the early thirteenth century. Dante himself and the *Divine Comedy* were powerfully influenced by the historical vision of Joachim.

In the late sixteenth and early seventeenth centuries another historical vision was introduced, by Francis Bacon, the vision of a better order in earthly affairs through scientific control over the functioning of the natural world, a vision that was first articulated as the doctrine of "progress" by Bernard Fontenelle in the following century. This vision found its fulfillment in the industrial age of the past two centuries. Whatever their differences, both liberal capitalism and Marxist socialism committed themselves totally to this vision of industrial progress which more than any other single cause has brought about the disintegration that is taking place throughout the entire planet. By a supreme irony this closing down of the basic life systems of the earth has resulted from a commitment to the betterment of the human condition, to "progress."

If these earlier patterns of historical interpretation have arisen in times of stress to guide and inspire the course of human affairs, so now a new historical vision is emerging to guide us on our way to a more creative future. This time the issue at stake is not the fall of a civilizational period, such as the Fall of Rome, nor is it the decline in morals envisaged by Joachim, nor is it the need to extricate humans from the controlling forces of the natural world.

The issue now is of a much greater order of magnitude, for we have changed in a deleterious manner not simply the structure and functioning of human society: we have changed the very chemistry of the planet, we have altered the biosystems, we have changed the topography and even the geological structure of the planet, structures and functions that have taken hundreds of millions and even billions of years to bring into existence. Such an order of change in its nature and in its order of magnitude has never before entered either into earth history or into human consciousness.

These events, no less than the Fall of Rome, require a new historical vision to guide and inspire a new creative period not only in the human community, but also in the functioning of the earth itself, for our world is a world of historical realism. If India is the world of transcendent spiritual vision, if the East Asian world is sensitized to the deepest rhythms of the cosmos, our world is the world of time and history and emergent evolutionary processes that extend from the first fiery energies of the universe through some billions of years to the shaping of the earth, to the emerging of life, and to the appearance of human consciousness.

The position assumed in these essays is that such a new age and such a historical vision do exist, that a period of mutually enhancing human-earth relationships is being established. Already this renewal of the earth is in process. As soon as we demand environmental impact statements on new projects affecting the environment, we are beginning to move beyond democracy to biocracy, to the participation of the larger life community in our human decision-making processes. Also, the United Nations has recognized the significance of the natural world in the conduct of human affairs—in the World Charter for Nature passed by the Assembly in 1982.

As Augustine's vision of a better world was achieved by a positive commitment to the course of history, so now—as the crashing of the tropical rain forests resounds about us, as the sun is dimmed in the day and the stars at night by the hovering pollution in the atmosphere, as the great hydrological cycles are disturbed in their vast role of watering the continents and bringing forth the greenery of the land, as a multitude of living species become extinct throughout the earth—even amid all these events, there is a resilience, a hope, and even an expectation for a surviving abundance of life upon earth, if only the human community will respond to the urgency with the insight and the vigor that distinguished these other historical periods.

The essays in this book are written against the background of this new historical vision, the vision of an intimate earth community, a community of all the geological, biological, and human components. Only in recent times has such a vision become possible. We never knew enough. Nor were we sufficiently intimate with all our cousins in the great family of the earth. Nor could we listen to the various creatures of earth, each telling its own story. The time has now come, however, when we will listen or we will die. The time has come to lower our voices, to cease imposing our mechanistic patterns on the biological processes of the earth, to resist the impulse to control, to command, to force, to oppress, and to begin quite humbly to follow the guidance of the larger community on which all life depends. Our fulfillment is not in our isolated human grandeur, but in our intimacy with the larger earth community, for this is also the larger dimension of our being. Our human destiny is integral with the destiny of the earth.

This context must be kept in mind in reading these essays—on creative energy, technology, ecology, economics, education, spirituality, patriarchy, bioregionalism, the Hudson River Valley, the Indian future, and peace—for while each of the essays concerns a particular phase of this new historical vision, each also carries the full force of the larger pattern of historical interpretation that I am suggesting. Only by such separate presentation could these reflections be kept from becoming too generalized, too academic, or too abstract. Yet the world of particularity would itself become meaningless if it were not caught up in some larger scheme of historical interpretation. I hope to have supplied in these reflections some indication of this larger context of meaning without neglecting the particular events in which life finds its expression in the phenomenal world about us.

Of special import, of course, is the essay "The Dream of the Earth." In it I am concerned with the earth not as the object of some human dream, but with the earth itself and its inherent powers in bringing forth this marvelous display of beauty in such unending profusion, a display so overwhelming to human consciousness that we might very well speak of it as being dreamed into existence. Our own dreams of a more viable mode of being for ourselves and for the planet Earth can only be distant expressions of this primordial source of the universe itself in its full extent in space and in the long sequence of its transformations in time.

Such a fantastic universe, with its great spiraling galaxies, its supernovas, our solar system, and this privileged planet Earth! All this is held together in the vast curvature of space, poised so precisely in holding all things together in the one embrace and yet so lightly that the creative expansion of the universe might continue on into the future. We ourselves, with our distinctive capacities for reflexive thinking, are the most recent wonder of the universe, a special mode of reflecting this larger curvature of the universe itself. If in recent centuries we have sought to collapse this larger creative curve within the horizons of our own limited being, we must now understand that our own well-being can be achieved only through the well-being of the entire natural world about us. The greater curvature of the universe and of the planet Earth must govern the curvature of our own being. In the coincidence of these three curves lies the way into a creative future.

·1·

Returning to
Our Native Place

We are returning to our native place after a long absence, meeting once again with our kin in the earth community. For too long we have been away somewhere, entranced with our industrial world of wires and wheels, concrete and steel, and our unending highways, where we race back and forth in continual frenzy.

The world of life, of spontaneity, the world of dawn and sunset and glittering stars in the dark night heavens, the world of wind and rain, of meadow flowers and flowing streams, of hickory and oak and maple and spruce and pineland forests, the world of desert sand and prairie grasses, and within all this the eagle and the hawk, the mockingbird and the chickadee, the deer and the wolf and the bear, the coyote, the raccoon, the whale and the seal, and the salmon returning upstream to spawn—all this, the wilderness world recently rediscovered with heightened emotional sensitivity, is an experience not far from that of Dante meeting Beatrice at the end of the *Purgatorio,* where she descends amid a cloud of blossoms. It was a long wait for Dante, so aware of his infidelities, yet struck anew and inwardly "pierced," as when, hardly out of his childhood, he had first seen Beatrice. The "ancient flame" was lit again in the depths of his being. In that meeting, Dante is describing not only a personal experience, but the experience of the entire human community at the moment of reconciliation with the divine after the long period of alienation and human wandering away from the true center.

Something of this feeling of intimacy we now experience as we recover our presence within the earth community. This is something more than working out a viable economy, something more than ecology, more even than Deep Ecology, is able to express. This is a sense of presence, a realization that the earth community is a wilderness community that will not be bargained with; nor will it simply be studied or examined or made an object of any kind; nor will it be domesticated or trivialized as a setting for vacation indulgence, except under duress and by oppressions which it cannot escape. When this does take place in an abusive way, a vengeance awaits the human, for when the other living species are violated so extensively, the human itself is imperiled.

If the earth does grow inhospitable toward human presence, it is primarily because we have lost our sense of courtesy toward the earth and its inhabitants, our sense of gratitude, our willingness to recognize the sacred character of habitat, our capacity for the awesome, for the numinous quality of every earthly reality. We have even forgotten our primordial capacity for language at the elementary level of song and dance, wherein we share our existence with the animals and with all natural phenomena. Witness how the Pueblo Indians of the Rio Grande enter into the eagle dance, the buffalo dance, and the deer dance; how the Navajo become intimate with the larger community through their dry-paintings and their chantway ceremonies; how the peoples of the Northwest express their identity through their totem animals; how the Hopi enter into communication with desert rattlesnakes in their ritual dances. This mutual presence finds expression also in poetry and in story form, especially in the trickster stories of the Plains Indians in which Coyote performs his never-ending magic. Such modes of presence to the living world we still carry deep within ourselves, beyond all the suppressions and even the antagonism imposed by our cultural traditions.

Even within our own Western traditions at our greater moments of expression, we find this presence, as in Hildegard of Bingen, Francis of Assisi, and even in the diurnal and seasonal liturgies. The dawn and evening liturgies, especially, give expression to the natural phenomena in their numinous qualities. Also, in the bestiaries of the medieval period, we find a special mode of drawing the animal world into the world of human converse. In their symbolisms and especially in the moral qualities associated with the various animals, we find a mutual revelatory experience. These animal stories have a playfulness about them, something of a common language, a capacity to care for each other. Yet these movements toward intensive sharing with the natural world were constantly turned aside by a spiritual aversion, even by a sense that humans were inherently cut off from any true sharing of life. At best they were drawn into a human context in some subservient way, often in a derogatory way, as when we projected our own vicious qualities onto such animals as the wolf, the rat, the snake, the worm, and the insects. We seldom entered their wilderness world with true empathy.

The change has begun, however, in every phase of human activity, in all our professions and institutions. Greenpeace on the sea and Earth First! on the land are asserting our primary loyalties to the community of earth. The poetry of Gary Snyder communicates something of the "wild sacred" quality of the earth. In his music Paul Winter is responding to the cry of the wolf and the song of the whale. Roger Tory Peterson has brought us intimately into the world of the birds. Joy Adamson has entered into the world of the lions of Africa; Dian Fossey the social world of the gentle gorilla. John Lilly has been profoundly absorbed into the consciousness of the dolphin. Farley Mowat and Barry Lopez have come to an intimate understanding of the gray wolf of North America. Others have learned the dance language of the bees and the songs of the crickets.

What is fascinating about these intimate associations with various living forms of the earth is that we are establishing not only an acquaintance with the general life and emotions of the various species, but also an intimate rapport, even an affective relationship, with individual animals within their wilderness context. Personal names are given to individual whales. Indeed, individual wild animals are entering into history. This can be observed in the burial of Digit, the special gorilla friend of Dian Fossey's. Fossey's own death by human assault gives abundant evidence that if we are often imperiled in the wilderness context of the animals, we are also imperiled in the disturbed conditions of what we generally designate as civilized society.

Just now one of the significant historical roles of the primal people of the world is not simply to sustain their own traditions, but to call the entire civilized world back to a more authentic mode of being. Our only hope is in a renewal of those primordial experiences out of which the shaping of our more sublime human qualities could take place. While our own experiences can never again have the immediacy or the compelling quality that characterized this earlier period, we are experiencing a postcritical naiveté, a type of presence to the earth and all its inhabitants that includes, and also transcends, the scientific understanding that now is available to us from these long years of observation and reflection.

Fortunately we have in the native peoples of the North American continent what must surely be considered in the immediacy of its experience, in its emotional sensitivities, and in its modes of expressions, one of the most integral traditions of human intimacy

4

with the earth, with the entire range of natural phenomena, and with the many living beings which constitute the life community. Even minimal contact with the native peoples of this continent is an exhilarating experience in itself, an experience that is heightened rather than diminished by the disintegrating period through which they themselves have passed. In their traditional mystique of the earth, they are emerging as one of our surest guides into a viable future.

Throughout their period of dissolution, when so many tribes have been extinguished, the surviving peoples have manifested what seems to be an indestructible psychic orientation toward the basic structure and functioning of the earth, despite all our efforts to impose on them our own aggressive attitude toward the natural world. In our postcritical naiveté we are now in a period when we become capable once again of experiencing the immediacy of life, the entrancing presence to the natural phenomena about us. It is quite interesting to realize that our scientific story of the universe is giving us a new appreciation for these earlier stories that come down to us through peoples who have continued their existence outside the constraints of our civilizations.

Presently we are returning to the primordial community of the universe, the earth, and all living beings. Each has its own voice, its role, its power over the whole. But, most important, each has its special symbolism. The excitement of life is in the numinous experience wherein we are given to each other in that larger celebration of existence in which all things attain their highest expression, for the universe, by definition, is a single gorgeous celebratory event.

·2·

The Earth
Community

It is important that we be mindful of the earth, the planet out of which we are born and by which we are nourished, guided, healed—the planet, however, which we have abused to a considerable degree in these past two centuries of industrial exploitation. This exploitation has reached such extremes that presently it appears that some hundreds of thousands of species will be extinguished before the end of the century.

It is indeed true that species become extinct in the natural processes whereby the great variety of lifeforms have developed over the centuries, for there is a violent as well as a benign aspect of nature. Yet in the larger pattern of life development over hundreds of millions of years, new species have appeared in ever-greater florescence. There is reason to believe that the earth was never more resplendent than it was when human consciousness awakened in the midst of the unnumbered variety of living forms that swim in the seas and move over the land and fly through the air.

When the agricultural civilizations began some ten thousand years ago, the human disturbance of the natural world was begun in a serious way. It may be said in general that these early Neolithic and the later classical civilizations had some deleterious effects on the regions they occupied. The extent varied according to geographical location and cultural traditions, but in the larger perspective the damage was sustainable.

In our times, however, human cunning has mastered the deep mysteries of the earth at a level far beyond the capacities of earlier peoples. We can break the mountains apart; we can drain the rivers and flood the valleys. We can turn the most luxuriant forests into throwaway paper products. We can tear apart the great grass cover of the western plains and pour toxic chemicals into the soil and pesticides onto the fields until the soil is dead and blows away in the wind. We can pollute the air with acids, the rivers with sewage, the seas with oil—all this in a kind of intoxication with our power for devastation at an order of magnitude beyond all reckoning. We can invent computers capable of processing ten million calculations per second. And why? To increase the volume and the speed with which we move natural resources through the consumer economy to the junk pile or the waste heap. Our managerial skills are measured by the competence manifested in accelerating this process. If in these activities the topography of the planet is damaged, if the environment is made inhospitable for a multitude of living species, then so be it. We are, supposedly, creating a technological wonderworld.

It is not easy to know how to respond to this attitude; its consequences are so overwhelming. We must, however, reflect on what is happening. It is an urgent matter, especially for those of us who still live in a meaningful, even a numinous, earth community. We have not yet spoken. Nor even have we seen clearly what is hap-

7

pening. The issue goes far beyond economics, or commerce, or politics, or an evening of pleasantries as we look out over a scenic view. Something is happening beyond all this. We are losing splendid and intimate modes of divine presence. We are, perhaps, losing ourselves.

Some years ago, in 1975, in the cathedral of John the Divine in New York, there was a public discussion on technology and the natural world by Edgar Mitchell, the astronaut; Eido Roshi, the Zen master; and Lame Deer, the Sioux Indian. When Lame Deer spoke, he stood with the sacred pipe in his hands and bowed in turn to the four directions. Then, after lifting his eyes to survey the vast cathedral, he turned to the audience and remarked on how overpowering a setting it was for communication with divine reality. Then he added that his own people had a different setting for communion with the Great Spirit, a setting out under the open sky, with the mountains in the distance and the winds blowing through the trees, with the earth under their feet, surrounded by the living sounds of the birds and insects. It is a different setting, he said, a different experience, but one so profound that he doubted that his people would ever feel entirely themselves or would ever be able to experience the divine adequately in any other setting.

It made an overwhelming impression on me and still lingers in my mind, causing me often to reflect on what we have gained and what we have lost in the lifestyle that we have adopted; on the encompassing technocratic, manipulative world that we have established; even on the sense of religion that we have developed. We must not overromanticize primitivism, as has been done on occasion; yet when we witness the devastation we have wrought on this lovely continent, and even throughout the planet, and consider what we are now doing, we must reflect. We must reflect especially on the extinction of species we are bringing about. It is estimated by highly regarded biologists that between now and the year 2000, in slightly more than ten years, in our present manner of acting, we will extinguish possibly between one-half and one million species out of the five to ten million species that we believe presently exist.

Extinction is a difficult concept to grasp. It is an eternal concept. It's not at all like the killing of individual lifeforms that can be renewed through normal processes of reproduction. Nor is it simply diminishing numbers. Nor is it damage that can somehow be remedied or for which some substitute can be found. Nor is it something that simply affects our own generation. Nor is it something that could be remedied by some supernatural power. It is rather an absolute and final act for which there is no remedy on earth or in heaven. A species once extinct is gone forever. The passenger pigeon is gone and will never return. So, too, the Carolina parakeet. However many generations succeed us in coming centuries, none of them will ever see a passenger pigeon in flight or any of the other living forms that we extinguish.

The Red Books of threatened and endangered species published by the International Union for Conservation of Nature and Natural Resources are sobering books to look through. The book of vertebrates includes some eight hundred species of higher animals that are presently imperiled in their wilderness habitat. The listing includes some of the most gorgeous expressions of life that have ever been present on the earth: the great whales, the Asian elephant, the magnificent snow leopard, the polar bear, the grizzly bear, the jaguar, the cheetah, the California pronghorn antelope, the giant ibis, the California condor, the black-necked swan, the whooping crane, the Mississippi sandhill crane, the golden eagle, the southern bald eagle, the paradise parrot, the ivory-billed woodpecker. The list could go on and on merely among the vertebrates, but then we would need to begin the list of those splendid insects upon which so much of life depends, and then the plant world, especially the flowering plants that are endangered, and the woodlands.

Not only are we bringing about the extinction of life on such a vast scale, we are also making the land and the air and the sea so toxic that the very conditions of life are being destroyed. As regards basic natural resources, not only are the nonrenewable resources being used up in a frenzy of processing, consuming, and disposing, but we are also ruining much of our renewable resources, such as the very soil itself on which terrestrial life depends. A long list of particular statements could be made concerning this assault of the earth, the sea, and the air, but much of this information is already known, and further emphasis on the details is not exactly what is needed. What is needed, and what can appropriately be considered here, is the deeper meaning of the relationship between the human community and the earth process.

Most often we think of the natural world as an economic resource, or as a place of recreation after a wearisome period of work, or as something of passing interest for its beauty on an autumn day when the radiant colors of the oak and maple leaves give us a moment of joy. All these attitudes are quite legitimate, yet in them all there is what might be called a certain trivializing attitude. If we were truly moved by the beauty of the world about us, we would honor the earth in a profound way. We would understand immediately and turn away with a certain horror from all those activities that violate the integrity of the planet.

That we have not done so reveals that a disturbance exists at a more basic level of consciousness and on a greater order of magnitude than we dare admit to ourselves or even think about. This unprecedented pathology is not merely in those more immediate forms of economic activity that have done such damage; it is even more deeply imbedded in our cultural traditions, in our religious traditions, in our very language, in our entire value system.

The ultimate impact of these conditions was restrained so long as our power was limited. But no longer is our power limited or our cunning thwarted. We have subverted the basic biological law that every lifeform shall have other lifeforms or conditions that limit its expansion, so that no single lifeform or group of lifeforms should suffocate the other lifeforms. The power of our technologies is now such, however, that nature cannot prevent us from doing whatever we decide in diminishing the splendor and vigor and variety of life upon the earth.

We should be clear about what happens when we destroy the living forms of this planet. The first consequence is that we destroy modes of divine presence. If we have a wonderful sense of the divine, it is because we live amid such awesome magnificence. If we have refinement of emotion and sensitivity, it is because of the delicacy, the fragrance, and indescribable beauty of song and music and rhythmic movement in the world about us. If we grow in our life vigor, it is because the earthly community challenges us, forces us to struggle to survive, but in the end reveals itself as a benign providence. But however benign, it must provide that absorbing drama of existence whereby we can experience the thrill of being alive in a fascinating and unending sequence of adventures.

If we have powers of imagination, these are activated by the magic display of color and sound, of form and movement, such as we observe in the clouds of the sky, the trees and bushes and flowers, the waters and the wind, the singing birds, and the movement of the great blue whale through the sea. If we have words with which to speak and think and commune, words for the inner experience of the divine, words for the intimacies of life, if we have words for telling stories to our children, words with which we can sing, it is again because of the impressions we have received from the variety of beings about us.

If we lived on the moon, our mind and emotions, our speech, our imagination, our sense of the divine would all reflect the desolation of the lunar landscape.

The change that is taking place on the earth and in our minds is one of the greatest changes ever to take place in human affairs, perhaps *the* greatest, since what we are talking about is not simply another historical change or cultural modification, but a change of geological and biological as well as psychological order of magnitude. We are changing the earth on a scale comparable only to the changes in the structure of the earth and of life that took place

11

during some hundreds of millions of years of earth development.

While such an order of magnitude can produce a paralysis of thought and action, it can, we hope, also awaken in us a sense of what is happening, the scale on which things are happening, and move us to a program of reinhabiting the earth in a truly human manner. It could awaken in us an awareness of our need for all the living companions we have here on our homeland planet. To lose any of these splendid companions is to diminish our own lives.

To learn how to live graciously together would make us worthy of this unique, beautiful, blue planet that evolved in its present splendor over some billions of years, a planet that we should give over to our children with the assurance that this great community of the living will lavish upon them the care that it has bestowed so abundantly upon ourselves.

·3·

Human Presence

Our relationship with the earth involves something more than pragmatic use, academic understanding, or aesthetic appreciation. A truly human intimacy with the earth and with the entire natural world is needed. Our children should be properly introduced to the world in which they live, to the trees and grasses and flowers, to the birds and the insects and the various animals that roam over the land, to the entire range of natural phenomena.

Such intimacy with the universe we find with the Omaha Indians. When a child is born, the Omaha declare its newborn presence to the entire universe. First they address the sun, the moon, the stars, and every being that moves in the heavens, declaring: "Into your midst has come a new life. Consent ye, we implore! Make its path smooth, that it may reach the brow of the first hill."

Then to the atmospheric world, to the winds, clouds, rain, mist, and all that moves in the air. Then to the hills, valleys, rivers, lakes, trees, and grasses. Finally, "Ye birds, great and small, that fly through the air. Ye animals, great and small, that dwell in the forest. Ye insects that creep among the grasses and burrow in the ground, I bid ye all to hear me. Consent ye all, we implore! Make its path smooth. Then shall it travel beyond the four hills."

This is an entrancing ritual for introducing a child to the world into which the child has been born. In our own thinking we are coming back to this once more out of our new mode of understanding the universe. We now experience ourselves as the latest arrivals, after some 15 billion years of universe history and after some 4.5 billion years of earth history. Here we are, born yesterday. We need to present ourselves to the planet as the planet presents itself to us, in an evocatory rather than a dominating relationship. There is need for a great courtesy toward the earth.

This courtesy we might learn from the Iroquois. Their thanksgiving ritual is one of the most superb ceremonies that humans have ever known. Too long to present in its entirety, it does have a refrain that is relevant here: "We return thanks"—first to our mother, the earth, which sustains us, then on to the rivers and streams, to the herbs, to the corn and beans and squashes, to bushes and trees, to the wind, to the moon and stars, to the sun, and finally to the Great Spirit who directs all things.

To experience the universe with such sensitivity and such gratitude! These are primary experiences of an awakening human consciousness. Such stupendous moments reveal a striking sense of the alluring earth. An intimacy wonderfully expressed in the famous Western Inscription of Chang Tsai, an eleventh-century administrative official in China. This inscription, placed on the west wall of his office, so that he would constantly have it before him, reads quite simply: "Heaven is my father and earth is my mother and even such a small creature as I finds an intimate place in its midst. That which extends throughout the universe, I regard as my body

14

and that which directs the universe, I regard as my nature. All people are my brothers and sisters and all things are my companions."

Also, Wang Yang-ming, an early sixteenth-century Chinese writer, tells us that a truly developed person is someone who realizes that we form one body with heaven, earth, and all living things. He mentions "everything from ruler, minister, husband, wife, and friends to mountains, rivers, heavenly and earthly spirits, birds, animals, and plants; all should be truly loved in order to realize my humanity which forms a unity, and then my clear character will be completely manifested and I will really form one body with heaven, earth, and the myriad things."

India, too, has an intimacy with the natural world, as expressed in the epic poem, *The Ramayana,* with its touching scenes of Rama and Sita in exile, wandering in the forest with its flowering plants, fruit-bearing bushes, elephants, monkeys, deer, and brightly plumed birds. Also in India there are the familiar animal tales of the *Hitopadesa,* the teaching of wisdom through playful narratives of forest life.

Everywhere intimacy, the mutual presence of the life community in all its numinous qualities. We, too, have something of this in our own transcendental and romanticist traditions that arose in Germany in the late eighteenth century and came to the English-speaking world through Coleridge in England and Emerson in America. Within this context, we developed our own American feeling for the natural world, expressed in the writings of Walt Whitman, Henry Thoreau, and John Muir. These are the archetypal personalities whose work is continued in writers Aldo Leopold, Loren Eiseley, Mary Austin, Joseph Wood Krutch, Gary Snyder, Edward Abbey, Annie Dillard, Barry Lopez, and so many others, and through a multitude of artists and musicians.

With the more recent nature writers a new understanding of the universe begins to take shape. Our scientific understanding of the universe, when recounted as story, takes on the role formerly fulfilled by the mythic stories of creation. Our naturalists are no longer simply romanticists or transcendentalists in their interpretative vision; they have absorbed scientific data into their writings. A new intimacy with the universe has begun within the context of our scientific tradition. This is the most distinctive contribution presently being made toward renewal of our presence to the earth. Science is providing some of our most powerful poetic references and metaphoric expressions. Scientists suddenly have become aware of the magic quality of the earth and of the universe entire.

The physicist Brian Swimme tells us, "The universe shivers with wonder in the depths of the human." From the tiniest fragment of matter to the grand sweep of the galactic systems, we have a new clarity through our empirical modes of knowing. We are more intimate with every particle of the universe and with the vast design of the whole. We see it and hear it and commune with it as never before. Not only in its spatial extension, but in its emergent process, we are intimate with the world about us. We experience an identity with the entire cosmic order within our own beings. This sense of an emergent universe identical with ourselves gives new meaning to the Chinese sense of forming one body with all things.

This identity is expressed by physicists in terms of the anthropic principle. In this perception the human is seen as a mode of being of the universe as well as a distinctive being in the universe. Stated somewhat differently, the human is that being in whom the universe comes to itself in a special mode of conscious reflection. That some form of intelligent reflection on itself was implicit in the universe from the beginning is now granted by many scientists. The difficulty presently is with the mechanistic fixations in the human psyche, in our emotions and sensitivities as well as in our minds. Our scientific inquiries into the natural world have produced a certain atrophy in our human responses. Even when we recognize our intimacy, our family relations with all the forms of existence about us, we cannot speak to those forms. We have forgotten the language needed for such communication. We find ourselves in an autistic situation. Emotionally, we cannot get out of our confinement, nor can we let the outer world flow into our own beings. We cannot hear the voices or speak in response.

Yet the beginning of an intimacy can be observed. The very intensity of our inquiry into the structure and functioning of the natural world reveals an entrancement with this natural world. This attraction to the primordial splendor of the universe, however betrayed by our industrial exploitation, remains an overwhelming experience. We are constantly drawn toward a reverence for the mystery and the magic of the earth and the larger universe with a power that is leading us away from our anthropocentrism to this larger context as our norm of reality and value.

Perhaps nothing is more difficult for those of us who live within the Western biblical-classical tradition. Throughout the entire course of this tradition, the autism has deepened with our mechanism, our political nationalism, and our economic industrialism. Presently a new interpretation of the Western historical process seems to be indicated. Neither the liberal progressive nor the conservative traditionalist seems to fit the situation. The only suitable interpretation of Western history seems to be the ironic interpretation. This irony is best expressed, perhaps, by the observation that our supposed progress toward an ever-improving human situation is bringing us to wasteworld instead of wonderworld, a situation that found its finest expression in *Endgame* by Samuel Beckett.

The intimacy expressed in the Omaha celebration of a new life born into the earth community and in the Seneca thanksgiving ritual, in the Chinese feeling of presence to the universe—these experiences that formerly were so strangely distant and unreal—now begins to fascinate us with the promise of healing our estranged situation. This estrangement, however, must be overcome within our own sense of a time-developmental, as well as in a seasonal-renewing, universe. We have a new story of the universe. Our own presence to the universe depends on our human identity with the entire cosmic process. In its human expression the universe and the entire range of earthly and heavenly phenomena celebrate

17

themselves and the ultimate mystery of their existence in a special mode of exaltation.

It has taken the entire course of some fourteen billion years for the universe, the earth, and all its living creatures to attain this mode of presence to itself through our empirical modes of knowing. Such is the culmination of the scientific effort. This endeavor over the past three centuries might be considered among the most sustained meditations on the universe carried out by any cultural tradition. Truly the Yoga of the West. If our science has gone through its difficulties, it has cured itself out of its own resources. Science has given us a new revelatory experience. It is now giving us a new intimacy with the earth.

In accord with the groping processes of nature itself, science has proceeded by an intense inquiry into the deep recesses of the universe by a special quality of empirical observation, analysis, and interpretation. This has brought us into the far depths of the heavens and into the inner spaces of the atom. Through this knowledge the very structure and functioning of life itself have been so affected that we can do very little anymore without this type of scientific understanding.

One of the finest moments in our new sensitivity to the natural world is our discovery of the earth as a living organism. This was clear in ancient times as an instinctive insight into the nature and functioning of the earth. But such insight expressed in mythic terms is no longer sufficient for an age of scientific inquiry. Quite naturally our scientific observation reveals first the physical aspects of the planet and its living forms. The genius of our sustained inquiry into the inner functioning of the planet finally brought us beyond a microphase perception into the larger macrophase awareness that the entire planet is a single organic reality that needs to be addressed in its spirit and person qualities as well as in its physical aspects.

Here the ancient mythic insight and our modern scientific perceptions discover their mutual confirmation. Personal designation of the earth as Gaia is no longer unacceptable in serious discussion.

In considering the larger patterns in the earth functioning, we are now able to identify its five major components: the geosphere, the hydrosphere, the atmosphere, the biosphere, and the noosphere. These are present to each other in a comprehensive manner and are all infolded in the light and radiance of the sun. In this context we have a new mode of understanding our own intimacy with the earth and also of our total dependence on these other modes of earth expression. How appropriate, then, the traditional invocation of all these powers in any human endeavor. Appropriate, also, is our continuing gratitude to these powers for bringing us into being and for sustaining us in existence.

How great a marvel that these five forces in the light of the sun should bring forth the seas and the continents, the winds and the rain, and the profusion of blossoming flowers and other living forms that inhabit the earth. A magic world! Enchanting.

But while we present these thoughts, we need to reflect especially on the mindsphere—the latest of these five powers that constitute the earth functioning. The landsphere and the other three powers that formerly functioned with such exuberant creativity seem now to have given over to the mindsphere the major share of directing the course of earth development. The earth that directed itself instinctively in its former phases seems now to be entering a phase of conscious decision through its human expression. This is the ultimate daring venture for the earth, this confiding its destiny to human decision, the bestowal upon the human community of the power of life and death over its basic life systems.

Such an event is clearly something more than historical change or cultural transformation such as we have known them in the prior course of human history, much more than the change from the Paleolithic to the Neolithic or the rise of the classical civilizations. Perhaps nothing so significant has happened since the original shaping of the earth, the rise of life itself, or the appearance of the human. Something strange indeed is happening to the entire process, and we must wonder at ourselves and what we are doing and what is happening to the larger destinies of the earth, even perhaps of the universe.

Such consideration brings us back to the ancient sense of Logos in the Greek world, of rita in Hinduism, or dharma in Buddhism, of tao, ch'eng, and jen in the Chinese world. These are the ancient perceptions of the ordering, or the balancing, principles of the universe, the principles governing the interaction of all those basic forces constituting the earth process. To recognize and act according to these principles was the ultimate form of human wisdom.

What is remarkable throughout the Asian world is that terms designating supremely affectionate qualities carry ultimate cosmological significance. So in the Chinese world, *jen,* a term translated as love, benevolence, or affection, is not only an emotional-moral term, it is also a cosmic force. This can be said also of the virtue of *ch'eng,* translated as sincerity or integrity. In India the term *bhakti,* devotional love, was a cosmological as well as a spiritual force. In Buddhist tradition the term *karuna,* compassion, is a supreme cosmic power. Thus we find a pervasive intimacy and compassionate quality in the very structure of the universe and of the earth itself.

Our own quest for a more intimate and benevolent human presence to the earth in our times might reflect these precedents. But even more, perhaps, we might consider our intimate and compassionate presence to the earth as originating ultimately in the curvature of space, as it is presented in modern science. The entire earth community is infolded in this compassionate curve whereby the universe bends inwardly in a manner sufficiently closed to hold all things together and yet remains sufficiently open so that compassion does not confine, but fosters, the creative process.

This curve that finds its first expression in the physical bonding of the universe and later in the living process of the earth finds its most intimate expression in human thought and affection, as well as in our art, music, and dance. We can hear anew *The Creation* of Haydn and the *Ode to Joy* of Beethoven. We can read anew

20

Leaves of Grass by Walt Whitman. We can understand the great intuitions the ancients had of the universe. We can dance anew to the rhythms of the earth.

This reenchantment with the earth as a living reality is the condition for our rescue of the earth from the impending destruction that we are imposing upon it. To carry this out effectively, we must now, in a sense, reinvent the human as species within the community of life species. Our sense of reality and of value must consciously shift from an anthropocentric to a biocentric norm of reference.

This anthropocentrism is largely consequent on our failure to think of ourselves as species. We talk about ourselves as nations. We think of ourselves as ethnic, cultural, language, or economic groups. We seldom consider ourselves as species among species. This might be referred to in biology, but it has never meant that much in real life. We must now do this deep reflection on ourselves. What earlier peoples did immediately and intuitively in establishing their human identity, we must do deliberately.

Although we are integral with the complex of life communities, we have never been willing to recognize this in law, economics, morality, education, or in other areas of human endeavor. We must do this now in the context of an emergent universe. What earlier peoples were doing, they were doing in a limited human world and in a spatial mode of consciousness. We have our experience in a dominant time-developmental mode of consciousness and with our empirical instruments of understanding. Within this context we can recognize ourselves not simply as a human community, but as genetically related to the entire community of living beings, since all species are descended from a single origin.

Perception of the earth itself as a living organism was first presented with scientific evidence by Lynn Margulis and James Lovelock. The idea itself, however, is not new. It has appeared in different cultural traditions at different historical periods. Although this belief was never central to Western thought tradition, it maintained itself consistently on the borders of Western consciousness as the *anima mundi* concept, "the soul of the world" concept of Plato. The influence of this concept continued through the hermetic teachings of Ficino, Pico della Mirandola, and Giordano Bruno. Later it passed on to the Cambridge Platonists of England. In Germany another expression of this vitalist tradition is found in the work of Silesius, Goethe, and Schelling, eventually reaching Bergson and all those influenced by him. Foremost among these were Vladimir Vernadsky and Teilhard de Chardin. Although these latter were primarily scientists and biologists, they were also deeply involved in the more profound philosophical currents of the West.

The scientific term *biosphere* was used in 1875 by an Austrian professor of geology, Edward Seuss (1831–1914). Later, also, he used the term in his four-volume study, which was completed in 1909—it was translated into English as *The Face of the Earth*. According to Jacques Grinevald in an unpublished paper entitled "The Forgotten Sources of the Concept of Biosphere," Teilhard read the work of Seuss in its French translation in 1920 and wrote a review of it in 1921. Already in the 1920s Vernadsky, Eduard Le Roy, and Teilhard were in contact with one another in Paris. Of these, Vernadsky was the one who wrote the first extensive treatise, entitled *La Biosphère,* in 1929. This term was quickly associated with the other term, *noosphere,* which was invented by Le Roy, but popularized by Teilhard. Later it was adopted by Vernadsky, who considered human thought as a "biospherical phenomenon."

Thus our general sense of the earth as a living planet has a twofold source. One is more visionary, the other more empirical. Even when the various cultures accepted the earth as a living entity, there were significant differences in their experiences. Grand as the other cultural traditions may be, and however helpful, they are not quite what we need presently in dealing with this question. We need the insight given by our own scientific study of the earth, for the planet is severely affected. Precisely as a living planet, the earth needs attention.

What is needed on our part is the capacity for listening to what the earth is telling us. As a unique organism the earth is self-directed. Our sense of the earth must be sufficiently sound so that it can support the dangerous future that is calling us. It is a decisive moment. Yet we should not feel that we alone are determining the future course of events. The future shaping of the community depends on the entire earth in the unity of its organic functioning, on its geological and biological as well as its human members.

·4·

Creative Energy

Awareness of an all-pervading mysterious energy articulated in the infinite variety of natural phenomena seems to be the primordial experience of human consciousness, awakening to an awesome universe filled with mysterious power. Not only is energy our primary experience; energy, and its multiple modes of expression, is also the primary concern of modern physics, its ultimate term of reference in describing the most fundamental reality of the universe. Physics is establishing contact with energy events rather than with substances of atomic or subatomic dimensions. These energy events extend in size all the way from subatomic particles to galactic systems. The universe can be seen as a single, if multiform, energy event, just as a particle such as the photon is itself perceived in its historical reality as an energy event.

24

Belief in a personal creative energy principle is the primary basis of Western spiritual tradition. Thus the creed opens with a reference to power as the distinguishing attribute of the creative principle of heaven and earth and all things. Unfortunately Western religious traditions have been so occupied with redemptive healing of a flawed world that they tend to ignore creation as it is experienced in our times. Consequently one of the basic difficulties of the modern West is its division into a secular scientific community, which is concerned with creative energies, and a religious community, which is concerned with redemptive energies. So concerned are we with redemptive healing that once healed, we look only to be more healed. We seldom get to our functional role within the creative intentions of the universe.

In an earlier phase of human development, creation mythologies provided the basic context for personal and social existence. In accord with these great mythic statements, the various cultural forms were established. These cultural forms themselves were energy expressions recognized primarily as subjective and psychic rather than physical in nature. The truly great society was the society of the divine, the natural, and the human. Each of these communicated energy to and evoked energy from the others. The Great Wheel turned, the Great Cosmic Wheel of the universe.

Within this context the human community was energized by the cosmic rituals wherein ultimate meaning was attained, absolute mysteries were enacted, human needs were fulfilled. An abundance of energy flowed into the human when these monumental celebrations took place; human psychic transformation found its proper instrument and expression. The variety of human societies was formed.

This was the archetypal period of history, the divine age of Vico, the period when the great goddesses and gods emerged in human consciousness; the imaginative powers attained heights never again to be rivaled. The pyramids were built. The Ming T'ang palace of the Chinese took shape. The Parthenon gave expression to the serene depths of the Greek mind. The Mayan and Aztec altars were raised. Borobodur rose majestically into the Indonesian sky.

Here was energy on a vast scale. We hardly know whether to refer to it as divine or cosmic or human energy. It was in reality one energy shared by all three in terms of subjective attribution. Primarily a numinous psychic energy, it found expression not only in monumental architecture, but also in the hierarchical structure of the great societies. Ritual codes were established on a firm basis. The human venture moved into the larger phase of its own structuring. *The Book of Ritual* of the Chinese was composed, and the *Code of Manu* in India. These ritual codes were the main instruments for sustaining and channeling the energies needed by the community.

In all of these societies spiritual movements took place, indicating that the ritual celebrations and the codes of conduct needed to be supplemented by an interior intensity equal to the elaborate exterior enactments. At the center and along the margins of these classical ritual civilizations, spiritual movements appeared in order to intensify the energy resources of both the individual and the society and to enable them to function in a properly human mode. To maintain these spiritual movements required a personal presence that only the most disciplined personalities with almost unlimited interior power could fulfill. Thus the sages, rishis, yogis, gurus, priests, philosophers, prophets, heroes, and divine kings of antiquity: Confucius, Buddha, Ignathon, Moses, Isaiah, Darius, Ch'in Shih Huang Ti, Asoka, Plato, Christ, and, later, Mohammed. These archetypal personalities have been followed by an unending sequence of others who have been instrumental in keeping the energy level of the various civilizations sufficient to carry on the basic functions required for their continuance.

These ancient ritual patterns and the personal spiritual disciplines were sufficient to keep the great societies within their proper energy cycles. Because entropy made itself felt and a running down of the system was experienced, a new world age was periodically in-

26

augurated. All that was diminished was made new and full and vigorous at the annual new year or springtime festivals.

During the period of classical cultures, this basic energy structure continued. Classical culture itself was a kind of energy pulsating in and through sacred liturgies carried out in seasonal life periods, as well as in the personal life cycle from birth to maturity to death. There was no functional awareness of an irreversibly unfolding universe within developmental historical time. The basic pattern of existence was experienced as movement and change within a contained and seasonally renewed world. Things might pass through multiple forms, but those forms of the real were themselves fixed in their structure.

There was a basic consistency in all of this that was not radically disrupted until the modern period when the entire order of things was shaken by the new historical mode of thinking the world. The true reality of things, and even the universal and liberating goal of human striving, came to be seen as a development within the historical process. This process was seen not as the set alteration of the seasons or as adjustment to any established structure of the natural or the social order. The world was a one-time emerging world. There was no established cosmos, no abiding society, only a cosmogenesis and a sociogenesis. The evocation of energies continued within the ancient patterns, but these patterns themselves came to be interpreted within a new historical context.

A new axis for the expression of energy was created. The emphasis shifted from the seasonal rhythms of the universe and from the transcendent liberation experiences to a shaping of the time process toward some ultimate fulfillment within the historical order. This new sense of a shape and destiny to be progressively realized within the historical order would ultimately bring about the most significant energy revolution that has taken place in the human process from its earliest phases. The story of how this has taken place is the story of Western civilization, even the story of the human community.

27

The destinies not only of the human, but also of the earth itself, were to be determined by this shift in the energy system of the human enterprise. The very purpose of this new energy was not to maintain the existing system nor to spiritually transcend the natural systems, but to change the system itself in its deepest meaning and the entire modality of its functioning. While significant changes had already taken place in the rise of the various civilizational developments, none of these was capable of affecting the structure and functioning of the earth in such a decisive manner.

Although this new vision was first set forth in the prophetic writings and in the apocalyptic visions of Daniel, it found its most effective presentation in the Revelation of John the Divine, especially in his reference to the "millennium," the thousand years at the end of the historical process when the great dragon would be chained up, when peace and justice would appear, and when the human condition would be decisively surmounted. This millennial vision is the source of what may be the most powerful psychic energies ever released on the earth, psychic energies that have eventually taken extensive control over the physical functioning of the planet and are now entering into control of its biological systems.

This vision at first concerned only the spiritual development of the human community. The natural world remained an unchanging world. Then, with the development of the empirical sciences, a new sense of historical process emerged. First the human mind was experienced as being perfected over the centuries. Then the earth itself was perceived as the product of an evolutionary sequence of changes. In the nineteenth century, through Lamarck, Darwin, and Wallace, the biosystems of the earth were seen as evolutionary processes. Finally, in the twentieth century, the universe revealed itself as an emergent evolutionary process, not as cosmos, but as cosmogenesis.

This in itself might not have been so revolutionary in its consequences were it not for the entrancing vision of a future millennial fulfillment beyond the human condition. When this vision of the future was joined with a feeling of the surging energies of the galactic systems, with the earth-shaping powers, and with the irrepressible fecundity of life in all its forms, then we were simultaneously propelled by the past and drawn by the future in such absolute fashion that resistance would have been the last absurdity.

There is a difference, however, between this impetus from the past and the attraction of the future. The movement of the universe from its first fiery stages, through its various transformations, on to the earth, life, and to our human mode of being, is beyond our control. Even in our earlier civilizational phases we were following a somewhat instinctive process of our development. We had minimal control over the natural world or over our own lives. But now this has changed.

With our new knowledge we can participate more fully in the emergent processes of the present and the shaping of the future. Yet the primary determinant in our activities is our sense of millennial fulfillment in whatever form it presents itself. In the last few centuries the millennium has appeared as the Enlightenment, the democratic age, the nation-state, the classless society, the capitalist age of peace and plenty, and the industrial wonderworld.

It is a supreme irony of history that the consequences of these millennial expectations have been the devastation of the planet—wasteworld rather than wonderworld. Of special significance is the fact that these entrancements and the consequent devastation exist on a worldwide scale. The earth entire and the human community are bound in a single destiny, and that destiny just now has a disintegrating aspect. The disintegration is so threatening because both the psychic and the physical energy levels were so high, the consequences generally irreversible. The modern question has always been the control of energy that exists on an order of magnitude many times greater than what was available in prior periods of history. Whatever the direction taken by the human community in modern times, its consequences will be vast beyond the imagining of any former generations. That we ourselves see only

29

the immediate microphase consequences of our energy systems and almost completely miss the larger, macrophase, consequences of these systems is an indication of our need to be extremely cautious in any use of the energies available to us.

The industrial context in which we presently function cannot be changed significantly in the immediate future. Our immediate survival is bound up in this context, with all its beneficial as well as its destructive aspects. What is needed, however, is a comprehensive change in the control and direction of the energies available to us. Most of all we need to alter our commitment from an industrial wonderworld achieved by plundering processes to an integral earth community based on a mutually enhancing human-earth relationship. This move from an anthropocentric sense of reality and value to a biocentric norm is essential.

The ideal of a human habitat within a natural setting of trees and fields and flowering plants, of flowing streams and seacoasts and those living forms that swim through the waters and move over the land and fly through the air—a world of nontoxic rain and noncontaminated wells, of unpolluted seacoasts with their fertile wetlands—the ideal of a human community integral with such a setting, if properly understood with all the severity of its demands on its human occupants, would seem to be our only effective way into a sustainable and humanly satisfying future.

This is, of course, a mythic vision, highly romanticized if it is taken too literally. Yet it is considerably less idealized than the wonderworld vision that supports our present industrial system. In both cases we recognize that the mythic vision is what evokes the energies needed to sustain the human effort involved. The important thing is that the mythic vision lead to a sustainable context for the survival and continued evolution of the earth and its living forms. The ecological vision that we are proposing is the only context that is consistent with the evolutionary processes that brought the earth and all its living beings into that state of florescence that existed prior to the industrial age. Because this earlier

30

situation made serious demands upon the human in return for the benefits given, the industrial age was invented to avoid the return due for the benefits received. The burdens imposed upon the human in its natural setting, generally referred to as the human condition, established a situation unacceptable to an anthropocentric community with its deep psychic resentment against any such demands imposed upon it, hence the entire effort of the industrial society to transform the natural world into total subservience.

So effective has this been that only fragments of this earlier natural world survive, and those are being extinguished at an astonishing rate each day, even though the industrial world itself cannot sustain itself apart from the resources taken from the very same natural world. Even so, a deep psychic fixation exists that inhibits any effort at mitigating this destructive process. So far, the energy evoked by the ecological vision has not been sufficient to offset the energies evoked by the industrial vision—even when its desolation becomes so obvious as it is at the present time. The various peoples of the earth find themselves caught between a dissolving industrial economy and a ruined natural environment. Immediate survival seems to be with the pervasive industrial processes. Millennial expectations are reduced to endurance in a desolated natural world.

Yet the psychic energies sustaining the industrial illusion are now dissolving in confrontation with the problems of water for drinking, air for breathing, nontoxic soil for food production. A new energy is beginning to appear. Already a pervasive influence throughout the North American continent, this energy is finding expression in more than ten thousand ecologically oriented action groups on this continent; it is distributed through all the professions and through all the various forms of economic, political, educational, religious, literary, and media enterprise.

If this movement has not yet achieved its full efficacy in confrontation with the industrial vision, it is not primarily because of the economic or political realities of the situation, but because of the mythic power of the industrial vision. Even when its consequences in a desolate planet are totally clear, the industrial order keeps its control over human activities because of the energy generated by the mythic quality of its vision. We could describe our industrial society as counterproductive, addictive, paralyzing, manifestation of a deep cultural pathology. Mythic addictions function something like alcohol and drug addictions. Even when they are obviously destroying the addicted person, the psychic fixation does not permit any change, in the hope that continued addiction will at least permit momentary survival. Any effective cure requires passing through the agonies of withdrawal. If such withdrawal is an exceptional achievement in individual lives, we can only guess at the difficulty on the civilizational or even the global scale.

Advances in ecological activities can be observed throughout every continent at the present time. The World Charter for Nature was approved by the United Nations Assembly in 1982. The World Strategy for Conservation and Development was drawn up and approved in 1980 by more than seven hundred scientists from more than one hundred different nations. A variety of projects are being initiated in Europe, Asia, Africa, and South America, as well as in North America. The way is now clear. In North America the directions have been established in all the basic professions and activities. In economics, energy, food production, law, medicine, education, religion, ethics—in every aspect of life—the ecological pattern of functioning is now established. What is needed presently is more-adequate elaboration of the mythic phase of the ecological process.

As has been mentioned, the main difficulty in replacing the industrial order is not the physical nature of the situation, but its psychic entrancement. This mythic commitment preceded the actuality of the industrial achievement. It was, rather, a condition for, not the consequence of, the industrial achievement. So, too, with the ecological pattern: the myth is primary, although its early realization must be achieved and valid indications established of its possibilities for the future. A taste for existence within the functioning of the natural world is urgent. Without a fascination with the grandeur of the North American continent, the energy needed for its preservation will never be developed. Something more than the utilitarian aspect of fresh water must be evoked if we are ever to have water with the purity required for our survival. There must be a mystique of the rain if we are ever to restore the purity of the rainfall.

This evocation of a mystique is the role that is fulfilled by the poets and natural history essayists. In a country such as the Philippines, which is being devastated, where the rain forests are being eliminated, the soil eroded, the mangrove swamps destroyed, the coral reefs blasted, the streams polluted, there is a primary need to strengthen the mystique of the land. If a mystique of the land existed in some instinctive manner in the past, it is no longer sufficient. Beyond the country's political and economic needs, and possibly a prior condition for any sustainable political structure or functional economy, is the need for a mystique of the land such as is supplied by the nature poets, essayists, and artists; for educators and religious teachers with a sense of the islands as revelation of the divine; for lawyers with a sense of the inherent rights of natural beings. The mythic dimension, the sacred aspect of the Philippines, is needed if anything significant is to be done to remedy the devastation already present and to activate a program of renewal. Only in a viable natural world can there be a viable human world.

In every country, then, a mystique of the land is needed to counter the industrial mystique. This mystique must be associated with the three basic commitments of our times: commitment to the earth as irreversible process, to the ecological age as the only viable form of the millennial ideal, and to a sense of progress that includes the natural as well as the human world. Only by fulfilling these conditions can we evoke the energies that are needed for future survival in a setting of mutually enhancing human-earth relationships.

The mythic dimension of the ecological age is neither a romanticism nor an idealism. It is rather a deep insight into the structure and functioning of the entire earth process. This includes its seasonal rhythms as well as its historical transformations, its global coherence as well as its bioregional diversity, its revelatory communication as well as its pragmatic functioning. The revelatory aspect of the ecological age finds expression in the ecological archetype which finds its most effective expression in the great story of the universe.

This story presents the organic unity and creative power of the planet Earth as they are expressed in the symbol of the Great Mother; the evolutionary process through which every living form achieves its identity and its proper role in the universal drama as it is expressed in the symbol of the Great Journey; the relatedness of things in an omnicentered universe as expressed by the mandala; the sequence of moments whereby each reality fulfills its role of sacrificial disintegration in order that new and more highly differentiated forms might appear as expressed by the transformational symbols; and, finally, the symbols of a complex organism with roots, trunk, branches, and leaves, which indicate the coherence and functional efficacy of the entire organism, as expressed by the Cosmic Tree and the Tree of Life.

These archetypal symbols are the main instruments for the evocation of the energies needed for our future renewal of the earth. They provide not only the understanding and the sense of direction that we need, they also evoke the energy needed to create this new situation. This energy must be of a unique order of magnitude, since never before has the planet or the human community been confronted with questions of ultimacy supported by such a powerful mythology and combined with such capacity for exploiting the natural world. It needs to be repeated continually that we are not now dealing with another historical change or cultural modification such as those that have been experienced in the past. The changes we are dealing with are changes on a geological and biological order of magnitude. The four great components of the earth—the landsphere, the watersphere, the airsphere, and the lifesphere—are being decisively and permanently altered in their composition and their functioning by the more recent sphere, the mindsphere, altered, that is, in a deleterious, irreversible manner.

Here we need to realize that the ultimate custody of the earth belongs to the earth. The issues we are considering are fundamentally earth issues that need to be dealt with in some direct manner by the earth itself. As humans we need to recognize the limitations in our capacity to deal with these comprehensive issues of the earth's functioning. So long as we are under the illusion that we know best what is good for the earth and for ourselves, then we will continue our present course, with its devastating consequences on the entire earth community.

Our best procedure might be to consider that we need not a human answer to an earth problem, but an earth answer to an earth problem. The earth will solve its problems, and possibly our own, if we will let the earth function in its own ways. We need only listen to what the earth is telling us.

·5·

The Ecological Age

As we think our way through the difficulties of this late twentieth century, we find ourselves pondering the role of the human within the life systems of the earth. Sometimes we appear as the peril of the planet, if not its tragic fate. Through human presence the forests of the earth are destroyed. Fertile soils become toxic and then wash away in the rain or blow away in the wind. Mountains of human-derived waste grow ever higher. Wetlands are filled in. Each year approximately ten thousand species disappear forever. Even the ozone layer above the earth is depleted. Such disturbance in the natural world coexists with all those ethnic, political, and religious tensions that pervade the human realm. Endemic poverty is pervasive in the Third World, while in the industrial world people drown in their own consumption patterns. Population increase threatens all efforts at improvement.

Such a description of our human presence on the earth tends to become paralyzing. While that is not my intention, it is my intention to fix our minds on the magnitude of the task before us. This task concerns every member of the human community, no matter what the occupation, continent, ethnic group, or age. It is a task from which no one is absolved and with which no one is ultimately more concerned than anyone else. Here we meet as absolute equals to face our ultimate tasks as human beings within the life systems of the planet Earth. We have before us the question not simply of physical survival, but of survival in a human mode of being, survival and development into intelligent, affectionate, imaginative persons thoroughly enjoying the universe about us, living in profound communion with one another and with some significant capacities to express ourselves in our literature and creative arts. It is a question of interior richness within our own personalities, of shared understanding with others, and of a concern that reaches out to all the living and nonliving beings of the earth, and in some manner out to the distant stars in the heavens.

This description of personal grandeur may seem an exaggeration, a romantic view of human possibilities. Yet this is the basis on which the human venture has been sustained from its very beginning! Our difficulty is that we are just emerging from a technological entrancement. During this period the human mind has been placed within the narrowest confines it has experienced since consciousness emerged from its Paleolithic phase. Even the most primitive tribes have a larger vision of the universe, of our place and functioning within it, a vision that extends to celestial regions of space and to interior depths of the human in a manner far exceeding the parameters of our own world of technological confinement.

It is not surprising, then, that when a more expansive vision of the human breaks upon us at this time it should come as a shock, as something unreal, insubstantial, unattainable. Yet this is precisely what is happening. The excessive analytical phase of science is over. A countermovement toward integration and interior subjective processes is taking place within a more comprehensive vision of the

37

entire universe. We see ourselves now not as Olympian observers against an objective world, but as a functional expression of that very world itself.

What has fascinated the scientist is a visionary experience that is only now coming to conscious awareness in the scientific mind. It can hardly be repeated often enough that the driving force of the scientific effort is nonscientific, just as the driving force of the technological endeavor is nontechnological. In both instances, a far-reaching transforming vision is sought that is not far from the spiritual vision sought by the ancient tribal cultures, as well as by the great traditional civilizations of the past. Only such a visionary quest could have sustained the efforts made these past two centuries in both science and technology. Nor could anything less than entrancement have so obscured for scientists and technicians the devastating impasse into which they have been leading the human venture.

Not until Rachel Carson shocked the world, in the 1960s, with her presentation of the disasters impending in the immediate future was there any thorough alarm at the consequences of this entrancement. That is what needs to be explained—our entrancement with an industrially driven consumer society. Until we have explained this situation to ourselves, we will never break the spell that has seized us. We will continue to be subject to this fatal attraction.

To bring about the closing down of the life systems of the planet on such an order of magnitude is obviously not something that originated yesterday or something that arises out of some trivial miscalculation, academic error, or ideology such as the Enlightenment, or even out of the industrial age itself. These are all symptoms and consequences of a vast turn in human consciousness that originated deep in the origins of the human process itself. It must indeed have been associated with those revelatory experiences that we consider the most profound experiences ever to take place in human intelligence, experiences so profound that we consider them to come from some divine reality. Our deepest convictions arise in this contact of the human with some ultimate mystery whence the universe itself is derived.

Some insight may be gained into these issues if we consider that in our early tribal period we lived in a world dominated by psychic power symbols whereby life was guided toward communion with our total human and transhuman environment. We felt ourselves sustained by a cosmic presence that went beyond the surface reality of the surrounding natural world. The human sense of an all-pervasive, numinous, or sacred power gave to life a deep security. It enabled us over a long period of time to establish ourselves within a realm of consciousness of high spiritual, social, and artistic development. This was the period when the divinities were born in human consciousness as expressions of those profound spiritual orientations that emerged from the earth process into our unconscious depths, then as symbols into our conscious mind, and finally into visible expression. All that we have done since then has taken the same course. The divinities have been changed, the visible expression has been altered, but the ultimate source of power still remains hidden in the dynamics of the earth and in the obscure archetypal determinations in the unconscious depths of the human mind.

These primordial determinations were further developed in the age of the great traditional civilizations of the Eurasian and American worlds, the age of Confucian China, of Hindu India, of Buddhist Asia, of the ancient Near East, of Islam, of medieval Europe, of the Toltec, Mayan, Aztec, Pueblo and Incan civilizations of Central and South America. The human structure of life in all these civilizations had many similarities: the sense of the divine, ritual forms, social hierarchies, basic technologies, agricultural economies, the temple architecture and sculpture. The great volume of civilizational accomplishments came in this period, especially in the development of the spiritual disciplines whereby human life was shaped in the image of the divine.

But then in the Western world a new capacity for understanding and controlling the dynamics of the earth came into being. While former civilizations established our exalted place within the seasonal sequence of the earth's natural rhythms and established those spiritual centers where the meeting of the divine, the natural, and the human could take place, the new effort, beginning in the sixteenth- and seventeenth-century work of Francis Bacon, Galileo Galilei, and Isaac Newton, was less concerned with such psychic energies than with physical forces at work in the universe and the manner in which we could avail ourselves of these energies to serve our own well-being.

By the mid-eighteenth century the invention of new technologies had begun whereby we could manipulate our environment to our own advantage. At this time also an "objective world" was born—a world clearly distinct from ourselves and available not as a means of divine communion, but as a vast realm of natural resources for exploitation and consumption. These scientific attitudes and technological inventions became the modern substitutes for the mystical vision of divine reality and the sympathetic evocation of natural and spiritual forces by ritual and prayerful invocation.

Yet, though differing in its method, the historical drive of Western society toward a millennium of earthly beatitude remained the same. But the means had changed. Human effort, not divine grace, was the instrument for this paradisal realization. The scientists and inventors, the bankers and commercial magnates, were now the saints who would reign. This, then, was the drive in the technological age. It was an energy revolution not only in terms of the physical energies now available to us, but also in terms of the psychic energies. Never before had we experienced such a turbulent period, such a movement to alter the world, to bring about an earthly redeemed state, and, finally, to attain such power as was formerly attributed only to the natural or to the divine.

This achievement was associated with a sense of political and social transformation that would release us from age-old tyrannies. The very structure of existence was being altered. In this mood

America was founded, achieved independence, and then advanced throughout the nineteenth century to a position of world dominance in the early twentieth century. America took seriously the words written by Thomas Paine in 1775 in his pamphlet *Common Sense:* "We have it in our power to begin the world over again. A situation similar to the present hath not appeared since the days of Noah until now. The birthday of a new world is at hand . . . " Earlier the pilgrims had foreseen this continent as the setting for the new City on a Hill to which the universal human community could look for guidance into a glorious future. Throughout the founding years, even until the twentieth century, peoples crossed the Atlantic with a vivid sense that they were crossing the Red Sea from the slavery of Egypt to the freedom and abundance of the Promised Land.

With such expectation came a new exhilaration in our powers to dominate the natural world. This led to a savage assault upon the earth such as was inconceivable in prior times. The experience of sacred communion with the earth disappeared. Such intimacy was considered a poetic conceit by a people who prided themselves on their realism, their aversion to all forms of myth, magic, mysticism, and superstition. Little did these people know that their very realism was as pure a superstition as was ever professed by humans, their devotion to science a new mysticism, their technology a magical way to paradise.

As with all such illusory situations, the awakening can be slow and painful and filled with exaggerated reactions. Our present awakening from this enchantment with technology has been particularly painful. We have altered the earth and human life in many irrevocable ways. Some of these have been creative and helpful. Most have been destructive beyond imagination.

Presently we are entering another historical period, one that might be designated as the ecological age. I use the term *ecological* in its primary meaning as the relation of an organism to its environment, but also as an indication of the interdependence of all the

41

living and nonliving systems of the earth. This vision of a planet integral with itself throughout its spatial extent and its evolutionary sequence is of primary importance if we are to have the psychic power to undergo the psychic and social transformations that are being demanded of us. These transformations require the assistance of the entire planet, not merely the forces available to the human. Otherwise we mistake the order of magnitude in this challenge. It is not simply adaptation to a reduced supply of fuels or to some modification in our system of social or economic controls. Nor is it some slight change in our educational system. What is happening is something of a far greater magnitude. It is a radical change in our mode of consciousness. Our challenge is to create a new language, even a new sense of what it is to be human. It is to transcend not only national limitations, but even our species isolation, to enter into the larger community of living species. This brings about a completely new sense of reality and of value.

What is happening was unthinkable in ages gone by. We now control forces that once controlled us, or, more precisely, the earth process that formerly administered the earth directly is now accomplishing this task in and through the human as its conscious agent. Once a creature of earthly providence, we are now extensively in control of this providence. We now have extensive power over the ultimate destinies of the planet, the power of life and death over many of its life systems. For the first time we can intervene directly in the genetic process. We can dissolve the ozone layer that encircles the earth and let the cosmic radiation bring about distortions in the life process. We can destroy the complex patterns of life in the seas and make the rivers uninhabitable. And we could go on with our description of human power, even over the chemical constitution and the very topography of the planet.

In its order of magnitude, this change in our relation to the earth is much greater than that experienced when the first Neolithic civilizations came into being some twelve thousand years ago. Nothing since then, not even the great civilizational structures themselves, produced change on such a significant scale. Such change cannot be managed by partial accommodations or even by major adjustments within the civilizational contexts of the past. The context of survival is radically altered. Our problems can no more be resolved within our former pattern of the human than the problems that led to quantum physics could be dealt with by any adjustment within the context of the Newtonian universe.

No adequate scale of action can be expected until the human community is able to act in some unified way to establish a functional relation with the earth process, which itself does not recognize national boundaries. The sea and air and sky and sunlight and all the living forms of earth establish a single planetary system. The human at the species level needs to fulfill its functional role within this life community, for in the end the human community will flourish or decline as the earth and the community of living species flourishes or declines.

A primary allegiance to this larger community is needed. It will do little good for any nation to seek its own well-being by destroying the very conditions for planetary survival. This larger vision is no longer utopian. It directly concerns the hardest, most absolute reality there is: the reality of the water we drink, the air we breathe, the food we eat.

However ineffective in many of its activities, the United Nations and its constituent members have begun to understand this reality: thus a World Charter for Nature, approved by the Assembly in 1982; thus, also, the megaconferences on environment, technology, habitat, water, and all those basic elements of life that must now attain human protection and just distribution for the welfare not only of the human, but of every living species. Whether as nations or as species, we have a single destiny with the larger community of earthly life.

Much of our trouble during these past two centuries has been caused by our limited, our microphase, modes of thought. We centered ourselves on the individual, on personal aggrandizement, on a competitive way of life, and on the nation, or the community of nations, as the guarantor of freedom to pursue these purposes. A sense of the planet Earth never entered into our minds. We paid little attention to the more-comprehensive visions of reality. This was for the poets, the romanticists, the religious believers, the moral idealists. Now we begin to recognize that what is good in its microphase reality can be deadly in its macrophase development.

Much of human folly is a consequence of neglecting this single bit of wisdom. A few hundred automobiles with good roads may be a great blessing. Yet when the number increases into the millions and hundreds of millions, the automobile is capable of destroying the higher forms of life on the entire planet. So with all human processes: undisciplined expansion and self-inflation lead only to destruction. Apart from the well-being of earth, no subordinate life system can survive. So it is with economics and politics: any particular activity must find its place within the larger pattern, or it will die and perhaps bring down the larger life system itself. This change of scale is one of the most significant aspects in the change of consciousness that is needed.

The ecological age into which we are presently moving is an opposed, though complementary, age that succeeds the technological age. In a deeper sense this new age takes us back to certain basic aspects of the universe which were evident to the human mind from its earliest period, but which have been further refined, observed, and scientifically stated in more recent centuries. These governing principles of the universe have controlled the entire evolutionary process from the moment of its explosive origin some fourteen billion years ago to the shaping of the earth, the emergence of life and consciousness, and so through the various ages of human history. These principles, known in past ages by intuitive processes, are now understood by scientific reasoning, although their implications have not yet been acted upon in any effective way. The ecological age must now activate these principles in a universal context if the human venture is to continue.

These principles on which the universe functions are three: differentiation, subjectivity, and communion.

Differentiation is the primordial expression of the universe. In the fiery violence of some billions of degrees of heat, the original energy dispersed itself through vast regions of space not as some homogeneous smudge or jellylike substance, but as radiation and as differentiated particles eventually distributed through a certain sequence of elements, manifesting an amazing variety of qualities. These were further shaped into galactic systems composed of highly individuated starry oceans of fire. Everywhere we find this differentiating process taking place. In our own solar system, within the sequence of planets, we find the planet Earth taking shape as the most highly differentiated reality we know about in the entire universe. Life on planet Earth finds expression in an overwhelming variety of manifestations. So, too, with the human: as soon as we appear, we immediately give to human existence multiple modes of expression. These themselves change through the centuries.

The second primary principle is that of increased subjectivity. From the shaping of the hydrogen atom to the formation of the human brain, interior psychic unity has consistently increased along with a greater complexification of being. This capacity for interiority involves increased unity of function through ever more complex organic structures. Increase in subjectivity is associated with increased complexity of a central nervous system. Then comes the development of a brain. With the nervous system and the brain comes greater freedom of control over the activity of the organism. In this manner planet Earth becomes ever more subject to the free interplay of self-determining forces. With subjectivity is associated the numinous quality that has traditionally been associated with every reality of the universe.

A third principle of the universe is the communion of each reality of the universe with every other reality in the universe. Here our scientific evidence confirms, with a magnificent overview, the ancient awareness that we live in a *universe—a single, if multiform, energy event.* The unity of the entire complex of galactic systems is among the most basic experience of contemporary physics. Although this comprehensive unity of the universe was perceived by primitive peoples, affirmed by the great civilizations, explained in creation myths the world over, outlined by Plato in his *Timaeus,* and given extensive presentation by Newton in his *Principia,* nowhere was the full genetic relatedness of the universe presented with such clarity as by the scientists of the twentieth century.

To Isaac Newton we are especially indebted for our understanding of the gravitational attraction of every physical reality to every other physical reality in the universe, an attraction that finds its ultimate fulfillment in the affective attractions that exist throughout the human community. Without the gravitational attraction experienced throughout the physical world, there would be no emotional attraction of humans to one another. To Darwin we are indebted for our understanding of the genetic unity of the entire web of living beings. To Einstein and his theories of relativity we are indebted for a new awareness of how to think about the dynamics of relatedness in the universe.

The ecological age fosters the deep awareness of the sacred presence within each reality of the universe. There is an awe and reverence due to the stars in the heavens, the sun, and all heavenly bodies; to the seas and the continents; to all living forms of trees and flowers; to the myriad expressions of life in the sea; to the animals of the forests and the birds of the air. To wantonly destroy a living species is to silence forever a divine voice. Our primary need for the various lifeforms of the planet is a psychic, rather than a physical, need. The ecological age seeks to establish and maintain this subjective identity, this authenticity at the heart of every being. If this is so of the prehuman phase of life, it is surely true of the human also.

Only such a comprehensive vision can produce the commitment required to stop the world of exploitation, of manipulation, of violence so intense that it threatens to destroy not only the human city, but also the planet itself. If we would terminate this danger, we must create another, less-vulnerable, life situation. So far, this new world order has not had its adequate presentation. Yet when it comes, it will take the form of what we are designating as the ecological age. This age can provide the historical dynamism associated with the Marxist classless society, the age of plenty envisaged by the capitalist nations, and the millennial age of peace envisaged in the Apocalypse of John the Divine. At present, however, we are in that phase of transition that must be described as the groping phase. We are like a musician who faintly hears a melody deep within the mind, but not clearly enough to play it through. This is the inner agony we experience, especially when we consider that the music we are creating is the very reality of the universe.

It would be easier for us if we would remember that the earth itself, as the primary energy, is finding its way both to interior conscious expression in the human and to outer fulfillment in the universe. We can solve nothing by dreaming up some ephemeral structure of reality or by giving the direction of the earth over to our bureaucratic institutions. We must simply respond to the urgencies imposed on us by the energy that holds the stars within the galactic clusters, that shaped the planet under our feet, that has guided life through its bewildering variety of expression, and that has found even higher expression in the exotic tribes and nations, languages, literature, art, music, social forms, religious rituals, and spiritual disciplines over the surface of the planet. There is reason to believe that those mysterious forces that have guided earthly events thus far have not suddenly collapsed under the great volume of human affairs in this late twentieth century.

What is clear is that the earth is mandating that the human community assume a responsibility never assigned to any previous generation. We are involved in a process akin to initiation processes which have been known and practiced from earliest times. The human community is passing from its stage of childhood into its adult stage of life. We must assume adult responsibilities. As the maternal bonds are broken on one level to be reestablished on another, so the human community is being separated from the dominance of Nature on one level to establish a new and more mature relationship. In its prior period the earth acted independently as the complete controlling principle; only limited control over existence was assigned to ourselves. Now the earth insists that we accept greater responsibility, a responsibility commensurate with the greater knowledge communicated to us.

This responsibility has so far been more than we could use wisely, just as the new powers of a young adult are powers seldom used wisely without an intervening period of confusion, embarrassment, and juvenile mistakes. As the child eventually learns a mature mode of conduct, discipline, and responsibility, so now, as individuals and as a planetary community, we will, it is hoped, learn our earth responsibilities.

Our problem is, of course, the problem of recognizing the primacy of the natural world and its spontaneous functioning in all that we do. Our own actions can be truly creative only when they are guided by these deeper spontaneities. Human administration of the universe in any comprehensive manner is far too great a task for any controlled process on the part of humans, just as the movement of the arm to pick up and drink a cup of tea would hardly be possible if we were required to consciously manipulate each movement of the eye, the arm, the nervous system, the oxygen, and the blood flow. Yet we do the act spontaneously, with extensive awareness and control. There is deliberation, but also spontaneity. As with our earth in all its processes, so with the human community: there are inner, spontaneous, all-pervasive forces present which are gradually responding to this integral functioning of the total system. What we need, what we are ultimately groping toward, is the sensitivity required to understand and respond to the psychic energies deep in the very structure of reality itself. Our knowledge and control of the environment is not absolute knowledge or absolute control. It is a cooperative understanding and response to forces that will bring about a proper unfolding of the earth process if we do not ourselves obstruct or distort these forces that seek their proper expression.

I suggest that this is the ultimate lesson in physics, biology, and all the sciences, as it is the ultimate wisdom of tribal peoples and the fundamental teaching of the great civilizations. If this has been obscured by the adolescent aspect of our earlier scientific and technological development, it is now becoming clear to us on an extensive scale. If responded to properly with our new knowledge and new competencies, these forces will find their integral expression in the spontaneities of the new ecological age. To assist in bringing this about is the present task of the human community.

·6·

Technology
and the Healing
of the Earth

Of all the issues we are concerned with at present, the most basic
issue, in my estimation, is that of human-earth relations. A multitude
of interhuman issues at the national and international levels also
confront us; even at their worst we can probably survive them much
better than we can survive the continued degradation of the earth
in its basic life systems. The twentieth century has eliminated the
terror of the unknown darknesses of nature by devastating nature
herself.

Our ultimate failure as humans is to become not a crowning glory
of the earth, but the instrument of its degradation. We have con-
taminated the air, the water, the soil; we have dammed the rivers,
cut down the rain forests, destroyed animal habitat on an extensive scale. We have driven the great blue whale and a multitude

of animals almost to extinction. We have caused the land to be eroded, the rain to be acid. We have killed ten thousand lakes as habitat for fish.

We are playing for high stakes, the beauty and grandeur and even the survival of the earth in its life-giving powers. From being admired and even worshiped as a mode of divine presence, the earth has become despoiled by the human presence in great urban population centers and in centers of industrial exploitation. We have also trivialized nature in vacation areas.

In this context we must ask what are the real gains for the human? The automobile, our urban centers, our space exploits, our communication skills? What have we gained? A set of once-magnificent but now-decaying infrastructures that exhaust our energies, our finances, and the resources of the earth itself. Whereas the infrastructures of nature continually renew themselves from within, our infrastructures dissolve in the corrosive acids of the environment or break under the relentless strain imposed upon them.

Are we really moving into a wonderland so magnificent that it is worth such a destructive presence to the natural world? Is this the only way to survive, to provide the food and shelter and clothing and energy that we need? What benefit is worth giving up the purity of the air we breathe, the water we drink, the life-giving soil in which our food is grown?

This critical view of the technological age admittedly does not adequately recognize the gains in human knowledge and the mitigation or elimination of many human miseries achieved by our new sciences and technologies. While weighing these benefits, however, we must inquire into the new, and perhaps greater and more universal, difficulties we are causing.

Until recently we have never reflected in depth upon the larger consequences of our industrial processes or their real meaning. Some made fortunes, others obtained jobs. For all of us, these modern developments provided an expansion of life and understanding, although this enlargement often went with the extinction

51

of basic human sensitivities and the loss of contact with the world of natural forces, its spontaneities, and the expansion of mental and emotional life it offers us.

This is not to say that the preindustrial world is always benign, always responsive to human need. The natural world is a violent world of volcanic explosions, of withering drought and onrushing floods, of hurricanes that come in from the seas and set everything awash before them. There are the frightening winters and the enervating summers. All these must be factored into the equation that we are considering. How are we to choose our way without bringing on disasters greater than those we avoid?

Our tendency is to exalt the bright side of industry over the dark side of nature or to exalt the bright side of nature over the dark side of industry. In reality we need to compare bright with bright and dark with dark.

It can be said that during the one hundred years since the rise of the scientific technologies of the 1880s and the corporative enterprises such as Standard Oil, Westinghouse, General Electric, U.S. Steel, and the automotive, petrochemical, electrical, and communications industries, the human has ascended until, with the coming of the nuclear age, we have finally achieved the capacity to determine on an extensive scale whether the basic life systems of the earth will live or die.

A unique situation has developed. We are certainly more aware of the larger consequences of our actions, the real price we are paying for the technological-industrial processes that presently envelop our world. But these are still not getting the attention they deserve, even though we can now discuss the issue with greater understanding and less emotional reaction than we could ten years ago.

In mentioning our present situation, we must also note that since the rise of agriculture at the beginning of the Neolithic period, some ten thousand years ago, humans have been putting a certain stress on the natural world. This stress increased considerably with the rise of the classical civilizations of the Eurasian, African, and pre-Columbian American continents. The cutting down of the forests of China, begun more than 3,000 years ago, has continued ever since, with erosion of the soil so vast that the ocean off China for fifty miles is known as the Yellow Sea. While part of this erosion is due to natural causes, a major part is ultimately due to human intervention. Similarly, in the classical Mediterranean world of Palestine, North Africa, Greece, and Rome, human presence degraded the natural life systems to a disastrous degree.

The industrial system that developed in Europe and was then brought to North America increased the stress on the planet by several orders of magnitude. We are, then, concerned with the most recent and most virulent phase of a long-standing civilizational problem, that of human-earth relations, the most basic of all issues before us and the source of many of the interhuman problems that we must resolve.

Here is not exactly an American, or European, problem, but a species problem. How should humans live upon the earth in a mutually enhancing relationship? How can there be progress shared by all the components of the planet? Can there be any true or lasting progress if it is not shared on this comprehensive scale? Must legitimate human development necessarily degrade the natural world?

It would seem that the life systems of the earth did flourish prior to the human in the larger pattern of their development. Although this development involved the rise and disappearance of species, the sequence of life expression on the more comprehensive scale continued its florescence, even arching over periods of widespread species extinction at the end of the Paleozoic, some 220 million years ago, and the extinctions at the end of the Mesozoic, some 65 million years ago. In both these cases new developments took place that were remarkably successful in the expansion of living forms.

While some parallels can be drawn, the differences with our

present moment are so great that we must say that the extinction we are bringing about—in its scale, in its conditions, and in its consequences—is something quite apart from these earlier extinctions and cannot be judged by oversimplified comparisons. In any case we are now dealing with a unique problem, the problem of a species with human intelligence and its consequent powers for conscious interacting with the larger earth process, its powers for controlling this process, and its powers for negating this process in many of its aspects. We still have not discovered at what level of development the human and the natural can be present to each other in a mutually enhancing manner.

Whereas many studies have been made in biological science and in theoretical studies of the human species in its relation to other species, very few studies have been made of our more practical problems and our technologies at the species level. We discuss ethnic groups, cultures, nations, social groups; yet the problems we are concerned with here require, I think, a new and more radical reassessment. This reevaluation began in 1962 with the publication of Rachel Carson's book on the chemical poisoning of the North American continent, *Silent Spring*. Chemical engineering was central to all the basic technologies of that period. It was deadly. Responses to the situation can be summarized in terms of four groups that have arisen in the past two decades.

The New Entrepreneurs

The first, and by far the dominant, group is entranced with the sense of continuing progress, if not toward wonderland, then toward a constant improvement of the human condition through our scientific industrial processes. This group has almost no sensitivity to the degradation of the earth that has been taking place in the twentieth century, especially in the postwar years when chemical engineering, electronic and nuclear engineering, aeronautical and space engineering, and agricultural engineering took control of the North American continent and all its living forms. Benefits, surely, in abundance: inventions, jobs, washing machines, refrigerators, telephones, travel, education, entertainment, and the shaping of an industrial world.

This group seems devoid of any appreciation of the disturbance caused by brash human intrusion into the ecosystems of nature that were evolved with such care over some hundreds of millions of years. When faced with the dangers consequent on the industrial process, Julian Simon and the late Herman Kahn have said that we should press on even more with our industrial development. The argument is that the crisis is exaggerated, that each generation in this country has had a better life than the preceding generation— even with our national debt rising beyond two trillion dollars, with our failing infrastructures, our declining forests, our eroded soil, and tens of thousands of hazardous waste sites. Even so, they insist, we should press on in our existing patterns of production and consumption.

Earlier industrial leaders such as Rockefeller, Vanderbilt, Carnegie, Hill, Gould, Morgan, and Mellon set up the corporate and financial context for the industrial establishment at the end of the nineteenth century and the beginning of this century. This was the period of the railroads, of U. S. Steel, of Standard Oil, of the expansion of Westinghouse, General Electric, Ford, General Motors, Du Pont, and Dow. After the second World War came the expansion of I.B.M., Burlington Mills, and the space and military industries along with the food industries, all exploitive and dependent on new technologies.

In just the past few years a new mystique of the corporate enterprise has come upon the scene. Chronicled by Thomas Peters and Robert Waterman in their book *In Search of Excellence,* it is a glorification of the so-called humanistic corporation. In Lawrence Miller's *American Spirit* we find another version of the lure of the corporate mystique for business in our country. This mystique is absorbing all the mythic and cultural language, and even the attitudes and emotions formerly associated with our religious and humanist traditions. There is mention of the corporate "culture," the "mythic meaning" of the enterprise, the "soul" of the establishment, the "spirit" of the corporation, the "belief" structures—all of this in an effort to overcome an instinctive awareness that the corporation is in the business of seducing the consumer while plundering natural resources and poisoning the environment. We must recognize, however, that not all those plundering the earth are crassly indifferent to the consequences of what they are doing. Many good, intelligent, competent persons dedicated to the improvement of the human situation simply do not understand the actual consequences of their actions—totally committed persons, simply catastrophic in their judgment.

This sharp critique of the industrial process needs to be mitigated only slightly by recognizing certain efforts to limit the damage being done to the environment. Some beginnings have been made to lessen the pollution, to neutralize toxic or hazardous wastes, or to contain the wastes until they lose their potency. Governmental agencies are still consistently failing, however, to enforce the regulations already enacted. Yet the documents are there and constitute a warning that penalties can be imposed. No longer can industrial sites be built without regard for their impact on the environment.

Engineers, during their professional training, and corporations are beginning to learn that human activity is most effective and most enduring when it is in accord with the natural functioning of the ecosystem into which it is inserted. If, so far, it is only the merest beginning, this process will never be able to return to its former attitude of total irresponsibility. On occasion leading figures in the corporative structures of our society are meeting with professional ecologists and with specialists in various fields of the natural sciences to consider the gains and losses involved in carrying out the industrial enterprise. Such is the case with Inform Inc., a research organization in New York that is concerned with practical actions for protection and conservation of natural resources.

The series of Globescope Conferences is also involved in bringing together executives from the industrial establishment and professional persons concerned with the integral functioning of the natural world.

That the World Bank, a major influence in the international economy and the industrialization of the Third World, should begin such an extensive reassessment of its own projects is indicative of a change in mood and the beginning at least of creating more acceptable values. The address of the president of the World Bank, Barber B. Conable, to the World Resources Institute in May 1987 contained pledges for activities directed toward worldwide protection of rain forests and for limiting the advance of the desert and the destruction of the forests of Africa. We await the fulfillment of these pledges, but already a change in its choice of projects is a beginning, however late this may be.

We all bear a certain amount of guilt for our present situation, since our American society has from its beginning supported the industrial process with enthusiasm. With few exceptions our society has considered the industrial route as the way into the future. We have been entranced with the progress myth, unlimited progress, progress that would lead beyond the existing human condition to something infinitely better, to wonderland. Such is the seductive theme of almost all our advertising.

As a result, our entire society is caught in a closed cycle of production and consumption that can go on until the natural resources are exhausted or until the poisons inserted into the environment are fed back into the system. We are so committed to this industrial cycle, so alienated from the needed knowledge or the competence to return to the ever-renewing cycle of the natural world, that even when we begin to experience the impending peril, we feel that we must cling to these "established" or "traditional" ways, ways that have become, as it were, a kind of salvific process. We feel that we must become even more dedicated to the cause; we must intensify our efforts. Thus, a kind of industrial-technological "fundamentalism" becomes prevalent, a fundamentalism that has led to the Reagan political regime. This fundamentalism expresses itself especially in magnifying our military establishment in order to defend ourselves and our industrial mode of existence. The military-industrial establishment then generates an overwhelming support for the industrial-commercial cycle.

Advertising takes on exaggerated expression in its volume and in its seductive appeal to the deepest and most sacred archetypal forces of the individual. Its presence has become so all-pervasive that the populace is surrounded on all sides with appeals to buy and consume, appeals so urgent, so competitive, and so compelling that they begin to take on hysterical dimensions.

For those absorbed in the industrial process, however, these signs indicate a need to expand the industrial process rather than to integrate our economy into a sustainable relationship with the ever-renewing processes of nature. With all his commitment to an emerging information society, John Naisbitt, in his best-selling book, *Megatrends,* gives no indication of the need to re-create an enduring and sustaining contact with the spontaneities and ever-renewing powers of the earth itself. He speaks of the "sunrise industries" and the new information society, ending his book with the cheerleader phrase: "My God, what a fantastic time to be alive." Julian Simon, in his books *The Ultimate Resource* and *The Resourceful Earth,* applauds the process.

Such is how one group is dealing with human-earth relations. This is the group that is now in control of the earth and its resources, our consumption habits, our military and its destructive instrumentalities.

Humanist Critiques of Technology

A second response to our earth-human situation is critiques, some based on the humanist and others based on the social consequences of our technological-industrial processes. Among the most incisive of such critics is Jacques Ellul. In his *Technological Society* he outlines the invasion of the technocratic process into every phase of human life, the imposition of a technosphere on the biosphere, and even on the psychosphere, with its progressive devitalization and dehumanization of life.

Theodore Roszak, in *The Making of a Counter-Culture,* identified the youth revolt of the late 1960s, with its opposition to technocracy. His view that the technocratic process was giving way to a more organic sense of human-earth relations was later expressed in his book *Person/Planet.* Ivan Illich provides a stinging indictment of technological society in a series of writings concerned with the medical profession, education, energy production, and other aspects of contemporary life. Socialist programs as well as labor pronouncements and papal encyclicals—these constantly give expression to a moral judgment upon the inequality in the distribution of the burdens and benefits of the industrial order. Yet none of these critics seems concerned with the consequences of the industrial plundering of the natural world. The labor movement in capitalist countries, the socialist and the communist movements, as well as capitalism, are all heavily committed to the technological-industrial process. It is a question of jobs, of sharing the wealth, of a more equitable place in the society. Smokestacks mean work and money and housing, food and clothing, economic survival, and education for the children. The acid rain, the contamination of the rivers, the paving over of the land, the toxic waste, the dying of the fish and the birds—these are distant and marginal concerns. If that is the condition for survival in the real world, then so be it. Romantic idealism toward the natural world belongs to a former world of dreams, illusion, and escape from reality.

The Integrity of Nature

A third way of dealing with human-nature relations is represented by those who criticize our technological-industrial society because of its disturbance of the natural world in its most basic life systems.

The ultimate source of evil in the existing order of life is perceived as its commitment to human well-being at the expense of the natural world. This third group insists that nothing very helpful can be achieved until we move away from our conquering attitude to a more evocative attitude in our relations with nature.

A consciousness of our disturbed relationship with nature was expressed by J. Hector St. John de Crèvecoeur in his *Letters from an American Farmer,* published in 1782. This theme of human disruption and antipathy toward nature is dealt with also in the Leatherstocking tales of James Fenimore Cooper and in *Moby Dick* by Herman Melville.

The earliest clear suggestions in America of a truly intimate presence to the natural world are found in Henry Thoreau (1817–1862) and in John Muir (1838–1914). Both lived for long periods in natural surroundings. John Muir traveled deep into true wilderness areas. Thoreau and Muir, however, remained profoundly in communication with American society and its cultural traditions. Both believed that the human species was part of the larger community of life and that a mutually enhancing bond was necessary for the true enrichment of the human.

The American continent, from post–Civil War times until the present, has suffered a period of industrial ascendancy and the degradation of its basic life systems with minimal protest. The virulence of the years since World War II is marked especially by the advance of the chemical, agricultural, automotive, construction, electronic, nuclear, military, and space industries. In this late period the great transnationals arrived. The entire planet was inventoried, its resources exploited, its ecosystems upset, its primordial forests destroyed, its native economies disrupted.

The postwar phase is also the advent of increased ecological consciousness. In the 1960s we began to identify the disastrous consequences of chemical fertilizers, pesticides, and herbicides on the living world about us. In 1968 The Club of Rome held its first meeting to assess the global situation. In 1972 the initial report appeared as *The Limits to Growth* by Donella Meadows and others. Few books have had such a startling impact in awakening America to the absurdity of exponential rates of growth.

At about the same time Greenpeace and Earth First! began their use of confrontational tactics to save the threatened species and the wild places of the world. More recently Sea Shepherd has taken over a significant role in protection of sea life.

Biologists Anne and Paul Ehrlich tell us in their book *Extinction* that before the year 2000 we will likely extinguish more than 20 percent of all living species. Rain forests the size of Connecticut are being destroyed each year. Frederick Turner, in *Beyond Geography: The Western Spirit Against the Wilderness,* tells us of the deepest spiritual and humanist origins of our assault on the planet.

The effort to state and defend the biocentric norm of reality and value is in ascendancy. The strongest academic presentation of the biocentric view is found in the Deep Ecology movement, begun by Arne Naess and later taken up by George Sessions, Bill Devall, and a number of others concerned with a more integral life orientation.

In the international realm a series of important events took place in the 1970s and early 1980s. In 1980 the *World Conservation Strategy: Living Resource for Sustainable Development* was set forth by the International Union for Conservation of Nature and Natural Resources in alliance with the United Nations Environment Programme and the World Wildlife Fund. This document outlined a program for development in the Third World that would be so integral with the functioning of the natural world that both could continue on a sustainable basis into the future. Scientists from more than one hundred nations were associated with the program. The document on strategy was followed in 1984 by a remarkable conference held at Tufts University. The papers of eighteen participants were published in the volume entitled *Sustaining Tomorrow: A Strategy for World Conservation and Development.*

The World Charter for Nature, which was approved by the

United Nations Assembly in 1982, notes quite clearly that our human civilization is integral with the natural world and that its recognition and preservation is urgent if the human community itself is to survive in any vital way. Earlier, in 1972, the Stockholm Conference on the Environment had taken place without immediate results. Afterwards, however, on their return home, these representatives led the way in establishing environmental protection agencies in most of the nations of the world. Such are some of the main forces that have thrown their activities, their scholarship, and their life purpose into saving the living world from industrial-technological destruction.

The Healing of the Earth

In addition to these groups, there is a fourth, a group that is evolving the alternative programs needed for healing the earth and fostering more functional modes of food and energy production. These people see the need for confrontational methods such as those used by Greenpeace, Sea Shepherd, and Earth First!, but their emphasis is on the alternative programs that are needed. They wish to provide functional models of human-nature relations that could remedy, or at least modify, our current dysfunctional industrial patterns. The most effective of these new models are functioning with regard to food production, energy, housing, architecture, craft skills, waste disposal, sanitation, health maintenance, and forestry.

One of the principal differences between this fourth group and the industrial processes is that of scale. Little attention has been given in recent years to the monstrous aspects of factories that increase production in terms of quantitative measurements without perceiving the change in quality that goes with quantitative changes. This is evident with the automotive industry in its continual effort to increase production and sales, while paying no significant attention to what is happening to the society and the North American continent. Automobiles are now inefficient in the cities, poisonous to the air, deadly to the forests, subversive of neighborhood community, and prohibitive to other modes of travel, such as walking or bicycling.

These questions of scale have received extensive treatment by Peter Berg in his bioregional program for reinhabiting the earth, a program further elucidated by Kirkpatrick Sale in his book *Human Scale*. Since 1957, Leopold Kohr has been dealing with "the diseconomies of scale," a principle he explains fully in his book *The Overdeveloped Nations: The Diseconomies of Scale*. It was followed in 1975 by Edward Schumacher's book *Small Is Beautiful*.

A number of other writers have also dealt with this sense of scale and with the recent tendencies toward local, limited patterns of production, distribution, and the technologies appropriate for lifestyles based on bioregional development. Innovative modes of interaction between microphase and macrophase functions need to be developed, with a fitting variety of such technologies.

Turning to specific issues, we might begin with the shift in agriculture away from monocultural, high-energy, petrochemical techniques to more emphasis on organic processes, mixed crops, local markets, permacultures, and year-round food production in solar-heated bioshelters. In this context subsistence gardening would be done by a large part of the population. Even metropolitan areas would, in alliance with nearby regions, become largely self-supporting in their food supply. Since many metropolitan areas are near the coastline, seafood would become available to them once the sources of ocean pollution were removed.

These new methods of food growing would diminish the exploitation of land in Third World countries by the more affluent countries, and would also assist countries all over the world to grow their own food. There are few peoples in the world who could not grow their own food if their own land were available to them, if food were not exported for the foreign exchange, if the land were properly cultivated, and if expensive packaging and transportation were avoided. The evidence for this has been presented by Frances Moore Lappé in her book *Food First.*

Promising developments in achieving such integral use of land and natural processes have been made by Wes Jackson at the Land Institute in Salina, Kansas; by John and Nancy Jack Todd at the New Alchemy Institute on Cape Cod; by Robert Rodale with his Regeneration Project in Emmaus, Pennsylvania; by Bill Mollison with his Permaculture Program; by Masanobu Fukuoka with his *One-Straw Revolution,* presented as a revolution of both farming and life itself.

Robert Rodale's Regeneration Project is especially concerned with our food supply. Rodale believes that food should be grown and consumed locally as far as is appropriate and that the fossil energy expenditure be lessened in growing and processing, packaging, preserving, transporting, and marketing.

Such timely agricultural processes involve a sensitivity to natural forces, which carry out their work spontaneously and freely. The worms work for free and with delight, the sun pours out its light and warmth and energy in abundance, seeds sprout of themselves if given a chance. Ecosystems evolve.

If these programs could carry out their promise, we would finally begin to heal the disruption of the earth that began in the Neolithic period and was continued throughout the course of the classical civilizations until it reached its ultimate destructive impact in the pathology of twentieth-century American agribusiness. The very absurdities of such aggression against the soil reveal the true nature and effects of our entire technocratic system. Our chemical, transportation, and energy technologies are all involved in this method of agriculture, the educational system, the social ideals, the health system, and the entire society. Aware of all this, Wendell Berry wrote his classic treatise, *The Unsettling of America: Culture and Agriculture,* in 1978.

In the energy field Amory Lovins has shown the need for on-site production of energy at end-use levels rather than production exclusively through regional power grids, enormous generating plants, massive dams, and nuclear reactors. *Soft Energy Paths,* his most widely read work, provides abundant information on the subject, followed by another incisive study, *Brittle Power.*

Agenda for an Ecological Age

Rather than outline additional specific programs, it might be best here to suggest some basic principles to guide us in developing technologies that would mutually enhance both the human community and the earth process.

First, human technologies should function in an *integral relation with earth technologies,* not in a despotic or disturbing manner or under the metaphor of conquest, but rather in an evocative manner. The spontaneities of nature need to be fostered, not extinguished. Nature has, during some hundreds of millions of years through numberless billions of experiments, worked out the ecosystems that were flourishing so abundantly when humans and human civilizations emerged into being. It is a brash and destructive thing for humans to intrude on this system without carefully observing just how these ecosystems function and how humans are best present within this context.

Second, we must be clear concerning *the order of magnitude* of the changes that are needed. We are not concerned here with some minor adaptations, but with the most serious transformation of human-earth relations that has taken place at least since the classical civilizations were founded. The industrial age has so alienated and so conditioned the human that survival outside the industrial bubble is difficult. Yet we must learn survival in more intimate relations with the natural world, since the industrial bubble cannot long endure in its present mode of functioning. The urgency is even greater when we consider that humans, through technological cunning, have now for the first time attained the power of life and death over the planet in many of its most basic life systems.

Third, sustainable progress must be progress for *the entire earth community*. Every component of the community must participate in the process. For humans to advance by eliminating, degrading, or poisoning other life systems is not only to diminish the grandeur of earthly existence, but also to diminish the chances for human survival in any acceptable mode of fulfillment. One example of integral progress is found in the soils of northern Europe and England. These soils, after millennia of cultivation, were at the beginning of the twentieth century more fertile than they had been originally. Only rarely has this accomplishment been equaled in the civilizational story.

Fourth, our technologies need to be integral. *They need to take care of their waste products.* Waste disposal should be associated with the process, either the immediate process or a related process. This law of integrity is among the most widely violated. The brazenness of industrial establishments is difficult to understand; they blast their refuse into the atmosphere or pour it into streams or dump their trash onto the fertile wetlands. It is strange that the chemical industry has been so little concerned with what happens to its chemicals once they are used for some isolated or limited purpose. What finally happens to those deadly substances seems not to concern the industries that produce them. This refusal to deal with their own waste is one of the most universal, consistent, and repulsive aspects of our contemporary technologies.

Fifth, there is need for a *functional cosmology,* a cosmology that will provide the mystique needed for this integral earth-human presence. Such a mystique is available once we consider that the universe, the earth, the sequence of living forms, and the human mode of consciousness have from the beginning had a psychic-spiritual as well as a physical-material aspect. We do not need such extrinsic spiritual interpretations of the earth process as are sometimes proposed. What we need is a sense of reverence such as we find with the great naturalists, or such as we find with some of the foremost scientists of our times, scientists such as Freeman Dyson, Sir Bernard Lovell, Brian Swimme, or Ilya Prigogine. Until technologists learn reverence for the earth, there will be no possibility of bringing a healing or a new creative age to the earth.

Sixth, nature is violent as well as benign. Our technologies have a *defensive role* to play. Nature—with its frequent droughts, its devastating floods, its hurricane winds, its termites ready to destroy our dwellings, its plague-bearing animals, its malarial infections— assaults and challenges us, and we need all our skills and effective technologies to defend ourselves against such forces that are ever ready to destroy us. But while these assaults on the human are all-pervasive, nature has so arranged its balance of forces that the remedy is already available. Much of the assault that we perceive as natural is really human in origin. By cutting forests we invite floods; by practicing extensive monocultural agriculture, we invite pest infestation on a massive scale; by pouring chemicals on the land, we kill the soil and invite erosion. We could extend the list endlessly. Nature is both benign and terrible, but consistently creative in the larger patterns of her actions. The difficulty with our technologies is not that they have a dark aspect, but that this dark aspect is so sterile that it terminates rather than enhances further life development.

Seventh, our new and healing technologies need to function within *a bioregional context,* not simply on a national or global scale. The functional divisions of the human should accord with the functional divisions of the earth itself and its lifeforms. The earth is not given to us in a single global sameness. The earth articulates itself in arctic and tropics, in seacoast and mountain regions, in plains and valleys, in deserts and woodlands.

Everywhere life is established on a functional community basis. These distinctive communities can be designated as *bioregions,* that is, regions with mutually supporting life systems that are generally self-sustaining. Future technologies must function primarily within such bioregional patterns and on the bioregional scale.

Road-building technologies need to take into consideration the region and the integration of its life systems. Roads that go along a stream or river are dangerous barriers to those living beings who need to get to the water. Many bird species cannot fly across a four-lane highway. A bioregional roadway would allow walking, bicycling, and horseback riding, and would accommodate animal-drawn carriages. The tyranny of the automobile can no longer be accepted.

An agriculture proper to the region would be developed and the land cared for so that the woodlands and the living inhabitants could once again feel secure. Monocultures would be eliminated as both unnatural and counterproductive.

Bioregional architecture involves using local materials, with reference to the climatic conditions, the numbers of people, and the community context; appropriate construction and materials and design technologies would appear. All this would be in accord with principles of designing with nature, not in alienation from or in opposition to nature.

The integrating element in a bioregional context would be the bioregional culture—its poetry and song, as well as its architecture and painting. Construction and transportation would take on the distinctive features of the bioregion. The norm would not be the boxes of Gropius, but the more intimate forms suggested by Ian McHarg and Gary Coates. The earth itself would be seen as the primary model in architecture, the primary scientist, the primary educator, healer, and technologist, even the primary manifestation of the ultimate mystery of things.

A person cannot doubt that the technologists of the present are becoming increasingly aware of the nobility and urgency of their work. Nor can we doubt their competence to fulfill their role in the creative tasks that are before us. Neither they nor ourselves can be entirely clear on the specific details of what needs to be done. What we do know is that the mechanistic patterns of the past are not adequate to solve the biological problems of the present. We also know that further imposition of our human technologies on the natural world, with such disdain for the technologies of nature, can lead only to a further impasse in the entire earth venture. We know further that our sciences and technologies are needed more urgently than ever: we can do nothing adequate toward human survival or toward the healing of the planet without our technologies. Extensive scientific research is needed if we are to appreciate the integral functioning of the basic life systems of the planet and enter into a mutually enhancing relationship.

After the distancing a new intimacy; after the mechanistic a greater biological sensitivity; after damaging the earth a healing. We need only look at the surrounding universe in its more opaque material aspects—look at it, listen to it, feel and experience the full depths of its being. Suddenly its opaque quality, its resistance, falls away, and we enter into a world of mystery. What seemed so opaque and impenetrable suddenly becomes radiant with intelligibility, powerful beyond imagination.

The work of the scientist has been spoken of by Brian Swimme in terms of the shamanic journey into a strange and distant world. In our times technologists are discovering ways of interacting with this awesome inner world of mysterious forces. What we might hope for is not that technologists refuse to enter this world, but that, as they participate in its powers, they become increasingly sensitive to those larger patterns of life into which its powers are organized, not simply into individual lifeforms, but also into those living communities that are indeed resilient, and also extremely vulnerable to disruption by insensitive humans.

We might sometimes reflect and recall that the purpose of all our science, technology, industry, manufacturing, commerce, and finance is celebration, planetary celebration. That is what moves the stars through the heavens and the earth through its seasons. The final norm of judgment concerning the success or failure of our technologies is the extent to which they enable us to participate more fully in this grand festival.

·7·

Economics as
a Religious Issue

Economics as a religious issue can be dealt with in different ways.
One way is to begin with the religious quest for justice. In this context we have a special concern that the well-being of the society
be shared by all, especially that the basic life necessities be available
to the less privileged. Such an approach emphasizes our social and
political responsibilities to ensure that the weak and less gifted are
not exploited by the strong and the competent.

The moral-religious critique in this country generally concerns
the issue of our capitalist market economy that neglects its social
responsibilities. The remedy offered, in accord with biblical and
moral principles, is to incorporate everyone into the functioning
and benefits of the economy. Admirable as this approach may be,
it may bring about only temporary improvement since the more

basic difficulty may not be the social issue, but the industrial economy itself. At least in its present form, the industrial economy is not a sustainable economy.

Another way of dealing with economics as a religious issue is to begin with the present economy and inquire into its deeper implications from within its own functioning, and that is how we proceed in this inquiry. We begin with a few observations concerning the reality of the present economy, its capacity to sustain itself, and the consequences not only for the well-being of the human community, but also for the life systems of the earth upon which a sustainable economy depends in a very direct manner.

The reality of our present economy is such that we must have certain forebodings, not simply as regards the well-being of the human community, but even of the planet itself in its most basic life systems. Economic dysfunction is generally expressed in terms of deficit expenditure: income does not balance outflow. In the natural world there exists an amazing richness of life expression in the ever-renewing cycle of the seasons. There is a minimum of entropy. The inflow of energy and the outflow are such that the process is sustainable over an indefinite period of time. So long as the human process is integral with these processes of nature, the human economy is sustainable into the future.

The difficulty comes when the industrial mode of our economy disrupts the natural processes, when human technologies become destructive of earth technologies. In such a situation the productivity of the natural world and its life systems is diminished. When nature goes into deficit, then we go into deficit. When this occurs to a limited extent on a regional basis, it can often be remedied. The difficulty is when the entire planetary system is affected. The earth system is most threatened when the human economy goes out of balance and frantic efforts toward a remedy lead to a reckless plundering of the land, spending our capital as our interest diminishes.

If we look at the specific data available on the U.S. economy, we find that we now have a gross national product of more than

$4 trillion. In the year 1987 we also had a national debt of more than $2 trillion, an annual budgetary deficit of some $150 billion, an infrastructure disintegration requiring repairs of $750 billion, a trade deficit of more than $150 billion, Third World financial loans unlikely to be repaid of more than $200 billion, and annual military expenditures of $300 billion. All of these can be considered in some manner as financial deficits, leading eventually to what I have termed *earth deficit.*

Seldom does anyone speak of the deficit involved in the closing down of the basic life system of the planet through abuse of the air, the soil, the water, and the vegetation. As we have indicated, the earth deficit is the real deficit, the ultimate deficit, the deficit in some of its major consequences so absolute as to be beyond adjustment from any source in heaven or on earth. Since the earth system is the ultimate guarantee of all deficits, a failure here is a failure of last resort. Neither economic viability nor improvement in life conditions for the poor can be realized in such circumstances. These can only worsen, especially when we consider the rising population levels throughout the developing world.

This deficit in its extreme expression is not only a resource deficit, but the death of a living process, not simply the death of *a* living process, but of *the* living process, a living process which exists, so far as we know, only on the planet earth. That is what makes our problem definitively different from those of any other generation of whatever ethnic, cultural, political, or religious tradition, or of any other historical period. For the first time we are determining the destinies of the earth in a comprehensive and irreversible manner. The immediate danger is not *possible* nuclear war, but *actual* industrial plundering.

Economics on this scale is not simply economics of the human community, it is economics of the earth community in its comprehensive dimensions. Nor is it a question of profit or loss in terms of personal or community well-being in a functioning earth system. Economics has invaded the earth system itself. Forests are dying on every continent. The seas are endangered. The soil is poisoned with chemicals. The rain is acid.

So the litany could go on. In this country we are losing more than four billion tons of topsoil each year. The great aquifers of the Plains region are diminished beyond their capacity for refilling. Industrial agriculture is no longer the participation in the productive cycles of the natural world; it is the extinction of the very conditions on which these productive cycles depend.

While it is unlikely that we could ever extinguish life in an absolute manner, we are eliminating species at a rate never before known in historic time and in a manner never known in biological time. Destruction of the tropical rain forests of the planet will involve destroying the habitat of perhaps half the living species of earth. Although its strictly economic implications have still not been worked out, it should be clear: an exhausted planet is an exhausted economy.

The earth deficit in its resources and in its functioning has been documented in a long series of specialized studies and in more-general evaluations in ever-increasing volume over the past twenty years. The first thorough scientific study of the situation was Rachel Carson's *Silent Spring.* In 1970 Paul Ehrlich edited a comprehensive study entitled *Ecoscience: Population, Resources, Environment.* Then came the comprehensive survey of the planet Earth as a complex of life systems, *The Limits to Growth,* a work based, in its method, on the earlier *World Dynamics* by Jay Forrester, 1971. In 1976 an unappreciated work originally published in 1952 was republished, the work by Edward Hyams entitled *Soil and Civilization,* an extraordinary study of the difficulties encountered in establishing sustainable human relations with the land in various civilizations, even suggesting that the destruction of the natural environment in the Mediterranean world by the classical civilizations contributed significantly to their decline.

One of the most helpful of these general studies was edited by Norman Myers in 1984, *Gaia: An Atlas of Planet Management.* In that same year Lester Brown, with the resources of Worldwatch Institute, started an annual publication entitled *State of the World.* Already in 1982 the MacArthur Foundation had funded the Institute for World Resources. Their annual reports on the planetary situation began in 1986. Much earlier the International Union for Conservation and Natural Resources began putting out their Red Books listing the threatened and endangered plant and animal species.

There are in-depth inquiries into why this assault on the earth is taking place, such as Carolyn Merchant's study *The Death of Nature,* published in 1980. There are special studies in different fields, such as the studies of agriculture by Rodale Press. All of these indicate that the planet cannot long endure present modes of human exploitation.

Until recently both textbook economics and corporation practices have ignored the implications of such data or have given it minimal attention. Deficits in nature were simply external or unreal costs of doing business, costs that were not entered into the bookkeeping records until social protest brought about environmental impact statements, limits on pollution of the environment, cleanup of waste sites, and liability for personal and physical damage resulting from toxic disruption of the basic life systems. Even the existence of such sites that need cleanup is telling us something: that the industrial system itself is a failing system. Whatever fictions exist in Wall Street bookkeeping, the earth is a faithful scribe, a faultless calculator, a superb bookkeeper; we will be held responsible for every bit of our economic folly.

Only now do we begin to consider that there is an economics of the human as a species as well as an economics of the earth as a functional community. The primary objective of economic science, of the engineering profession, of technological invention, of industrial processing, of financial investment, and of corporation management must be the integration of human well-being within the context of the well-being of the natural world. Only within the ever-renewing processes of nature is there any future for the human community. Not to recognize this is to make economics a deadly affair.

The exploitation itself was and still is experienced by the commercial enterprise not as deterioration of the planet, but as a creative process leading to a wonderworld existence. This is "progress," a belief so entrancing for the modern world that no doubt of its validity is permitted. Even though this belief has long ago been severely critiqued and its limitations indicated, it remains the functional basis of our economy. The GNP must increase each year. Everything must be done on a larger scale, with little awareness of the built-in catastrophe involved in the exponential rate of increase. However rational modern economics might be, the driving force of economics is not economic, but visionary, a visionary commitment supported by myth and a sense of having the magical powers of science to overcome any difficulty encountered from natural forces.

The erratic consequences of this visionary approach can be seen in our constant anxiety over the industrial economy, the daily rising and falling levels of stock market quotations, the shifting of currency values, the formation of the great conglomerates, the mystique of the entrepreneur. As Peter Drucker indicates, we are moving from a managerial economy to an entrepreneurial economy. Lee Iacocca is among the most recent archetypal figures in the entrepreneurial mode. Along with Michael Novak and Julian Simon, *The Wall Street Journal* is still encouraging us to continue our established way into the future, confident that our scientific insight, technological competence, and economic discernment, despite all the temporary upset, are leading us into an even better life. These people argue that every generation in modern times has lived better than the prior generation, that there is no serious problem, that we must not lose our nerve, that science can resolve our difficulties.

Presently there is a glut of food in America and throughout western Europe. In Third World countries there is a glut of basic money crops. There is an increase in land under cultivation throughout the world, so why worry about the loss of topsoil? Our American vision of wonderworld is being fulfilled. Already *The Wall Street Journal* identifies itself as "The Daily Diary of the American Dream." This commitment to progress and the partial success of the business-world-opposed ecological movement in the 1970s has led to a resentment toward the entire environmental movement. This resentment has found expression in the books *Progress and Privilege* by William Tucker and *The Environmental Protection Hustle* by Bernard J. Frieden.

Thus the mythic drive continues to control our world even though so much is known about the earth, its limited resources, the interdependence of life systems, the delicate balance of the ecosystems, including the consequences of disturbing atmospheric conditions, of contaminating the air, soil, waterways, and seas. The drive continues despite the limited quantity of fossil fuels in the earth and the inherent danger of chemicals discharged into natural surroundings. Although all this has been known for generations, neither the study nor the commercial-industrial practice of economics has shown any capacity to break free from the mythic commitment to progress, or any awareness that we are in reality creating wasteworld rather than wonderworld.

This mythic commitment to continuing economic growth is such that none of our major newspapers or newsweeklies considers having an ecological section equivalent to the sports section or the financial section or the arts section or the comic section or the entertainment section, although ecological issues are more important than any of those, even more important than the daily national and international political news. The real history that is being made is interspecies and human-earth history, not nation or internation history. The real threat is from the retaliatory powers of the abused earth, not from other nations.

If this assault on the earth were done by evil persons with destructive intentions, it would be understandable. The tragedy is that our economy is being run by persons with good intentions under the illusion that they are bringing only great benefits to the world and even fulfilling a sacred task on the part of the human community. "We bring good things to life." "Progress is our most important product." "Fly the friendly skies." "The heartbeat of America." Millennial dreams for moving into new frontiers of economic accomplishment, for the fulfillment of the high purposes of the universe itself.

Nor has the real situation been appreciated by social reformers or by those concerned with the needs of the poor and dispossessed. Whether socialist or capitalist in orientation, they wish mainly to assist the poor in finding their place in the industrial world. Whether privately or socially controlled, the industrial process itself is generally accepted.

Nor have our moral theologians been able to deal with our abuse of the natural world. After dealing with suicide, homocide, and genocide, our Western Christian moral code collapses completely; it cannot deal with biocide or geocide. Nor have church authorities made any sustained protest against the violence being done to the planet.

The new sense of what economics is all about has emerged from the naturalist Aldo Leopold in his essay "A Land Ethic," from the economist Nicholas Georgescu-Roegen in *The Entropy Law and the Economic Process,* and from Herman Daly in *A Steady-State Economy.*

Georgescu-Roegen had a profound sense of the economic implications of the second law of thermodynamics. Before his time no modern economic system had any realization of the earth system itself as the primary functional context of life in all its aspects. Every modern economic system—from the mercantile and physiocrat theories of the seventeenth and eighteenth centuries, through the free-enterprise system of Adam Smith, through the socialist economics, to the supply-demand theories of Keynes—is anthropocentric and exploitive in its programs. The natural world is considered a resource for human utility, not a functioning community of mutually supporting life systems within which the human must discover its proper role.

The basic critique of Georgescu-Roegen is that economists were caught in a mechanistic world that could be understood simply from within its own economic data. Within such a limited context, derived from Newtonian cosmology, the economists in their theories and the corporations with their practices sought to manage the economic world. Economics was a closed process of commercial transactions, with reference only to the production and exchange of goods. As Georgescu-Roegen indicates: "Economists do speak occasionally of natural resources. Yet the fact remains that, search as one may, in none of the economic models in existence is there a variable standing for nature's perennial contribution." He also notes, "The fact that biological and economic factors may overlap and interact in some surprising ways, though well established, is little known among economists."

Even now, corporations feel imposed upon when they are required to make environmental impact statements concerning their intrusion into the natural world, when they are required to refrain from scattering industrial waste over the land, when they are required to inform their workers of the toxic nature of the materials they are working with, or when they are required to list the chemical contents of their products.

There is a certain pathos in social reform movements and in the efforts made to improve the living conditions of the impoverished within the context of such a dysfunctional and nonsustainable economy. This is understandable, however, since life's necessities— air and water, food, clothing and shelter—are demanded presently. Tomorrow is too late. Whatever the existing economy, human needs must be supplied, even though food today for the few may be starvation tomorrow for the many. This means jobs within the existing context. No immediate alternative seems available.

Even so, an awareness should exist that the present system is too devastating to the natural fruitfulness of the earth to long supply human needs. Alternative programs are being elaborated and be-coming functional. If the moral norm of economics is what is happening to the millions of persons in need, then these more-functional economic developments are required not only by those excluded from the present system, but also by the entire nation community, by the entire human community, and by the entire earth community.

This is not a socialism on the national scale, nor is it an interna-tional socialism, it is planetary socialism. It is a socialism based on the *Summa Theologica* of Saint Thomas, wherein he deals with the diversity of creatures. Beyond planetary socialism he proposes an ultimate universal socialism where he says that because the divine goodness "could not be adequately represented by one creature alone, he produced many and diverse creatures, that what was want-ing to one in the representation of the divine goodness might be supplied by another. For goodness, which in god is simple and uniform, in creatures is manifold and divided; and hence the whole universe together participates the divine goodness more perfectly, and represents it better than any single creature whatever."

From this we could argue that the community of all the com-ponents of the planet Earth is primary in the divine intention. Even biologically it is evident that the well-being of the earth itself is a primary consideration if there is to be a well-being of the various components of the earth. The trees of the Appalachian Mountains will not be healthy if the rain is acid. Nor will the soil be fertile. Nor will humans have their proper nourishment. Nor will imagina-tion be activated to its grand poetic visions. Nor will our sense of the divine be so exalted if the earth is diminished in its glory. It is all quite clear. If we pull the threads, the fabric falls apart—the human fabric, especially—in both its religious and economic aspects.

We come to the essential problem of economics as a religious issue when we consider that the present threat to both economics and religion is from a single source: the disruption of the natural world. If the water is polluted, it can neither be drunk nor used for baptism. Both in its physical reality and in its psychic symbolism, it is a source not of life, but of death.

Obviously economics and religion are two aspects of a single earth process. If the economy is more immediately the cause for disruption of the natural world, the ultimate sources for this mode of economic activity may be found in the religious-cultural context from which our present economy emerged.

This may well be the reason, at this time, when threatened in the very source of our sense of the divine and in our sacramental forms, there is no sustained religious protest or moral judgment concerned with the industrial assault on the earth, the degradation of its life systems, or the threatened extinction of its most elaborate modes of life expression. Even more important: why did this process develop in a civilization that emerged out of a biblical-Christian matrix?

This most urgent theological issue, so far as I know, has never been dealt with in any effective manner, although the accusation has been made by Lynn White, Jr., that Christianity bears "an immense burden of guilt" for the present ecological crisis. Many answers have been written, a few by theologians, but mostly brief articles not entirely convincing because of their inadequate consideration of those dark or limited aspects of Christianity that made our Western society liable to act so harshly toward the natural world.

While none of our Christian beliefs individually is adequate as an explanation of the alienation we experience in our natural setting, they do in their totality provide a basis for understanding how so much planetary destruction has been possible in our Western tradition. We are radically oriented away from the natural world. It has no rights; it exists for human utility, even if for spiritual utility.

Because our sense of the divine is so extensively derived from verbal sources, mostly through the biblical scriptures, we seldom notice how extensively we have lost contact with the revelation of the divine in nature. Yet our exalted sense of the divine itself comes from the grandeur of the universe, especially from the earth, in all the splendid modes of its expression. Without such experience we would be terribly impoverished in our religious and spiritual development, even in our emotional, imaginative, and intellectual development.

Even our sense of divine immanence tends to draw us away from the sacred dimension of the earth in itself. This is not exactly the divine presence. We go too quickly from the merely physical order of things to the divine presence in things. While this is important, it is also important that we develop a sense of the reality and nobility of the natural world in itself. Saint Thomas dedicated his efforts in great part to defending the reality and goodness and efficacy intrinsic to the natural world. The natural world is not simply object, not simply a usable thing, not an inert mode of being awaiting its destiny to be manipulated by the divine or exploited by the human.

The natural world is subject as well as object. The natural world is the maternal source of our being as earthlings and the life-giving nourishment of our physical, emotional, aesthetic, moral, and religious existence. The natural world is the larger sacred community to which we belong. To be alienated from this community is to become destitute in all that makes us human. To damage this community is to diminish our own existence.

If this sense of the sacred character of the natural world as our primary revelation of the divine is our first need, our second need is to diminish our emphasis on redemption experience in favor of a greater emphasis on creation processes. Creation, however, must now be experienced as the emergence of the universe as a psychic-spiritual as well as a material-physical reality from the beginning. We need to see ourselves as integral with this emergent process, as that being in whom the universe reflects on and celebrates itself. Once we begin to experience ourselves in this manner, we immediately perceive how adverse to our own well-being psychically and spiritually as well as economically is any degradation of the planet.

We must also develop a way of thinking about "progress" that would include the entire earth community. If there is to be real and sustainable progress, it must be a continuing enhancement of life for the entire planetary community. It must be shared by all the living, from the plankton in the sea to the birds above the land. It must include the grasses, the trees, and the living creatures of the earth. True progress must sustain the purity and life-giving qualities of both the air and the water. The integrity of these life systems must be normative for any progress worthy of the name. Already these three commitments—to the natural world as revelatory, to the earth community as our primary loyalty, and to the progress of the community in its integrity—constitute the new religious-spiritual context for carrying out a change of direction in human-earth development. For, indeed, this is the order of magnitude of the task that is before us. If the industrial economy (which well nigh done us in) in its full effects has been such a massive revolutionary experience for the earth and the entire living community, then the termination of this industrial devastation and the inauguration of a more sustainable lifestyle must be of a proportionate order of magnitude.

The industrial age itself, as we have known it, can be described as a period of technological entrancement, an altered state of consciousness, a mental fixation that alone can explain how we came to ruin our air and water and soil and to severely damage all our basic life systems under the illusion that this was "progress."

But now that the trance is passing we have before us the task of structuring a human mode of life within the complex of the biological communities of the earth. This task is now on the scale of "reinventing the human," since none of the prior cultures or concepts of the human can deal with these issues on the scale required.

One of our main concerns must also be with human habitation that does not disrupt the habitation requirements of the other species that inhabit this planet. Here much important work has been

done by architects aware of the new requirements for more intimate, more functional, and more viable communities. Ian McHarg
has outlined some of the basic elements in designing habitats for
human affairs in harmony with the functioning of the natural world.
Gary Coates has also contributed significantly in this general area,
especially with the information he has presented on community
efforts recently begun in various parts of the country. His study,
Resettling America, presents a number of such community projects. There we find such chapter titles as Rural New Towns for
America, An Ecological Village, The Rise of New City-States, Urban
Agriculture, Goals for Regional Development. In his book *Ecocity
Berkeley* Richard Register has presented some of the most challenging ideas on designing cities that have yet appeared.

In addition to these projects, fifty-some of the larger nature- and
ecology-oriented organizations in the United States joined together
a few years ago to defend the North American continent from
governmental neglect in carrying out its responsibilities for protection of the ecosystems of the continent. All of these efforts are
outside the professional or official establishments. Objections to
ecological activities exist not only in economics and industry, in
boardrooms and research laboratories, but also in education, law,
medicine, and religion. Having become part of the bureaucratic
process, they all find serious difficulty in adapting to change of the
order of magnitude that is required.

For the past hundred years the great technical engineering schools,
the research laboratories, and the massive corporations have dominated the North American continent, and even an extensive por-
tion of the earth itself. In alliance with governments, the media,
the universities, and with the general approval of religion, they have
been the main instruments for producing acid rain; hazardous waste;
chemical agriculture; the horrendous loss of topsoil, wetlands, and
forests; and a host of other evils the natural world has had to endure from human agency. The corporations should be judged by
their own severe norms. What exactly have they produced? What

83

kind of world have they given us after a century of control?

Feeling threatened now by the rising movements for change, they are seeking to strengthen their position. The surge of economic activity throughout the world; the vast volume of exchange transactions; the enormous assets that now rise above the hundred-billion-dollar level; the global extent of exploitation; the new ease of information gathering, analysis, and communication—all these function like a great exhilarating wave of activity in corporate consciousness. The feeling of euphoria that recently pervaded the business world has been sobered by the stock market crash of October 1987. We now have deep forebodings concerning the future of the industrial enterprise. Since growth, however, is the central fact of contemporary economics, a sudden confrontation with the inherent limits of earth development is coming as a sobering experience indeed.

Before this moment arrives, however, an extensive series of confrontations can be expected. Already these are occurring in every aspect of human endeavor—in all our institutions, professions, and activities. The successes in environmental legislation in the 1970s that set up regulatory agencies and norms concerning the quality of air and water and waste disposal were the occasion for a later resentment by industry and the corporate enterprise. Increasing difficulty is experienced in meeting standards, but even greater difficulty is experienced in enforcing standards. In many instances the situation is fairly clear concerning what needs to be done. The difficulty for government, for industry, and for the citizenry is accepting the consequences of the changes required, for we are involved in changes in the deep structure of our sense of reality and of value as well as in the practical adaptation to lifestyles less extravagant in their demands on the environment.

In other instances we must be aware of how difficult our present situation is for everyone, even when there is a willingness to deal effectively with the issues before us. The scientific determination of acceptable standards in environmental purity is enormously difficult. The technologies for meeting these standards, their cost to the society, the sensitivity of the citizenry—all these are difficult. By entering into an industrial economy, we may have taken on a task beyond human capabilities for both judgment and execution. The arrogance of our engineering intrusion into nature is only now being manifest, our arrogance and our naiveté concerning our rational skills and our inventive genius. The difficulty is that the arrogance continues even when its deleterious consequences are so evident. President Ronald Reagan foils the efforts of the Environmental Protection Agency to fulfill its official mandate. Such attitudes evoke confrontational movements by activist ecologists, lawsuits initiated by the National Resources Defense Council, and extensive lobbying in state legislatures and in Congress. Along with these actions are the great variety of spontaneous protest movements and a great volume of newsletters, reports, and periodicals that are making demands on industrial and political establishments. Presently they are finding a way to sustain influence on the society through Green movements in various fields of social life, but especially in politics. In several countries Green parties are beginning to function.

In the United States, also, a Green political organization called the Green Committees of Correspondence has been in process for several years, often in alliance with the bioregional movement, and now has more than one hundred local groups. The spiritual dimension of Green politics has been articulated in this country through the work of Charlene Spretnak. Her sense of the deeper spiritual foundations needed for an effective reorientation of the political life of contemporary society is providing a more integral context in which the customary left-right conflict can be surmounted. Another American contribution to the international Green movement is the writings of Murray Bookchin on Social Ecology. In New England the Green movement is establishing itself as the successor to the diminished socialist parties, principally through the work of the New England Committees of Correspondence. In Vancouver, center of the British Columbia Green party, the Green movement in its commercial-financial phase is finding expression in the Local Exchange Trading System devised by Michael Linton.

Among these significant movements, the one with the most immediate concern for the integral presence of the human to the natural world is the bioregional movement. This movement, fostered originally by Raymond Dasmann, Gary Snyder, Peter Berg and the Planet Drum Foundation, and David Haenke, is particularly strong in North America. It is based on a realization that the earth expresses itself not in some uniform life system throughout the globe, but in a variety of regional integrations, in bioregions. These can be described as identifiable geographical areas of interacting life systems that are relatively self-sustaining in the ever-renewing processes of nature. As we diminish our commitment to our present industrial context of life with its nonselfrenewing infrastructures, we need to integrate our human communities with the ever-renewing bioregional communities of the place where we find ourselves.

We need to realign human dwelling and human divisions of the earth with the local biosystems. These provide a primary biological identity rather than a primary political or social or ethnic identity. Our cultural development within this context could have a new vigor derived from such intimate association with the dynamism and artistic creativity of nature. Much more can be said of the bioregional movement in both its confrontational and in its creative aspects. Its power is in its integration of the human within the cosmological process. In this manner it achieves what a number of new-age activists and writers fail to achieve.

Besides the work of Marilyn Ferguson, presenting new-age thinking in *The Aquarian Conspiracy,* there are other writers with a similar sense of an exciting new period in human development, such as John Naisbitt and Alvin Toffler. Both present amazing amounts of information on every aspect of contemporary life. Peter Drucker, with his concentration on the managerial role, contributes considerably to our understanding of the controlling processes of our corporative institutions. Robert Heilbroner gives us a more profound insight into the governing principles and ideals of our economy.

But all of these writers fail ultimately in judging the present and in outlining a program for the future because none is able to present data consistently within a functional cosmology. Neither humans as a species nor any of our activities can be understood in any significant manner except in our role in the functioning of the earth and of the universe itself. We come into existence, have our present meaning, and attain our destiny within this numinous context, for the universe in its every phase is numinous in its depths, is revelatory in its functioning, and in its human expression finds its fulfillment in celebratory self-awareness. Neither the psychological, sociological, nor theological approaches is adequate. The controlling context must be a functional cosmology.

At this time the question arises regarding the role of the traditional religions. My own view is that any effective response to these issues requires a religious context, but that the existing religious traditions are too distant from our new sense of the universe to be adequate to the task that is before us. We cannot do without the traditional religions, but they cannot presently do what needs to be done. We need a new type of religious orientation. This must, in my view, emerge from our new story of the universe. This constitutes, it seems, a new revelatory experience that can be understood as soon as we recognize that the evolutionary process is from the beginning a spiritual as well as a physical process.

The difficulty so far has been that this story has been told simply as a physical process. Now, however, the scientists themselves are awakening to the wonder and the mystery of the universe, even to its numinous qualities. They begin to experience also the mythic aspect of their own scientific expressions. Every term used in science is laden with greater mythic meaning than with rational comprehension. Thus science has overcome its earlier limitations out of its own resources. As Brian Swimme notes concerning the scientists, "Their experience with the most awesome realities of the universe revealed a fantastic dimension that exceeded, exploded, and destroyed the language of the everyday realm." He notes further, "To speak of the diaphanous quality of matter or to speak of the cosmic dawn of the universe is to treat questions that every culture throughout history has confronted."

We are entering into a period that might be identified as the period of the Third Mediation. For a long period the divine-human mediation was the dominant context not only of religion, but of the entire span of human activities. Then, for some centuries of industrial classes and nation-states, a primary concern has been inter-human mediation. Now the dominant mediation can be identified as earth-human mediation. The other two mediations will in the future be heavily dependent on our ability to establish a mutually enhancing human-earth presence to each other. The great value of this approach is that we have in the earth an extrahuman referent for all human affairs, a controlling referent that is a universal concern for every human activity. Whether in Asia or America or the South Sea Islands, the earth is the larger context of survival.

All human professions, institutions, and activities must be integral with the earth as the primary self-nourishing, self-governing and self-fulfilling community. To integrate our human activities within this context is our way into the future.

·8·

The American
College in
the Ecological Age

The American college may be considered a continuation, at the
human level, of the self-education processes of the earth itself:
universe education, earth education, and human education are
stages of development in a single unbroken process. We cannot
adequately discuss any stage of the development without seeing
it within this comprehensive context.

By universe education I do not mean universal education or
university education, but the education which identifies with the
emergent universe in its variety of manifestations from the beginning until now. So, too, by earth education I do not mean education about the earth, but the earth as the immediate self-educating
community of those living and nonliving beings that constitute the
earth. I might also go further and designate earth as the primary

educational establishment, or the primary college, with a record of extraordinary success over some billions of years.

Such fundamental issues need to be discussed because we must be absolutely clear about what we designate as "education" and what we are concerned with when we talk about "college." Our difficulty in appreciating the earth community as primary educator is that we have little sense of or feeling for the natural world in its integral dimension. Serious attention in terms of real values seems to be given to the spiritual world or to the human world. Our concern for the natural world is one of utility or as an object to satisfy intellectual curiosity or aesthetic feeling.

A sense of the earth and its meaning is particularly urgent just now, for the different sciences have developed an immense volume of information about the natural world in its physical aspects, and a corresponding power to control it. Yet the earth is still seen as so much quantified matter. Life and consciousness as integral and pervasive dimensions of the earth have until recently found little appreciation except as more advanced phases of a mechanistic process. Because of this, the human community, the psychic component of the earth in its most complete expression, has become alienated from the larger dynamics of the planet and thereby has lost its own meaning. That we are confused about the human is a consequence of our confusion about the planet.

This disturbed situation is affecting our educational programs at their deepest levels. Some, looking for answers in the traditional civilizations, suggest that we rediscover our educational principles in the humanities. Some suggest that we turn more fervently to our spiritual-moral traditions. Some put their hope in pragmatic adaptation to the world through acceptance of its imperatives as known by physical sciences, politics, economics, or sociology. Some consider that our best guidance comes from psychology.

What is really needed is a functional cosmology. The difficulty is that the term *cosmology* is so exclusively physical in its accepted meaning that it does not indicate the integral reality of the universe.

For the same reason, the term *geology* does not indicate the integral reality of the earth, but only its physical aspects. Thus these terms are not usable terms for the subject under discussion. Indeed, we do not presently have a terminology suited to a serious consideration of the earth.

The earth is the central locus in the universe of the three later phases of the fourfold evolutionary process: first, the evolution of the galaxies and the elements; second, the evolution of the solar system and of the earth with its molecular and geological formations; third, the evolution of life in all its variety; and, fourth, the evolution of consciousness and the cultural developments of the human order.

It is especially important in this discussion to recognize the unity of the total process, from that first unimaginable moment of cosmic emergence through all its subsequent forms of expression until the present. This unbreakable bond of relatedness that makes of the whole a universe becomes increasingly apparent to scientific observation, although this bond ultimately escapes scientific formulation or understanding. In virtue of this relatedness, everything is intimately present to everything else in the universe. Nothing is completely itself without everything else. This relatedness is both spatial and temporal. However distant in space or time, the bond of unity is functionally there. The universe is a communion and a community. We ourselves are that communion become conscious of itself.

As regards the planet Earth, any adequate description must include its every aspect. The simpler elements are not known fully until their integration into more comprehensive modes of being is recognized. Later complex unities are not fully intelligible until their component parts are understood. We would not know the real capacities of hydrogen carbon, oxygen, and nitrogen were it not for their later expression in cellular life and indeed in the entire world of living beings, including the remarkable world of human consciousness. So with consciousness: the thoughts and emotions, the social forms and rituals of the human community, are as much "earth" as is the soil and the rocks and the trees and the flowers. We can reduce the flowers to the atoms or the atoms to the flowers. There are no atoms that are just atoms, no flowers that are just flowers. There is no earth without the human; no human without the earth. Any other earth or any other human is a pure abstraction.

Having said all this, we might come more directly to ourselves, to our identity and our function within this comprehensive context, if we are to achieve any adequate sense of what education is, or what a college is, or what the American college should be doing. These questions identify with the question of what the earth is, what it is doing presently, and what are its directions into the future. Human education is primarily the activation of the possibilities of the planet in a way that could not be achieved apart from human intelligence and the entire range of human activities. In this sense human education is part of the larger evolutionary process.

Coding: Genetic and Cultural

The earth's evolutionary process is planetary self-education. The planet out of its own spontaneities has, in a manner, taught itself the arts of life in the vast variety of their manifestations. The invention of such a fantastic complex of genetic codes, interrelated so that each depends upon all the others, is an accomplishment of supreme competence. And then to establish a genetic coding that determines a being to transgenetic cultural development is a much more amazing achievement.

The human in alliance with the earth is genetically mandated to invent a second level of its own being, a cultural realm, a realm freely developed in which the human gives itself its own identity in time and space and expands its activities in language and imagination and in that vast complex of activities that we indicate by the term *human culture*. To continue all these humanistic activities in association with the world of physical being and genetic determination has required special educational processes to communicate the cultural tradition from generation to generation. These educational processes must not only communicate some fixed cultural form, but also act as creative principles of further self-transformation for the human community and for the planet.

Whereas in other beings the genetic coding provides sufficient guidance for life activities with only minimal teaching after birth, in the human the genetic coding establishes only certain directions and the freedom and intelligence needed to activate these other realms of accomplishment in their particular determinations. These in turn give to life its human qualities. Human education can be defined, then, as a process whereby the cultural coding is handed on from one generation to another in a manner somewhat parallel to the manner by which the genetic coding of any living being is communicated to succeeding generations. This cultural coding is itself differentiated in a wide variety of patterns that characterize the various societies that are distributed over the planet.

There is also a historical sequence in cultural coding that is parallel to the evolutionary mutation of prehuman species. Thus we have not only the diverse patterning within a certain level of cultural development, but also historical change of cultural level. So far in the course of human development we can identify five basic phases of such transformation. These we might indicate as the Paleolithic, the Neolithic, the classical-traditional, the scientific-technological, and now the emerging ecological phase.

The educational problem is especially severe at these moments of change into a new mode of cultural patterning. The difference between the Neolithic and the great classical cultures is much greater than the difference between the Neolithic cultures among themselves. It is also greater than the difference between any of the greater classical cultures.

Transition from the classical cultural patterns to the scientific-technological cultural patterns has been especially severe, so severe indeed that we still do not comprehend just what has happened. The creators of the scientific-technological age had only minimal awareness of what they were doing. The industrial civilization that came to dominate this period has required some centuries of functioning before its creative and destructive aspects could be revealed in any effective manner.

The next transition, from the dominant scientific-technological period to the ecological period, is turbulent indeed. This turbulence establishes the context of our present educational discussions. In the scientific-technological period the central concern was the understanding of technological controls over earth's functioning. This period, which emerged first in the European context, spread throughout the entire world in the nineteenth and twentieth centuries, with its new mode of understanding and with its new powers for exploiting the planet. During this period an effort was made to keep the religious faith of the past, the moral and spiritual values, and the humanistic education.

As the cultural coding of this period established itself, however, it became progressively less oriented toward the numinous experience of the divine, more oriented toward secular values, exploitive in relation to the natural world, mechanistic in its conception of the universe, egalitarian in its social forms.

Education in this context became more an external conditioning than an interior discipline, more a training in manipulative techniques than initiation into religious rituals. The skills to be mastered were not the contemplative skills or imaginative capacities for dealing with numinous presence or with the aesthetic insight into the inner structure of reality; they were rather the skills needed by industry to bring forth the natural resources from the hidden depths of the planet, the skills to shape them in the manufacturing establishments and to make them available to a consumer-oriented society.

Behind the entire endeavor was the vast scientific effort to understand the universe in quantitative terms, mainly by an analytical reductionism of apparent wholes to their component parts. These component parts were seen as the true reality, with the design of the whole considered as secondary and adventitious. But while this quantitative universe, seen as the integral reality of things, was really an abstraction, it did alter human consciousness on a scale associated with religious experiences of the past whereby the earlier cultural codings had been established.

Strangely enough, the scientific venture has been unable to understand the significance of its own achievements. As a consequence, the cultural coding could not be established in an integral form; education remained dependent on its earlier structures for its humanistic meaning.

Meanwhile a frightening disruption was occurring in the natural world, and this on a geological and biological rather than simply on a human historical scale. As this situation becomes more aggravated, the demand for a further cultural mutation into an ecological context for human activities is being experienced. This period of cultural coding mandates a reintegration of the human process with the earth process. After generations of analytical preoccupation with taking the earth apart, the sciences begin a new phase of synthesis. We begin to appreciate the integral majesty of the natural world, the need that every form of life has for every other form, and the involvement of the human in the total process. Science has given us the basis for a metareligious vision that provides not only the intelligibility of the ecological period, but also the energy needed to bring it into existence.

Presently a multitude of countercultural movements are taking place throughout American society in all areas of human activities. These movements are taking place outside the formal establishments at a depth of human consciousness that is seldom reached by official training processes. These primordial-type movements are now transforming all our contemporary institutions and professions. The interaction taking place between the spontaneous and the trained is often dominated by the instinctive and intuitional modes of

95

awareness not bound by established dogmas of the existing professional worlds.

This mode of historical transformation is following the usual unpredictable paths whereby new codings take place in both the genetic and the cultural orders. Yet as soon as its influence is felt on this scale, there is a need for the spontaneous and intuitional to establish their own critical reflection. They must develop their own formal processes lest their achievements be dissipated or trivialized.

At such moments of cultural transformation, the educational process must go through a period of groping toward its new formal expression. This groping period has been especially difficult in recent times because of the magnitude of cultural change that is involved. Education in this context is precisely the subject of this chapter. Before we examine a detailed presentation of the educational program that is needed, we might note that the new cultural coding of the ecological age is already asserting itself in various areas of contemporary life, albeit in the confused and groping manner we have indicated.

This integration of the human with an organic functional world, after detaching the human from the mechanistic world can be considered among the most difficult of all historical transitions. The feel for life, the skills for creative interaction with the earth processes: these have been suppressed over a series of generations. The land is paved over, production is automated, the automobile has taken over the roadways. Walking has become dangerous. New forms of physical conditioning as well as cultural adaptation and technical training are required before this new relationship between the human and the earth can become fully functional.

Formal educational programs cannot fulfill all of these requirements. Education must be a pervasive life experience. Yet formal education must be transformed so that it can provide an integrating context for the total life functioning. Only in this way can we preserve the historical continuity needed for the integral development of the ecological age. Especially at the higher levels of formal education the needed processes of reflection on meaning and values must take place within this critical context.

Here we might consider the special role of the American college. College should be a center for creating the more encompassing visions as well as for communicating such visions to students. The college student in this late twentieth century needs to be involved in a significant historical as well as a significant personal process. Neither of these can function effectively without the other. College students should feel that they are participating in one of the most significant ventures ever to take place in the entire history of the planet.

The difficulty is so great because our present industrial coding is so extensively developed. We have attained such amazing insight into the mechanics of the earth and such control over its functioning that we have lost our ability to commune with the earth in an intimate manner. This alienation from the earth venture has led to confusion about the entire human venture. The college has no adequate context in which to function. Traditional colleges could always feel that somewhere in the background there was a meaningful world that could provide from without what was not available from within the college process itself. But this has not been an effective response.

The most common solution in cultural terms has been to reinstate past forms of humanistic studies in a core curriculum, a curriculum which includes philosophy, ethics, history, literature, religious studies, and perhaps some form of general science—all of these in a critical rather than a commitment context. Yet somehow these programs do not seem to take. A cultural canon does not emerge that could do for our world what the religious and cultural orientations of earlier religious cultures did for the societies of those centuries. The program does not activate the human energies that are needed for a vital human mode of being. There is an inability to bring together the scientific secular world with the religious believing world or with the humanist cultural world. Each of these feels impelled to go its own way. Consequently all three remain trivialized. No unifying paradigm emerges. Effective education does not take place. No larger context is established in which the college can envisage itself or its educational mission.

At such crisis moments we need to return to the story of the universe. The entire college project can be seen as that of enabling the student to understand the immense story of the universe and the role of the student in creating the next phase of the story. Discovering this story has been the high privilege and central meaning of the modern scientific venture. If our difficulties have emerged in this period, so too has the solution, at least in its basic outlines. Never before has the human community had such a profound understanding of the universe in its origin and development over the centuries. While this account is scientific, it is also mythic as a coherent presentation of the universe against backgrounds far beyond anything that rational intelligence can properly understand. Almost every term used by science carries with it more mystery than rational comprehension. Thus the all-pervading sense of the mythic at the heart of the scientific process. Thus, too, the role of myth and symbolism in scientific discovery.

Although as yet unrealized, this scientific account of the universe is the greatest religious, moral, and spiritual event that has taken place in these centuries. It is the supreme humanistic and spiritual as well as the supreme scientific event. The sublime mission of modern education is to reveal the true importance of this story for the total range of human and earthly affairs.

For the first time the peoples of the entire world, insofar as they are educated in a modern context, are being educated within this origin story. It provides the setting in which children everywhere— whether in Africa or China, in the Soviet Union or South America, in North America, Europe, or India—are given their world and their own personal identity in time and space. While the traditional origin and journey stories are also needed in the educational process, none

98

of them can provide the encompassing context for education such as is available in this new story, which is the mythic aspect of our modern account of the world. This story tells us how the universe emerged into being and of the transformation through which it has passed, especially on the planet Earth, until its present phase of development was realized in contemporary human intelligence.

What is needed, however, is the completion of the story of the physical dimensions of the universe by an account of the numinous and psychic dimensions of the universe. The primordial particles are already radiant with intelligibility and with unfathomable mystery as well as with the physical energy that is articulated within their structure.

While this integral story is the proper context of the entire educational process, it cannot be appreciated by students at elementary and high school levels in a reasoned, reflexive manner. It is the excitement of the college years. At that time the story can be understood in its more profound implications. It can become functional in every phase of those professional activities for which students are being prepared. This constitutes what might be called both a philosophy and a program for college education. A set of core courses could be indicated as the practical fulfillment of these suggestions.

A first course, perhaps the most difficult, would present the sequence of evolutionary phases of this functional cosmology: the formation of the galactic systems and the shaping of the elements out of which all future developments took place; the formation of the earth within the solar system; the emergence of life in all its variety upon the earth; the rise of consciousness and human cultural development.

This course, if related to the stars we see, the air we breathe, the water we drink, the food we are nourished by, the earth we stand on, the natural life of the environment as well as the cities we inhabit, could evoke a profound sense of mutual presence of the student and the universe to each other. But, most powerfully, the student, looking at his or her own hand and considering the time span of fourteen billion years that it took to produce such a hand, could feel a personal importance in the scheme of things. This would be further enhanced by consideration of those great moments when the universe found its way through the many apparent impasses that it faced.

Such a moment occurred when living forms had consumed the conditions of their own survival and life was threatened with extinction. At that moment photosynthesis was invented, the process upon which all future life development depended. A long series of such danger moments could be identified to communicate to the student the perilous adventures through which the universe and the planet Earth have passed in establishing a context for the emergence of life and the appearance of the human community. With this event the future of planet Earth became in a special manner dependent on the human members of the earth community.

Within this context the student could begin to appreciate something of our human responsibility for the destinies of the entire earth process, even of the universe process. The urgency for this type of a comprehensive course can hardly be exaggerated. Its value is enhanced when we consider that this interpretative context for the universe as well as for human existence is bound in only a minimal way to any prior cultural context. It is available to all the peoples of the world. It is at present the most powerful single intellectual force enabling more than 160 nations present on the earth to communicate with one another in a meaningful way.

This mode of experiencing the unity of the destinies of the universe with our human destiny can serve as a common basis of understanding for both the traditional religious-humanistic teaching and the modern scientific-technological teaching. While in earlier times scientists were unrelenting in their insistence on the mechanistic and purely random aspects of the universe, this is less true of the thinking scientist of the present. So, too, with the religious or humanist personality; while there has frequently been an aversion or an inability to understand the scientific presentation of the universe, there is now a greater appreciation for the imaginative power, the intellectual insight, and the spiritual quality of the scientific vision. The fruitful interaction between the scientific and the religious-humanist vision is our greatest promise for the future as well as the great task of the educator, both in comprehending for oneself and in communicating this vision to future generations of students.

A second course in the proposed curriculum could be a course on the various phases of human cultural development: the Paleolithic phase, the Neolithic village phase, the period of the great religious cultures, the scientific-technological phase, and the emerging ecological phase. This course would enable the student to envisage a comprehensive human development in its historical stages as well as in its cultural differentiation. Students could see the continuity of their own personal development in the prior development of the universe, of the earth, and of all human history. A feeling of identity with the entire human venture could be activated in the student. Thus a person could more easily appreciate the genius of the time when the languages of the human community took shape, when the religions and arts and social forms of the world were developed, when the great humanistic cultures were formed, when the elementary technologies were invented, as well as appreciate how the modern sciences emerged within the European cultural region, and the need now for a new adjustment of human modes of being and activity to the dynamics of the natural world. Such an overview would enable students to discover their personal identity in historical time and cultural space. It would assist the college generation in envisaging the historical mission of the times. This would provide meaning to life that might not otherwise be available.

A third course might deal with the period of the great classical cultures that has dominated human development over the past several thousand years and which has given to the human community its more elaborated patterns of linguistic expression, of religious formation, of spiritual disciplines; its critical understanding in the arts and sciences and literature; its political and social structures; its ethical and legal norms; its advanced craft skills; and its popular recreations.

While these cultures have been widely differentiated in the cultural patterns that cover the planet, they have achieved throughout the Eurasian, American, and African worlds certain basic expressions of the human that seem to be definitive achievements. Even though these expressions will surely be extensively modified in the future, they will always be present in the psychic structure of the human, at least for the foreseeable future. From these cultures the student should learn the powerful impact of the divine, the need for spiritual discipline, the majesty of art, the great literature and music and dance and drama which befits the human mode of being, as well as how to achieve economic well-being through technological skills.

While these traditions are now undergoing the most profound alteration they have experienced since they came into existence, they still account for, and in the immediate future will continue to supply, the main principles of civilized order known to the human community. These traditions are still the most formidable barriers to chaos that the human community possesses. The problem, of course, is that these traditions cannot remain static; they must enter into a new phase of their own history. No longer will each be isolated from the others, no longer will the economies of the various peoples be independent of the others.

One great difficulty of these civilizations, born in a dominant spatial experience of reality, is the difficulty of entering into a dominant evolutionary experience of reality. How to do this and be strengthened rather than disintegrated is the challenge to these cultures and to the societies in which these cultures have found their finest expression.

In different parts of the world, a special emphasis could be given to that special humanist-religious tradition to which the students generally are heirs. Since the American student lives within the humanist traditions of Western society, a certain emphasis needs to be given to this tradition, in all the richness of its development, in its spiritual as well as in its humanistic aspects. A serious understanding of Western traditions becomes especially important when we consider the extent to which the entire world of life and thought and values has been influenced by these Western cultural traditions. The tragedy is that the dark, destructive aspect of Western patriarchal civilization has become virulent just at this time when the influence of the West has become so pervasive throughout the human community and when its technological capacity for plundering the earth has become so overwhelming that all the basic life systems of the planet are being closed down.

A fourth course that might be proposed is the study of the scientific-technological phase of human development, culminating in the awakening of human consciousness to the time sequence in the story of the universe, of the earth, of life, and of the human community. This course should be especially concerned with the power that has come under human control in and through the technological inventions of recent centuries. The consequences of this new power, its helpful and harmful aspects, could be considered along with those social, economic, political, and cultural changes that we have witnessed in the past two centuries.

While this period has so far lasted only a few hundred years, in contrast to the several thousands of years of the classical civilizations, these centuries of science and technology deserve consideration more as a geological age than as a historical period; the topography of the planet, its chemistry, its biological functioning, have been so profoundly altered. This is the age of dominance of the human over the natural; it is also the period when the numinous presence pervading the universe was diminished in human awareness in favor of a dominant preoccupation with human reason, human power, and the sense of the machine as the dominant metaphor for understanding the reality of things.

Yet this is also the period when a profound social consciousness was developed. The globe was affected by political, social, economic, and religious adjustments that have shaken the planet with unique severity. It has been the period of medical advance, of increased human population, of release from many of the physical and social ills of former times.

A fifth course could deal with the emerging ecological age, the age of the growing intercommunion among all the living and nonliving systems of the planet, and even of the universe entire. A study of this age should concern itself with reestablishing the human within its natural context. Above all, it should deal with the integral functioning of the biosphere, the healing of the damage already done to the dynamics of the earth, the fostering of a renewable economic order by integration of the human within the ever-renewing cycles of the natural world as they are sustained by solar energy.

This course might also deal with the renewal of all human roles and all human institutions within this context, after the adventurism of the former period, which was dominated by the mechanistic and exploitive processes of science, technology, industry, manufacturing, and commerce.

Law in this new ecological context would function with a greater sense of the inherent rights of natural realities, that is, the rights of living beings to exist and not be abused or wantonly used or exterminated, whether directly or indirectly, by exploitive human processes. Consideration of natural beings simply as physical or material realities would be recognized as an inadequate or false perception, or even a criminal perception if made the basis of action.

Medicine in this context would envisage the earth as primary healer. It would also envisage integration with earth's functioning as the primary basis of health for the human being. The role of the physician would be to assist in interpreting the earth-human relationship and guiding the human community in its intercommunion with the earth, with its air and water and sunlight, with its nourishment and the opportunity it offers for the expression of human physical capacities.

Religion would perceive the natural world as the primary revelation of the divine, as primary scripture, as the primary mode of numinous presence. Christian religion would cease its antagonism toward the earth and discover its sacred quality.

Commerce would recognize that a base exploitation of the planet—the poisoning of earth, air, and water—cannot be justified as an acceptable mode of commercial or industrial activity. It is ultimately self-destructive for commerce as well as for the human community and constitutes an ultimate blasphemy against a sacred reality. The entire system of bookkeeping needs to be revised to bring it out of its fictional context into some relation with reality by including the cost to environment, the invaluable nature of irreplaceable resources, the awareness of the need to integrate the entire industrial-commercial enterprise with the ever-renewing cycle of the natural world.

These are a few of the issues that give urgency to courses on the ecological age. Mainly these courses should envisage activities already taking place, or in preparation, to establish centers of human occupation in terms of biocultural regions, that is, identifiable geographical regions where the economic and cultural life of the human social group would be established in relation to the geological structure, the living forms, and the climatic conditions of a given place.

A sixth course could be a course on the origin and identification of values. This course would seek to discover within our experience of the universe just what can be a foundation for values. Such a foundation for values should supply in our times what was supplied in medieval times by the doctrine of natural law. This becomes especially urgent since we no longer accept the earlier doctrine of the fixed nature of things, which in former times determined the natural goodness or evil of things or actions. Obviously we cannot simply transpose values from the medieval to the modern period. We need to discover the values indicated by reality itself as we experience it.

In terms of the educational process as we have been discussing

105

it, we will find these values in the self-emergent processes of the universe, which are the self-governing processes of the universe and also the value manifestations of the universe. The universe emerges as a differentiation process. Without differentiation there is no universe, there is no existent reality. From the beginning, after its brief period of almost formless radiation, the universe articulated itself in unique, identifiable, intelligible energy constellations, or patterns. Reality is not some infinitely extended homogeneous smudge. Each articulation is unrepeatable and irreplaceable at whatever level, from the subatomic to the galactic, from the iron core of the earth to the flower, from the eagle in flight to the human persons who walk over the land. Each of these is a unique expression of the total earth presence. At the human level the individual becomes almost a species, the unique quality of the individual becomes such a commanding presence. This, then, is the first value.

The second value is subjectivity. Not only is the articulation of the individual reality so absolute in reference to otherness, this identity carries with it an interior depth, a special quality, a mystery that expresses not only a phenomenal mode, but also an archetypal realization. This enables each articulation of the real to resonate with that numinous mystery that pervades all the world. This quality of things is universal, but its activation in the human order provides the creative dynamics of the thinker, the poet, the writer, the scientist, the farmer, the craftsman, the political leader, the trader, the educator, and whichever other role is fulfilled by human beings in the functioning of the universe.

A third basis of value is communion, for every reality of the universe is intimately present to every other reality of the universe and finds its fulfillment in this mutual presence. The entire evolutionary process depends on communion. Without this fulfillment that each being finds in beings outside itself, nothing would ever happen in the entire world. There would be no elements, no molecules, no life, no consciousness.

This law of communion finds its most elementary expression

in the law of gravitation whereby every physical being in the universe attracts and is attracted to every other physical being in the universe. Gravitation at this elementary level finds an ascending sequence of realizations through the variety of lifeforms and their modes of generation up to human affection in its most entrancing forms.

The universality and intensity of this communion indicate its immense value. But even more evident is the fact that human survival depends so immediately and absolutely on this capacity for intimate human relationships, a capacity that requires a high level of human development for its proper human fulfillment. Thus, the need for extensive interior discipline and development if this value is to be realized in any satisfying human form.

One of the difficulties experienced by the human, one of the causes of our planetary, human, and educational disarray, is that we have not adequately developed this capacity for communion. We have been especially delinquent in fulfilling this law of communion in relation to the natural world, a failure that this proposed college program is intended to remedy.

Much else might be said here. I will end, however, with a view that the first college to announce that its entire program is grounded in the dynamics of the earth as a self-emerging, self-sustaining, self-educating, self-governing, self-healing, and self-fulfilling community of all the living and nonliving beings of the planet should have an extraordinary future.

Professional education should be based on awareness that the earth is itself the primary physician, primary lawgiver, primary revelation of the divine, primary scientist, primary technologist, primary commercial venture, primary artist, primary educator, and primary agent in whichever other activity we find in human affairs.

General education should likewise be explained on the basis of the courses that have been suggested. These could provide the cultural and historical context that students need to provide for themselves a functional identity.

Business education also should be grounded in this appreciation of the dynamics of the planet. The great need of the commercial-industrial-financial world is to escape from the inflationary processes that it has imposed upon the planet by wanton exploitation of both renewable and nonrenewable resources and by the excessive pressures it has exerted to force the earth to produce renewable resources beyond what the earth can reasonably bring forth on a sustainable basis. Business has a great mission to fulfill in establishing a viable economy for the human community by integrating the human economy within the renewable cycles of earth economy.

Liberal arts, the humanities, as they are called, can experience a grand renewal within this context. The deeply felt antipathies between the sciences and the humanities could be eliminated. The amazing new discovery by science of the story of the universe would be recognized as a supreme humanistic achievement and as providing a basis for the further expansion of all the traditional humanistic cultures.

The educational process itself would have through this program a cultural, historical, and cosmological context of meaning that can be accepted on a broad scale by persons of different ethnic and cultural backgrounds. Within this context the American college could understand in some depth its role in creating a future worthy of that larger universal community of beings out of which the human component emerged and in which the human community finds its proper fulfillment.

·9·

Christian
Spirituality and the
American Experience

The American experience can be presented in terms of enlightenment philosophy, post-Reformation Christianity, scientific competence, technological skill, commercial drive, and military might—all
let loose on what might be the richest, most benign, surely one
of the most beautiful and unspoiled, continents. After some four
centuries of the American experience, we have before us a still
beautiful and abundant land, but a land of roads and automobiles
and grimy cities, a land of acid rainfall, polluted rivers and endangered species, a land extensively plundered of its forests and
its mineral resources, a land with its human inhabitants somewhat
bewildered and rebellious against their role as the great consumer
people of earth.

Much has happened in these centuries; glory and wealth and

knowledge and power such as these have never been known before. Yet after these few centuries, we find ourselves on a continent impoverished and toxic beyond our capacities for renewal or purification. It's a story too confused to tell, the story of the American experience, although it is as exciting as any story of a comparable period of time. The Roman story is not greater, nor is the Chinese story, nor the story of any of the great classical ages. Indeed, the American story has about it a magnitude and a meaning that baffles all our efforts at understanding. Such power, such ideals of human freedom, such commercial cunning, such a sense of historical destiny—all are brought together in an attempt to bring the entire world into the millennial age.

Looking at America simply as historical drama, we can contemplate the human venture in one of its most spectacular phases. From the beginning the resources of the continent and the possibilities of life on this continent were to be activated. The land and everything on the land and under the land were to be transformed. Nothing was to be left in its primordial state. The view of Francis Bacon that human intelligence had as its primary purpose the understanding and control of nature found its fulfillment here.

We might reflect on the causes for this and its meaning and the relation it bears to traditional Christian spirituality and to the emerging spirituality of the future. Strangely enough, perhaps, we might consider the American experience itself as one of the great spiritualities. In this manner we could speak of three spiritualities: the traditional Christian spirituality, the more recent American spirituality, and the emerging spirituality that is the challenge of our present generation.

I have referred to the destructive aspect of the American experience because public spiritualities generally have a turbulent aspect, and I am primarily interested in public spirituality, which I describe as "the functional values and their means of attainment in an identifiable human community." This public spirituality is, I think, much more significant than the cultivated spirituality of

110

marginal groups or individuals engaged in intensive prayer and meditation apart from the dynamics of the larger human community. Their lives and their guidance are of significant import for the human venture, but the ultimate spiritual issues are those dealt with in the cruel and compassionate world of active human existence, in the marketplace, in the halls of justice and injustice, in the places where the populace lives and works and suffers and dies. The glory of an earlier period, as described by Paul Claudel, was the medieval cathedral that arched over the crossroads of the world, with all its surging energies of good and evil, whereas in later times the ideal of religion and spirituality frequently encountered is more that of the withdrawn place of worship, a place reflecting more personal intimacy than marketplace turmoil, a place of undisturbed goodness and divine presence. This is true even when extensive efforts are made in the evangelical tradition of mercy and social justice.

Even while we locate the area of our discussion as that of public spirituality, I would like to indicate that any realistic discussion of our subject must take place in the context of the supreme historical event of recent times: the discovery of a new origin story, the story of the universe as emergent evolutionary process over some fifteen billion years, a story that now provides our sense of where we are in the total context of the universe development. Our new consciousness of the universe and of the planet Earth can be understood as a revelatory experience of universal significance for the human community and for every phase of human activity.

So significant is this new story of the universe and so great its power for altering the structure and functioning of the earth that this event can be compared only with such changes as the great geological, climatic, or biological changes of the past. The earth itself has been disturbed in a manner never before known in the course of human history. The only comparable events in human history are events such as those when the great religions came into being. This is the order of magnitude of the change that is taking

111

place, although its effects are still delayed and its major impact is still to be recognized throughout most areas of life. This is to be expected of an event so momentous in its significance.

Presently we are caught in a transitional situation; our own experience of the universe as it comes to us through scientific observation and inquiry has given us the power that enables us to journey into space and to visit the moon. We can pick out of the surrounding air thousands of radio messages. We can hear presently, through microwave radiation, the sound of the early emergent universe back through some billions of years. We can devastate the earth with nuclear explosives. All this and much more could be listed, including our amazing capacity to understand and even to alter genetic coding. Yet with such a magical world as we have made, or discovered, we have no functional cosmology to guide and discipline our human use of all this knowledge and skill and all these energy resources.

We really do not understand the new story of the universe or its meaning. We have the scientific data. We can perform the magic. But the scientists themselves seldom manifest any sense whatsoever of what it all means. Interpretation compromises scientific inquiry. Indeed, during the great period of scientific inquiry after Newton, cosmology as a study diminished considerably in importance. Analytical processes alone provided true knowledge. After some centuries of neglect, scientific cosmology has come back into the area of serious consideration. Yet we are still probing our way into this subject, just as we are trying to comprehend the historical and human meaning of technology, how it relates to the biosphere, and its role in the total earth process. The limitations in our intellectual competence in regard to these critical issues are astounding, as they occur in scientists, technologists, and commercial persons.

The real tragedy, however, is that religious and spiritual persons themselves remain unaware of their need to provide for themselves and for the society a more significant evaluation of this larger context of our lives. On both sides, the scientific and the religious, there is a naiveté that is ruinous to the human community, to the essential functioning of the biosphere, and eventually disastrous to the earth itself.

While the positive aspects of Western spirituality can be seen throughout the American experience, there are also the negative, alienating, and even destructive aspects of these same spiritual traditions. That traditional Western spiritualities have not enabled their followers to mitigate or even to understand or protest the terrifying assault of American society on the natural world is evidence of a certain incompetence or lack of understanding in these traditions.

It might not be too much to say that our spiritual traditions not only provided much of the context in which this assault became possible, but they also provided a positive, if often indirect, support for this process. Without this background the course of the American experience might well have been quite different from what it has been. We must, however, be constantly aware that the American experience has resulted from a complex of forces and conditions beyond human calculation. We are not proposing that traditional spirituality is the only force involved, only that it is a pervasive force of great significance in understanding the total process.

When we inquire into the reasons for this inefficacy in our spiritual traditions, we might observe that our identification of the divine as transcendent to the natural world makes a direct human-divine covenant relationship possible, but also we negate the natural world as the locus for the meeting of the divine and the human. The natural world becomes less capable of communicating divine presence. This makes possible the conception of the natural world as merely external object.

A further difficulty results from our insistence that the human is a spiritual being with an eternal destiny which is beyond that of the other members of the created world. We were related to the divine by a special covenant. Our sense of being integral members of the earth community was severely weakened through both of these commitments. We thought that we were elevating the human when in reality we were alienating ourselves from the only context in which human life has any satisfying meaning.

A third difficulty came later, when not only the divine and the human were taken away from intimate presence to the natural world, but also when the inner principle of life in natural beings was taken away in the Cartesian period. The concept of crass matter emerged as mere extension, capable only of externally manipulated and mechanistic activity. We entered onto a mechanistic phase in our thinking and in our basic norms of reality and value. If this has proved to be enormously effective in its short-term achievements, it has been disastrous in its long-term consequences.

Another significant factor in the American experience is found in the Christian doctrine of an infrahistorical millennial age of peace, justice, and abundance to be infallibly attained in the unfolding of the redemptive order. This concept of the millennium is different from the idea of utopia, from that of paradise, and from that of arcadia. Utopia is an ideal model for human society that is never expected to be achieved in itself, but only to outline basic forms of human life and to assist in thinking through their functioning in the social and personal order. Paradise is that transcendent beatitude expressed in intimate forms of bodily and spiritual delight. Arcadia is a quiet pastoral ideal that comes down to us from Roman times and is associated with a certain serene, if poignant, sense of existence in a garden apart from the tragic world of time. While the millennium was originally considered as a spiritual condition to be brought about infallibly by divine providence, it was later interpreted simply as an age of human fulfillment to be brought about by human effort and human skill in exploiting the resources of the earth.

All of these ideals influenced America, although the millennial drive is the strongest. When this millennial age did not appear by divine grace, the American people felt an obligation to raise it up by human effort. This is the original dynamism of American political and economic life. It also provided the deeper inspiration of science and technology. Commercial and political programs as well as universal education were all means to millennial transformation of the earth.

Just as the doctrine of divine transcendence took away the pervasive divine presence to the natural world, so the millennial vision of a blessed future left all present modes of existence in a degraded status. All things were in an unholy condition. Everything needed to be transformed. This meant that anything unused was to be used if the very purpose of its existence was to be realized. Nothing in its natural state was acceptable.

This compulsion to use, to consume, has found its ultimate expression in our own times, when the ideal is to take the natural resources from the earth and transform them by industrial processes for consumption by a society that lives on ever-heightened rates of consumption. That consumption has something sacred about it is obvious from the central position it now occupies. This is all quite clear from the relentless advertising campaigns designed to convince the society that there is neither peace nor joy, neither salvation nor paradise, except through heightened consumption.

The sense of an untouched world, of primordial wilderness as divine presence to be left undisturbed by human interference, survived in a few persons such as Henry Thoreau and John Muir; but these were exceptional instances. Only such as these were aware that the diminishment of the grandeur and fertility of the natural world was not simply an economic loss, but also a weakening of the entire biosphere, elimination of a profound psychic experience, restriction of imaginative power, and ultimately the loss of unique modes of divine presence. Yet while Thoreau's and Muir's teachings were read with a certain respect, American determination to eliminate natural modes of being continued as the dominant attitude of the society.

The instrument for this was a technology that was also transcen-

115

dent, that is, a technology for which the natural world had no adequate limiting power. This phase of human cunning was too much for nature. The basic law of nature is that every expansive life force should have arrayed against it limiting forces that would prevent any single force or combination of forces from suffocating the other members of the life community. This law could not operate effectively in confrontation with these new technologies, although the natural world might eventually overwhelm human perpetrators with their own waste products, leading to a progressive degrading of the human quality of life.

The argument of Lynn White that the historical roots of this ecological disturbance lie in the deepest sources of Western spiritual tradition could be quite easily critiqued if we consider only its limited consequences. This has been done by René Dubos, who rightly points out that all the classical cultures abused their land and devastated their environment. Yet none of these other traditions had the millennial entrancement or the technological skills that exist in our Western religious traditions. This is what makes the devastation within our world so terrifying in its consequences.

Yet few, if any, apparently, could see that the ultimate basis of our ecological difficulties lay in our spirituality itself, as it has come down through the centuries, a situation that could be remedied only by a more intimate human association with the natural world in its evolutionary unfolding. There is no need to argue that the spirituality being taught was not the authentic tradition, that an earlier, pure, more valid, more integral tradition existed wherein these defective tendencies did not exist, that this earlier tradition would in time prevail in a spontaneous purifying reaction. This may be true, but it is difficult to accept a pure unspoiled form of any tradition.

There is, in this sense, no fixed identifiable religious or spiritual system. By definition any "tradition" is a process, not some established, contained, unchanging mode of believing, thinking, or acting. There is no definitive Christianity or Hinduism or Buddhism,

116

but only an identifiable Christian process, Hindu process, or Buddhist process. The historical reality is the reality of the tradition. All traditions have their grandeur and their limitations, their luminous and their dark aspects, their successes and their failures. These tend to be correlative. The specific mode of grandeur makes possible a corresponding mode of failure. Discipline can generally be associated with indulgence. What is important here is to recognize that traditions must constantly go beyond any existing expression of themselves to new forms of expression.

The time has come for the most significant change that Christian spirituality has yet experienced, but this change is itself part of a much more comprehensive change in human consciousness brought about by the discovery of the evolutionary process. Discovery of this unfolding process of the universe can be considered a moment of supreme significance not only for the human community, but also for the universe itself, especially in its expression on the earth as the only biospiritual planet that we know.

Just as the human body took its shape through some fourteen billion years of effort on the part of the universe and through some four and a half billion years of earth existence, so the human psychic structure and our spirituality have been taking shape over all these billions of years, beginning with the primordial atomic particles which held within themselves the destinies of all that has followed, even the spiritual shaping of the human. The formation of our psychic structure, originating at this mysterious level far beyond rational or empirical penetration, takes further shape in our genetic coding, but even more completely in the cultural coding that the human community has established.

In the period of the great classical religious civilizations, an extraordinary sense of the divine coexisted with a sense of social hierarchy, with sacrificial rituals, revelatory experience, and interior spiritual disciplines whereby the human activated the deepest level of its being. This cultural-spiritual phase was so fully developed, so powerful in its coding, so effective in its communication of this coding to successive generations, that any significant change in the future would of necessity appear as destructive, immoral, heretical, anarchistic. Any significant alteration of the knowing process would be seen as illogical and irrational.

Thus when we now look back at the earlier forms of our traditions, we can see a kind of a priori necessity for the scientific venture of the next period to appear as a needless destructive process that could only end in a devastating period for the human venture. There has indeed been sufficient groping into the new age, sufficient devastation to satisfy the adverse judgment invoked upon this new age, with its emphasis on scientific observation, quantitative measurement, mathematical reasoning, also with its aversion to hierarchy in favor of the democratic, its neglect of faith in favor of reason, its exaltation of technology as the instrument for the conquest of nature, its insistence on individual freedom.

Once the scientific-technological period established itself, however, the intensity of its own dedication to its objectives took on the characteristics of a religious attitude and of a spiritual discipline parallel with the religious dedication and spiritual discipline of the classical religious cultures that preceded it. This included a new sense of orthodoxy, a new dogmatic integrity not to be challenged by reasonable persons. Yet, as mentioned previously, neither the creators of this new situation nor the spiritual personalities of the period have known how to read the change that has taken place.

The full extent of the change escapes us perhaps because we have mistaken its order of magnitude. The proposition can be defended that these centuries of science and technology should be considered more as a geological age rather than simply as a historical period since we have, through our technology, within a few generations altered the planet in its physical structure and the biosphere in its most basic functioning on a scale that formerly took one hundred or two hundred million years. Much of this change has been destructive.

Yet this was seen by its human agents as a sublime human-spiritual accomplishment. These agents could, of course, see only what the cultural coding of the scientific-technological age permitted them to see, since our cultural coding establishes the perimeters of our values and our patterns of action. The negative side of our cultural determinations is generally hidden from consciousness. In this sense the culture depends on what might be called an altered state of consciousness, a trance state.

The industrial-commercial mode of consciousness in our society has coexisted with a traditional spiritual coding in the pattern of Western classical spirituality. These two patterns cause little trouble to each other because neither the modern scientific mode of consciousness nor our spiritual consciousness is concerned with the integral functioning of the earth community. Indeed, both modes of consciousness experience the human as Olympian ruler of the planet, the planet as naturalistic functioning, and earth's resources as objects for unlimited human exploitation.

We now begin to realize, however, that the planet Earth will not long endure being despised or ignored in its more integral being, whether by scientists, technologists, or saints; nor will it submit forever to the abuse it has had to endure. Already the earth is taking away the oxygen we breathe, the purity of the rain, our protection from cosmic rays, the careful balance of our climate, the fruitfulness of the soil. Finally we begin to recover a reverence for the material out of which we were born, for the nourishing context that sustains us, the sounds and scenery, the warmth of the wind and the coolness of the water—all of which delight us and purify us and communicate to us some sense of sacred presence. In the twentieth century this reverent attention hardly exists, nor can it exist in any vital mode until the spirituality of the new ecological age begins to function with some efficacy.

What might be proposed here is that one of the historical roles now being assigned to our generation is the role of creating, in its main outlines, the spiritual context of the ecological age, the next great cultural coding that is presently taking on its effective form.

Yet all peoples are ultimately involved in this new cultural coding, for the scientific basis of the new origin story is now being accepted as the context for education everywhere on the planet. For the first time in its history, the human community has a single origin story whereby it establishes its identity in the vast reaches of space and time.

The greatest single need at present is the completion of the story, as told in its physical dimensions by science, by the more integral account that includes the numinous and consciousness dimensions of the emergent universe from its primordial moment. Once that is done, a meaningful universe, a functional cosmology, is available as a foundation for the total range of human activities in the ecological age.

America should have a special affinity for this new cultural coding since American society has experienced so extensively the creative possibilities and the limitations of both the classical-religious and the scientific-technological periods. Now is the time to establish a cultural coding grounded in the intercommunion of all the living and nonliving components of the universe.

This universe itself, but especially the planet Earth, needs to be experienced as the primary mode of divine presence, just as it is the primary educator, primary healer, primary commercial establishment, and primary lawgiver for all that exists within this life community. The basic spirituality communicated by the natural world can also be considered as normative for the future ecological age. This spirituality is grounded in the basic characteristics of the universe as manifested from the beginning: the unique and irreplaceable qualities of the individual and the inseparable bonding with every other being in the universe. These constitute the ultimate basis of a functional spirituality for the human community just as they constitute the functional cosmology of the human community.

The interrelatedness of the universe in its every manifestation is what establishes the unity of the entire world and enables it to be a "universe." Every atomic particle is immediately present to every other atomic particle in a manner that enables us to say that the volume of each atom is the volume of the universe. This mutual presence is the immediate cause for the unfolding of the universe in the full complexity of its living and nonliving forms. Without such intercommunion nothing would ever happen. In this sense the gravitational attraction which holds every being in its identity and its relatedness finds its fulfillment in the meeting of individuals in the world of the living and in the full expression of affection at the level of human consciousness.

Here, too, we find the sublime expression of the deepest mystery of the universe: the revelation of the divine. To deepen this experience of the divine is one of the purposes of all spiritual discipline and of all spiritual experience. This sense of communion at the heart of reality is the central force bringing the ecological age into existence. Thus the birth of a new overwhelming spiritual experience at this moment of earth history.

To restore a sense of the earth as matrix of the human, as primary norm of all human values and activities, is a difficult change, but one which cannot but have its own validation in confrontation with the devastating consequences of the existing mode of cultural coding. This new coding, which might be designated as "ecological," might better be designated simply as a "functional cosmology." The integration sought is not simply an ideal put forward as an abstract goal, but as a process that is already taking place throughout America. It is presently the most vital phase of the American experience. Hundreds, even thousands, of movements in this direction are already taking place in every phase of American life: in law and medicine, in agriculture, in architecture, in commerce and industry, in education.

Some awareness for the wide range of activities that is supporting this new coding can be obtained by paging through the book by Marilyn Ferguson, *The Aquarian Conspiracy,* a work that surveys the transforming movements already taking place throughout the world, and especially in America.

Many religious and spiritual persons are beginning to understand the new context of their own future development as members of the planetary community, although Christian theologians and scripture scholars generally have so far remained unaffected in their study by the altered context of contemporary existence. Overattachment to the salvific role of our spiritual traditions seems to prevent any serious inquiry into a creation-oriented spirituality within the context of our present mode of experiencing the universe.

Soon, however, we can expect a change. The imperatives of life and thought are too urgent for us to remain at the present impasse. As the Fathers of the church gave a new expansiveness to Christianity through their association of Christian belief with Platonic philosophy, as Augustine and Dionysus gave a higher spiritual vision to Christianity through the insights of Neoplatonism, as Thomas gave new vigor to the Christian faith through his interpretation of Aristotle, so now a new vision and a new vigor are available to Christian tradition through our modern understanding of the origin and development of the universe and the emerging ecological age. If creating this new cultural coding of the ecological age is the next phase of the American experience, creating a spirituality integral with this coding may well be the next phase of the Christian tradition.

·10·

The New Story

It's all a question of story. We are in trouble just now because we do not have a good story. We are in between stories. The old story, the account of how the world came to be and how we fit into it, is no longer effective. Yet we have not learned the new story. Our traditional story of the universe sustained us for a long period of time. It shaped our emotional attitudes, provided us with life purposes, and energized action. It consecrated suffering and integrated knowledge. We awoke in the morning and knew where we were. We could answer the questions of our children. We could identify crime, punish transgressors. Everything was taken care of because the story was there. It did not necessarily make people good, nor did it take away the pains and stupidities of life or make for unfailing warmth in human association. It did provide a context in which life could function in a meaningful manner.

Presently this traditional story is dysfunctional in its larger social dimensions, even though some believe it firmly and act according to its guidance. Aware of the dysfunctional aspects of the traditional program, some persons have moved on into different, often new-age, orientations, which have consistently proved ineffective in dealing with our present life situation. Even with advanced science and technology, with superb techniques in manufacturing and commerce, in communications and computation, our secular society remains without satisfactory meaning or the social discipline needed for a life leading to emotional, aesthetic, and spiritual fulfillment. Because of this lack of satisfaction many persons are returning to a religious fundamentalism. But that, too, can be seen as inadequate to supply the values for sustaining our needed social discipline.

A radical reassessment of the human situation is needed, especially concerning those basic values that give to life some satisfactory meaning. We need something that will supply in our times what was supplied formerly by our traditional religious story. If we are to achieve this purpose, we must begin where everything begins in human affairs—with the basic story, our narrative of how things came to be, how they came to be as they are, and how the future can be given some satisfying direction. We need a story that will educate us, a story that will heal, guide, and discipline us.

Western society did have, in its traditional story of the universe, an agreed-upon functioning story up until somewhere around the fourteenth century. This religion-based story originated in a revelatory experience some three thousand years ago. According to this story, the original harmony of the universe was broken by a primordial human fault, and that necessitated formation of a believing redemptive community that would take shape through the course of time. Human history was moving infallibly toward its fulfillment in the peace of a reconstituted paradise.

This religious story was integrated with the Ptolemaic account of the universe and how it functioned, an abiding universe that endlessly renewed itself and its living forms through the seasonal sequence of time. The introduction of irreversible historical time onto this abiding cosmological scene is precisely the contribution of the Western religious tradition. However severe the turbulent moments of history through the late classical and early medieval periods, these at least took place within a secure natural world and within a fixed context of interpretation. Whatever the problems were, they were not problems concerning the basic human or spiritual values that were at stake. Those were clear.

The confusion and insecurity that we presently experience originated, to a large extent, in the fourteenth century when Europe experienced the plague known as the Black Death. Without making this event a simplistic explanation of all later history, we can say that it was a transition period. Even more, it was a central traumatic moment in Western history. It is estimated that this plague, which reached Europe in 1347, had by 1349 killed off perhaps one-third of the population. Almost half of the people of Florence died within a three-month period. Throughout the later fourteenth century there was a population decline in the whole of Europe. In London the last of the great plagues was in 1665.

In response to the plague and to other social disturbances of the fourteenth and fifteenth centuries, two directions of development can be identified—one toward a religious redemption out of the tragic world, the other toward greater control of the physical world to escape its pain and to increase its utility to human society. From these two tendencies the two dominant cultural communities of recent centuries were formed: the believing religious community and the secular community with its new scientific knowledge and its industrial powers of exploiting the natural world.

Since the people of these centuries had no knowledge of germs and thus no explanation of the plague, other than divine judgment on a wicked world, the answers most generally sought were in the moral and spiritual order, frequently outside the orthodox teachings of the church. The believing community in its various sectarian

125

expressions had recourse to supernatural forces, to the spirit world, to the renewal of esoteric traditions, and sometimes to pre-Christian beliefs and rituals that had been neglected in their deeper dynamics since the coming of Christianity. Even within traditional Christianity there was an intensification of the faith experience, an effort to activate supernatural forces with special powers of intervention in the phenomenal world now viewed as threatening to the human community. The sense of human depravity increased. The need for an outpouring of influences from the higher numinous world was intensified. Faith dominated the religious experience. Redemption mystique became the overwhelming form of Christian experience.

Such excessive emphasis on redemption, to the neglect of the revelatory import of the natural world, had from the beginning been one of the possibilities in Christian development. The creed itself is overbalanced in favor of redemption. Thus the integrity of the Christian story is affected. Creation becomes increasingly less important. This response, with its emphasis on redemptive spirituality, continued through the religious upheavals of the sixteenth century and on through the Puritanism and Jansenism of the seventeenth century. This attitude was further strengthened by the shock of the Enlightenment and Revolution periods of the eighteenth and nineteenth centuries.

The American version of the ancient Christian story has functioned well in its institutional efficiency and in its moral efficacy, but it is no longer the story of the earth. Nor is it the integral story of the human community. It is a sectarian story. At its center there is an intensive preoccupation with the personality of the Savior, with the interior spiritual life of the faithful, and with the salvific community. The difficulty is that we came to accept this situation as the normal, even the desirable, thing.

The other response to the Black Death was the reaction that led eventually to the scientific secular community of our times. That reaction sought to remedy earthly terror not by supernatural or

126

religious powers, but by understanding and controlling the earth process. Although those working in that trend were at first committed to the esoteric wisdom traditions and to Platonic idealism, they did emphasize the need for empirical examination of the phenomenal world and its expression in quantitative terms. Scientific inquiry became the controlling human preoccupation, pushed by obscure forces in the unconscious depths of Western culture. The telescope and microscope were invented. Calculus, the supreme instrument of modern science, was discovered. A scientific priesthood came to govern the thought life of our society. We looked at the earth in its physical reality and projected new theories of how it functioned. The celestial bodies were scrutinized more intently, the phenomenon of light was examined, new ways of understanding energy evolved. New sciences emerged. The *Novum Organum* of Francis Bacon appeared in 1620, the *Principia* of Isaac Newton in 1687, the *Scienza Nuova* of Giambattista Vico in 1725.

All of these led to an awareness that the human mind was advancing. This in turn led to the Enlightenment period of the eighteenth century and to the sense of absolute progress of the human mind as expressed by Condorcet in his 1793 volume entitled *Historical Survey of the Progress of the Human Mind.* In the nineteenth century the doctrines of social development appear with Fourier, Saint-Simon, and August Comte. Karl Marx brought this movement to its most realistic expression in his 1848 *Manifesto.*

While these changes in the mode of human perception and of social structure were taking place, evidence was appearing in the realms of geology and paleontology indicating that there was a time sequence in the very formation of the earth and of all lifeforms upon the earth. The earth was not the eternal, fixed, abiding reality that it had been thought to be. It suddenly dawned upon Western consciousness that earlier lifeforms were of a simpler nature than later lifeforms, that the later forms were derived from the earlier forms. The complex of life manifestations had not existed from the beginning by some external divine creative act setting all things

127

in their place. The earth in all its parts, especially in its lifeforms, was in a state of continuing transformation.

Discovery of this life sequence, with an explanation of how it came about, found expression in Darwin's *Origin of Species* in 1859. After Darwin, the physicists in their study of light and radiation came almost simultaneously to an understanding of the infra-atomic world and the entire galactic system. Insight into both the microphase and macrophase of the phenomenal world was obtained, and the great unity of the universe became apparent both in its spatial expansion and its time sequence.

Just at that moment, however, a sudden shift in the mode of consciousness took place. The scientists suddenly became aware that the opaqueness of matter had dissolved. Science was ultimately not the objective grasping of some reality extrinsic to ourselves. It was rather a moment of subjective communion in which the human was seen as that being in whom the universe in its evolutionary dimension became conscious of itself.

Thus a new creation story had evolved in the secular scientific community, equivalent in our times to the creation stories of antiquity. This creation story differs from the traditional Eurasian creation stories much more than those traditional stories differ one from another. This new creation story seems destined to become the universal story taught to every child who receives formal education in its modern form anywhere in the world.

The redemptive believing community, first dazzled by this new vision of developmental time, then frustrated by an inability to cope with the new data, lapsed unenthusiastically into its traditional attitudes. In recent centuries, indeed, the believing community has not been concerned with any cosmology, ancient or modern, for the believing community has its real values concentrated in the Savior, the human person, the believing church, and a postearthly paradisal beatitude.

There is, however, a surviving cosmology in which the redemption story takes place and which to some extent still plays a role in the Christian story. According to this story the cosmos, and every

128

being in the cosmos, reflects the divine examplar considered by Plato as the Agathon, the Good; by Plotinus as the One; by the Christian as God. All things are beautiful by this beauty. The supremely beautiful is the integrity and harmony of the total cosmic order, as Saint Thomas insists upon repeatedly.

The human mind ascends to the contemplation of the divine by rising through the various grades of being, from the physical forms of existence in the earth, with its mountains and seas, to the various forms of living things, and so to the human mode of consciousness, then to the soul, and from the inner life of the soul to God. This sequence, portrayed first in the *Symposium* of Plato, is presented in all its sublime qualities in the soliloquy of Augustine as he meditated with his mother by the window just prior to her death. So Bonaventure could write on the reduction of all the arts and sciences to theology, for all eventually depend upon the divine reference. So, too, the journey of Dante through the various spheres of reality up to the divine vision in itself. Initiation into the basic human and Christian values was initiation into this cosmology. Christian spirituality was built up in this manner. The mysteries of Christianity were integral with this cosmology.

The difficulty with this cosmology is that it presents the world simply as an ordered complex of beings that are ontologically related as an image of the divine. It does not present the world as a continuing process of emergence in which there is an inner organic bond of descent of each reality from an earlier reality.

Yet in their functional roles neither this traditional cosmology nor the new scientific cosmology has been of serious religious concern because of the shift in the Western religious tradition from a dominant creation mystique to a dominant redemption mystique. This Christian redemptive mystique is little concerned with the natural world. The essential thing is redemption out of the world through a personal savior relationship that transcends all such concerns. Even the earlier mystical experiences of ascending to the divine through the realms of created perfection are diminished.

Presently this excessive redemptive emphasis is played out. It cannot effectively dynamize activity in time because it is an inadequate story of time. The redemption story has grown apart not only from the historical story, but also from the earth story. Consequently an isolated spiritual power has eventuated that is being victimized by entropy.

If this is the impasse of the believing redemption community of America, the impasse of the secular scientific community, committed to a developmental universe, is the commitment to the realm of the physical to the exclusion of the spiritual. This has been the tough, the realistic, position. The Darwinian principle of natural selection involves no psychic or conscious purpose, but is instead a struggle for earthly survival that gives to the world its variety of form and function. Because this story presents the universe as a random sequence of physical and biological interactions with no inherent meaning, the society supported by this vision has no adequate way of identifying any spiritual or moral values.

We must not think that these two communities have no regard for each other. Extensive courtesies are extended; cooperation is offered. Persons in the scientific professions as well as in modern industrial and commercial pursuits have extensive regard for the religious dimension of life. Many are themselves religious personalities. Those in the religious community have their own esteem for scientific, technological, and commercial activities. Training in the professions takes place in religious schools and even dominates the curriculum. So what's the fuss about? The answer is that surface agreement is not depth communion or the basis of sound cosmic-earth-human values. The antagonisms are deeper than they appear. An integral story has not emerged, and no community can exist without a unifying story. This is precisely why the communication between these two is so unsatisfying. No sustaining values have emerged. Our social problems are not resolved. The earth continues to disintegrate under the plundering assault of humans.

Both traditions are trivialized. The human venture remains stuck in its impasse. Children who begin their earth studies or life studies do not experience any numinous aspect of these subjects. The excitement of existence is diminished. If this fascination, this entrancement, with life is not evoked, the children will not have the psychic energies needed to sustain the sorrows inherent in the human condition. They might never discover their true place in the vast world of time and space. Teaching children about the natural world should be treated as one of the most important events in their lives. Children need a story that will bring personal meaning together with the grandeur and meaning of the universe. The secular school as presently constituted cannot provide the mystique that should be associated with this story. Nor can the religious-oriented school that has only superficially adopted this new story of the universe evoke this experience in the child.

The tragedy of this situation is that schooling now fulfills a role in our society that is similar to the role of initiation ceremonies in earlier tribal societies. In those societies the essential mystery communicated to the youthful initiates was the story of the universe in its awesome and numinous aspects. The capacity for communing with and absorbing into their own beings these deeper powers of the natural world was bestowed on them. The pathos in our own situation is that our secular society does not see the numinous quality or the deeper psychic powers associated with its own story, while the religious society rejects the story because it is presented only in its physical aspect. The remedy for this is to establish a deeper understanding of the spiritual dynamics of the universe as revealed through our own empirical insight into the mysteries of its functioning.

In this late twentieth century that can now be done with a clarity never before available to us. Empirical inquiry into the universe reveals that from its beginning in the galactic system to its earthly expression in human consciousness the universe carries within itself a psychic-spiritual as well as a physical-material dimension. Otherwise human consciousness emerges out of nowhere. The human is seen as an addendum or an intrusion and thus finds no real place in the story of the universe. In reality the human activates the most profound dimension of the universe itself, its capacity to reflect on and celebrate itself in conscious self-awareness.

So far, however, spiritually oriented personalities have been pleased because the mechanistic orientation of the scientific world enables them to assume an aloof spiritual attitude that disdains any concern for the natural world. Scientists, on the other hand, are pleased since that attitude leaves them free to structure their world of quantitative measurements without the problem of spiritual values associated with human consciousness. Thus both scientists and believers remain disengaged from any profound understanding of the earth process itself. To remedy this situation, we need simply to reflect on the story itself.

The story of the universe is the story of the emergence of a galactic system in which each new level of expression emerges through the urgency of self-transcendence. Hydrogen in the presence of some millions of degrees of heat emerges into helium. After the stars take shape as oceans of fire in the heavens, they go through a sequence of transformations. Some eventually explode into the stardust out of which the solar system and the earth take shape. Earth gives unique expression of itself in its rock and crystalline structures and in the variety and splendor of living forms, until humans appear as the moment in which the unfolding universe becomes conscious of itself. The human emerges not only as an earthling, but also as a worldling. We bear the universe in our beings as the universe bears us in its being. The two have a total presence to each other and to that deeper mystery out of which both the universe and ourselves have emerged.

If this integral vision is something new both to the scientist and to the believer, both are gradually becoming aware of this view of the real and its human meaning. It might be considered a new revelatory experience. Because we are moving into a new mythic age, it is little wonder that a kind of mutation is taking place in the entire earth-human order. A new paradigm of what it is to be human emerges. This is what is so exciting, yet so painful and so disrupting. One aspect of this change involves the shift in earth-human relations, for we now in large measure determine the earth process that once determined us. In a more integral way we could say that the earth that controlled itself directly in the former period now to an extensive degree controls itself through us.

In this new context the question appears as to where the values are, how they are determined, how they are transmitted. Whereas formerly values consisted in the perfection of the earthly image reflecting an external Logos in a world of fixed natures, values are now determined by the human sensitivity in responding to the creative urgencies of a developing world. The scientist in the depths of the unconscious is drawn by the mystical attraction of communion with the emerging creative process. This would not be possible unless it were a call of subject to subject, if it were not an effort at total self-realization on the part of the scientists. As scientists, their taste for the real is what gives to their work its admirable quality. Their wish is to experience the real in its tangible, opaque, material aspect and to respond to that by establishing an interaction with the world that will advance the total process. If the demand for objectivity and the quantitative aspect of the real has led scientists to neglect subjectivity and the qualitative aspect of the real, this has been until now a condition for fulfilling their historical task. The most notable single development within science in recent years, however, has been a growing awareness of the integral physical-psychic dimension of reality.

The believing redemption community is awakening only slowly to this new context of understanding. There is a fear, a distrust, even a profound aversion, to the natural world and all its processes. It would be difficult to find a theological seminary in this country that has an adequate program on creation as it is experienced in these times. The theological curriculum is dominated by a long list of courses on redemption and how it functions in aiding humans to transcend the world, all based on biblical texts. Such a situation cannot long endure, however, since a new sense of the earth and its revelatory import is arising in the believing community. The earth will not be ignored, nor will it long endure being despised, neglected, or mistreated. The dynamics of creation are demanding attention once more in a form unknown for centuries to the orthodox Christian.

It is clear that the primordial intention of the universe is to produce variety in all things, from atomic structures to the living world of plant and animal forms, to the appearance of humans, where individuals differ from one another more extensively than in any other realm of known reality. This difference can be seen not only in individuals, but also in social structures and in historical periods of our development. But here, also, the difficulty in the human order, for there is no absolute model for the individual. Personal realization involves a unique creative effort in response to all those interior and exterior forces that enter into individual life. So, too, with each historical age and each cultural form, there is need to create a reality for which, again, there is no adequate model. This is precisely the American difficulty, a difficulty for which there is no complete answer, but only a striving toward. At each moment we must simply be what we are, opening onto a larger life.

Interior articulation of its own reality is the immediate responsibility of every being. Every being has its own interior, its self, its mystery, its numinous aspect. To deprive any being of this sacred quality is to disrupt the larger order of the universe. Reverence will be total or it will not be at all. The universe does not come to us in pieces any more than a human individual stands before us with some part of its being. Preservation of this feeling for reality in its depths has been considerably upset in these past two centuries of scientific analysis and technological manipulation of the earth and its energies. During this period, the human mind lived in the narrowest bonds that it has ever experienced. The vast mythic, visionary, symbolic world with its all-pervasive numinous qualities was lost. Because of this loss, we made our terrifying assault upon

134

the earth with an irrationality that is stunning in enormity, while we were being assured that this was the way to a better, more humane, more reasonable world.

Such treatment of the external physical world, deprived of its subjectivity, could not long avoid also encompassing the human. Thus we have the most vast paradox of all—ourselves as free, intelligent, numinous beings negating those very interior qualities by our own objective reasoning processes and subserving our own rationalizations. Yet, finally, a reversal has begun, and the reality and value of the interior subjective numinous aspect of the entire cosmic order is being appreciated as the basic condition in which the story makes any sense at all.

Here we come to the further realization that the universe is coherent within itself throughout the total extent of space and the entire sequence of its time development. This web of relationships throughout the universe is what first impinges on our waking consciousness. It is this deepening association within the universe that enables life to emerge into being. The living form is more individuated, with greater subjectivity and more intensive identity within itself and with its environment. All these factors are multiplied on a new scale of magnitude in the realm of consciousness. There a supreme mode of communion exists within the individual, with the human community, within the earth-human complex. Increased capacity for personal identity is inseparable from this capacity for mutual presence. Together this distance and this intimacy establish the basic norms of being, of life, of value. It is the mission of our present and all future generations to develop this capacity for mutual presence on new and more comprehensive levels.

In transmitting values through the sequence of generations, we no longer have the initiation techniques whereby the vision and values of earlier generations were transmitted to succeeding generations. Yet there is an abiding need to assist succeeding generations to fulfill their proper role in the ongoing adventure of the earth process. In the human realm education must supply what instinct supplies in the prehuman realm. There is need for a program to aid the young to identify themselves in the comprehensive dimensions of space and time. This was easier in the world of the *Timaeus,* where the earth was seen as an image of the eternal Logos. In such a world Saint Thomas could compose his masterful presentation of Christian thought, and the place and role of the human within that context. This could then be summarized in catechetical form and taught to succeeding generations.

Now a new way of understanding values is required. We are returning to a more traditional context of story as our source of understanding and value. It is somewhat fascinating to realize that the final achievement of our scientific inquiry into the structure and functioning of the universe as evolutionary process is much closer to the narrative mode of explanation given in the Bible than it is to the later, more philosophical mode of Christian explanation provided in our theologies.

It is of utmost importance that succeeding generations become aware of the larger story outlined here and the numinous, sacred values that have been present in an expanding sequence over this entire time of the world's existence. Within this context all our human affairs—all professions, occupations, and activities—have their meaning precisely insofar as they enhance this emerging world of subjective intercommunion within the total range of reality. Within this context the scientific community and the religious community have a common basis. The limitations of the redemption rhetoric and the scientific rhetoric can be seen, and a new, more integral language of being and value can emerge.

Within this story a structure of knowledge can be established, with its human significance, from the physics of the universe and its chemistry through geology and biology to economics and commerce and so to all those studies whereby we fulfill our role in the earth process. There is no way of guiding the course of human affairs through the perilous course of the future except by discovering our role in this larger evolutionary process. If the way of Western civilization and Western religion was once the way of election and differentiation from others and from the earth, the way now is the way of intimate communion with the larger human community and with the universe itself.

Here we might observe that the basic mood of the future might well be one of confidence in the continuing revelation that takes place in and through the earth. If the dynamics of the universe from the beginning shaped the course of the heavens, lighted the sun, and formed the earth, if this same dynamism brought forth the continents and seas and atmosphere, if it awakened life in the primordial cell and then brought into being the unnumbered variety of living beings, and finally brought us into being and guided us safely through the turbulent centuries, there is reason to believe that this same guiding process is precisely what has awakened in us our present understanding of ourselves and our relation to this stupendous process. Sensitized to such guidance from the very structure and functioning of the universe, we can have confidence in the future that awaits the human venture.

·11·

Patriarchy: A New Interpretation of History

A new interpretation of Western historical development is emerging through the concept of patriarchy. It is an interpretative pattern consisting of prepatriarchy, patriarchy, and postpatriarchy, terms that are frequently met with in recent writings on contemporary cultural issues. Prepatriarchy has special reference to the matricentric period of Old Europe, which flourished, apparently, from around 6500 B.C. until the Aryan invasions around 3500 B.C. Patriarchy is coterminous with the Western civilizational process for the past five thousand years. Postpatriarchy identifies with the ecological period of total participatory governance presently emerging as the context of future historical development of Western civilization and even of the global civilizational enterprise.

This sequence of historical periods might also be designated as the matricentric, patricentric, and omnicentric periods. By using the suffix "centric" rather than "archal," we move from the idea of dominion or rule to that of cultural integrity. The ecological period is designated as omnicentric, to indicate that ecosystems are a comprehensive participatory process. This period might also be termed the ecofeminist period since the spontaneities and nurturing qualities of the period might traditionally be designated as feminine. This is in contrast to the patricentric period, which is generally designated in its oppressive aspects as "patriarchy."

There is clearly a certain mythic dimension to such patterns of historical interpretation. Yet the context of interpretation in any area of human thought finds its best expression in terms with a high mythic content. History does not in reality divide into such neatly arranged sequences or into such symmetrical patterns. It is rather a continuous flow in its sequence of transformations. Yet to attain some intelligibility we resort to such patterns of interpretation as we are suggesting here.

This pattern of historical interpretation now takes its place in the account of Western historical interpretation that began with Augustine's six-age sequence, from creation to the millennium, as articulated in *The City of God*. In the twelfth century there was the three-age sequence of Joachim of Flores: the ages of the Father, the Son, and the coming age of the Holy Spirit. Then we have the three ages of Giambattista Vico: the divine, the heroic, and the human ages.

In the nineteenth century we have the sequence that passes from the mythic religious period, through the metaphysical period, to the positivist period, as these periods are presented in the work of Auguste Comte. In the same century, Marx presents us with a vision of history that moves from an original classless society through the feudal and bourgeois societies to terminate eventually in the classless society of communism. Other schemas of historical interpretation have also appeared, such as that of Oswald Spengler. In his view Western civilization has passed through its early creative development and its period of stabilization. Now, in the twentieth century, we have entered into the inevitable period of decline.

In this new way of identifying the Western historical sequence—in terms of the matricentric, patricentric, and omnicentric—we find that each of these periods can be fairly well delineated. The period of the prepatriarchal, or matricentric, cultural development has been extensively researched by archaeologists such as Marija Gimbutas in her study of the goddesses and gods of pre-Indo-European Old Europe. Charlene Spretnak has presented additional data on this matricentric period as it is manifested in the goddess-centered religion of early Greece. Reflection on the basic human values expressed in this earlier culture and their suppression by the patriarchal culture of the invading Aryan peoples is bringing about a reevaluation of the entire Western civilizational enterprise as it has developed over the past five thousand years.

When the apparent success of this earlier matricentric period is seen in contrast with the devastation of the earth resulting from the civilizational order that followed, we have a comprehensive critique of the Western civilizational process that has probably never been surpassed. We are confronted with a profound reversal of values. The entire course of Western civilization is seen as vitiated by patriarchy, the aggressive, plundering, male domination of our society. This condemnation is more severe in its implications than the secularist judgment of our religious culture as suppressive of basic human values. It is also greater than the Marxist condemnation of bourgeois oppression of the proletariat.

If we inquire into the driving forces that have evoked this critical reevaluation of Western civilization, we can identify them as the rising consciousness of women and the devastation of all the basic living forms of earth presently taking place in consequence of the male-dominated regimes that have existed during this period. The new mode of ecological consciousness now emerging sees the new period of the earth community as having a basic nurturing aspect that tends more toward traditional feminine than toward masculine qualities. There are indeed religious, cosmological, biological, and

140

historical reasons for considering the feminine as having a special role in our thinking about the earth.

The term *patriarchy,* used to designate the deepest and most destructive level of determination in the Western perception of reality and value, has not yet been formally adopted into the language. Yet this designation can be proposed as the most available and most appropriate term for this situation. The term itself has remarkable clarity and power for this expanded role that is now assigned to it. Indeed, few words have appeared so suddenly to fulfill such a critical and, at the same time, creative role. Through this term, as one of its main instruments, efforts are being made to identify the source and then to terminate the destructive course of human affairs that has emerged within the Western civilizational process and which now threatens the survival of the planet in all its basic life systems. If this term is not the one needed, then we must soon find a more effective term, lest the earth perish under its present controlling powers.

Evidence that the earth is in danger of perishing was presented by Peter Raven in his 1987 address—"We Are Killing the World"— to the American Association for the Advancement of Science. At no other moment in the story of the earth has there been devastation in this manner or at this order of magnitude. Even the extinctions at the end of the Permian period some 220 million years ago, when some 90 percent of all living species perished, was quite different and, in the larger arc of earth development, less significant than what is now threatened.

Immediately, when we discuss this situation in terms of patriarchy, it becomes evident that we have a dictionary as well as a practical problem, since we are not simply introducing a new use of the word *patriarchy* into the language. We are making this term something close to the central word about which the language itself must be adjusted. A postpatriarchal dictionary is needed, one that would establish a new sense of reality and value throughout the entire structure of the Western language.

141

If we begin with the term itself, we see that originally *patriarchy* meant simply the rule of a senior male person over an extended natural family or tribal people. Its original connotations of intimate family benevolence and protection disappeared amid the harsh realities that emerged within the familial and, later, more extended forms of human societies.

There is no article on *patriarchy* in Hastings' *Encyclopedia of Religion,* published in 1908. Nor is there any article in the *Encyclopedia of the Social Sciences,* published in 1948. In the latest Webster's dictionary, *patriarchy* is described simply as a family or tribe ruled by men. There is no reference to the use of the term as it is presently envisaged. In the latest (1975) edition of the *Encyclopaedia Britannica,* a brief article indicates that *patriarchy* is "a hypothetical social system based on the absolute authority of the father or an elderly male over the family group." We are also told that the word *patriarchy* "has fallen out of use among social scientists as a technical or categorical term." In the *Encyclopedia of Religion,* edited by Mircea Eliade and published in 1987, there is, again, no listing for *patriarchy,* although there is an impressive article on *feminine sacrality.* Thus the word that now carries such absolute significance in the determination of the human and earthly process is still not a functioning term within our standard reference sources.

Our most prominent illustration of male rule over the extended tribal family is found in the patriarchal period in the earliest biblical narratives, prior to establishment of separate roles for priest and prophet. Even more important in relation to the theme we are considering is the "patria potestas" in Roman law. In this period the father had absolute rights over his entire family, including the right to impose capital punishment. The extended family was a total possession. The father owned everything and decided everything. While our Western sense of authority over human affairs is derived not only from Roman precedent, but also from the incoming tribal peoples to the north and east of Europe, these earlier Mediterranean developments were of great significance. When joined with the heroic leadership ideals of the barbarian peoples, the tradition of rule by male warrior personalities was well established in the European world.

Ecclesiastically, *patriarchy* designates the supreme centers of prestige in the church. The four great patriarchies of the Eastern church are Constantinople, Jerusalem, Alexandria, and Antioch. In the West the supreme patriarchate is centered in Rome. Since religious authority in the West has always been exercised by a male priesthood and required immediate and total acceptance by the believing community, this, too, contributed mightily to the sense of patriarchal responsibility for the unfolding of Western history.

From these beginnings the term *patriarchy* has now been brought forward as a way of indicating the larger sources of responsibility for what is happening not only with women, but also with the total civilizational structure of our society and even with the planet itself. The sense of *patriarchy* has now evolved as the archetypal pattern of oppressive governance by men with little regard for the well-being or personal fulfillment of women, for the more significant human values, or for the destiny of the earth itself.

Choice of the term *patriarchy* for defining the basic pathology of Western civilization is being confirmed by historical evidence of an earlier, more benign civilizational period, a matricentric or matrifocal period, as this period is generally designated, although the term *matriarchal* is sometimes used. From her studies Judy Chicago concludes that "all archaeological evidence indicates that these matriarchal cultures were egalitarian, democratic, peaceful. But female-oriented agricultural societies gradually gave way to a male-dominated political state in which occupational specialization, commerce, social stratification, and militarism developed." This view is supported by the extensive research on this period done by Marija Gimbutas, Professor of European Archaeology of the University of California, Los Angeles. Although much further study is needed to clarify the distinctive characteristics and the historical

143

role of this period, sufficient evidence does exist to support the basic outlines such as we have them at present.

Change from this earlier period to a dominant patriarchal type of civilizational process took place in Old Europe, apparently, with the invading Aryan Indo-European peoples beginning around 4500 B.C., the period from which we have, until now, traced the most profound determinations of our Western mode of consciousness. In the words of Marija Gimbutas, "The earliest European civilization was savagely destroyed by the patriarchal element, and it never recovered, but its legacy lingered in the substratum which nourished further European cultural development." Those proposing this reversal of values are not arguing exactly from philosophical principles, but from historical realities and from our planetary peril as well as from the deepest realms of the human psyche.

We will understand very little of current feminist writers until we understand their use of such phrases as *this patriarchal planet, patriarchal history, the patriarchal bias of our society.* On other occasions we meet phrases such as *patriarchal logic* and *patriarchal culture.* In each of these contexts the term sweeps some of the most sensitive areas of traditional culture into a denunciatory context. Patriarchy becomes the original sin, the primordial and all-encompassing evil through all the generations of Western society during these past five millennia.

In this context of historical interpretation, the earlier matricentric period is more fully developed and plays a more extensive role than the earlier, primordial period of communal life plays in the historical vision of Marx. The reason for this may be that the feminist mode of consciousness gives a greater emphasis to the seasonal renewal rituals within a spatial mode of consciousness. Marxist consciousness is absolutely progressivist, until history culminates in the classless society. The feminist historical vision is more extensively committed to the seasonal sequence of time, with its ritual evocation of the powers of the universe. However creative the evolutionary modality of the universe in its prehuman and its earlier human phases, it is extremely flawed in its human expression during these past five millennia of Western historical development. Even on a wider scale the entire civilizational enterprise seems to have imposed unsustainable pressures on the biological functioning of the earth. The historical mission of the present is to introduce a more integral period of earth development, a period when a mutually enhancing human-earth relationship might be established—if indeed the human is to prove itself to be a viable species on a viable planet. That the human is nonviable in its present mode of patriarchal functioning seems to be quite clear.

Even in this period of patriarchal dominance the heritage of the earlier matricentric phase has continued as an undercurrent within Western cultural traditions. Matricentric ways of thinking and their associated rituals seem to be among the component elements of our submerged cultural traditions. They carry on an earlier wisdom associated with alchemy, astrology, the pagan nature rituals, and the hermetic teachings. These hidden traditions, considered destructive and unacceptable within the religious-humanist traditions of Western society, need reconsideration for the contributions they make to our understanding of the universe, its deeper modes of functioning, and the proper role of the human. They carry some of the most creative aspects of our civilization. In their symbolic modes of expression, especially, they enable us to go beyond the rational processes derivative from the classical philosophers and our later theologies. Through these traditions we have recovered our understanding of the archetypal world of the unconscious.

As we look back on the Western historical process, we can identify four patriarchal establishments that have been in control of Western history over the centuries. However benign our view of these establishments or however brilliant in some of their achievements, we must observe that they have become progressively virulent in their destructive powers, until presently they are bringing about the closing down of all the basic life systems of the planet.

These four establishments are: the classical empires, the ecclesiastical establishment, the nation-state, and the modern corporation. These four are exclusively male dominated and primarily for fulfillment in terms of the human as envisaged by men. Women had minimal if any consistent role in the direction of these establishments.

The classical empires had their precedent in the sacred rulers that appeared in Sumeria and in Egypt some five thousand years ago. In Egypt the ruler participated in divine status, while in Sumeria the ruler functioned as representative of the divine. In both cases we have an oppressive human situation associated with the first organized civilizations engaged in extensive irrigation and construction projects. These empires were identified by Karl Wittfogel in his study of Oriental despotism as "the harshest form of total power." When we look at the grandeur of these civilizations and at their successors in Assyria and Babylonia, we can only wonder at so much oppression coexisting with such stupendous achievements, just as later when we consider the Greek world and the "humanist" heritage from that world, we must reflect that they were achieved within a slave society. In terms of fully organized political rule over a diverse association of peoples, the earliest of the empires was the Persian Empire under Cyrus in the sixth century B.C. Then came the Macedonian Empire of Alexander and the Roman Empire in the Western world. In the East came the sequence of Chinese empires, from the earlier kingdoms of the Shang and the Chou, then the more functionally effective empires begun by Ch'in Shih Huang Ti in the last years of the third century B.C. In India the imperial process produced Asoka in the third century B.C., one of the most benign of the great rulers of the period.

This sequence of empires was succeeded in the West by the Byzantine Empire, the Holy Roman Empire in Europe, then the later empires with a dominant presence of the Spanish, the Portuguese, the Dutch, the French, and the British—all overseas— while the Russians expanded their empire throughout the Eurasian continent. Later even the nation-states become adventuresome in their rivalry for imperial dominion over the planet.

146

These empires took on cosmic symbols and established their power relationships either through the birth of the ruler as divine king, as incarnations of cosmic power, or through religious coronation ceremonies. The difficulty with patriarchy is precisely that it is something more than a social or political arrangement or institution. Patriarchy reaches far back into the cosmological structure of existence and even into the ritual, moral, and belief commitments of religion. Even in modern times Social Darwinism provides in its principle of natural selection something of an equivalent justification for the controls exercised by the nation-state and the modern corporation. In either case the imperial controls over human populations were carried out in the name of the divine and in association with the cosmological order of things. Rulers had cosmological as well as divine status.

The triumphal achievements of these imperial personalities were extolled in epic poetry, in the Homeric accounts of the *Iliad* and the *Odyssey,* in the *Aeneid* of Virgil. So, too, in the epic accounts of *Beowulf* and in the Germanic legends of heroic deeds. So in the *Cid,* the account of the Christian conflict with the invading Moslem warriors. These epic stories became the inspiration of succeeding generations. As Greek youth was educated through the Homeric stories, so the Western world was educated through Virgil, sometimes known as The Father of the West, and through the epic ideals of the knighthood and The Crusades. Only later would Dante tell a story that would bring judgment on the historical order in some comprehensive way, although even he thought it best if some saving ruler would seize both political and religious control of the European world. Finally Cervantes produced his commentary on the warring ideal as it existed in the later sixteenth and early seventeenth centuries. Although he collapsed the idealism of an earlier, more vigorous tradition, the warring process simply took on more realistic forms.

In Europe even up until the late-seventeenth-century reign of the Sun King, Louis XIV, this sense of functioning in a divine-cosmic context as well as in a human order survived. All these men ruled in terms of patriarchal norms of conquest, even when on rare occasions women were in the position of authority, as when Joan of Arc took up the sword in the service of the French dynasty. To doubt these ideals or to fail in enthusiasm for these wars, whether of defense or of conquest, would be to doubt not only the human process, but also the divine disposition of the universe. Virgil announced in the opening lines of the *Aeneid,* "I sing of arms and the man . . . hard driven on land and on the deep by the violence of heaven. . . . "

In the sacred writings of the Bible also we find a warring deity and warrior ideals. If a more peaceful teaching did arise in the gospels, it did not survive the challenge that arose in later centuries when conflict appeared as the way for survival. In the age of chivalry, efforts were made to mitigate the violence by a sense of dedicated strength in the service of the weak who were assaulted by the strong. Once the natural and human worlds were envisaged as inherently subject to the strife for power, the way of peace and pacifism was no longer available. As with any addiction, it could only become worse. The pathology was too deep and too universal to eradicate at the time. It could only continue until the bombs were dropped on Hiroshima and Nagasaki and industrial nations began construction of nuclear warheads sufficient to extinguish all the greater lifeforms on the planet.

The second patriarchal establishment, with even greater intellectual and spiritual impact, is the Western ecclesiastical establishment, with its religious and moral authority, an authority with more profound consequences than even the political empire. However much these two etablishments struggled against each other, both were enclosed within the same cultural boundaries. The church was the single comprehensive, transnational authority in the Western world for more than a thousand years. By baptism a person attained membership in both the civil and the religious society, a situation that endured until the time of the French Revolution and the rise of the nation-state.

The church controlled not only the religious belief and moral discipline of European society, but also its intellectual and cultural formation. If economics, law, and politics had some independent status, these, too, were subject to the interpretation given by the church. The Crusades, one of the central concerns of the medieval centuries, were sponsored by the church, which commissioned the various rulers to carry them out through their military forces.

The main determinant of reality and value in Western civilization was expressed in the belief structures presented by the church. These in turn were determined by the divine revelation contained in the Bible and in the living tradition, both subject to church interpretation. Here is the deepest source and support for the patriarchal tradition of Western civilization. It is also the most profound challenge in terms of the reversal taking place in our understanding of reality and value. The sense of the sacred in any civilization is precisely that which cannot be questioned, for the sense of the sacred is the unquestionable answer to all questions. Thus the psychic shock in the reassessment that is presently being made.

The biblical tradition begins with the creation narrative wherein the Earth Mother of the eastern Mediterranean is abandoned in favor of the transcendent Heaven Father. Later the relationship between the human and the divine is constituted in terms of a covenant between a chosen people and a personal transcendent creative Father deity. This becomes the context in which human-divine affairs are worked out over the succeeding centuries. The natural world is no longer the locus for the meeting of the divine and the human. A subtle aversion develops toward the natural world, a feeling that humans in the depth of their beings do not really belong to the earthly community of life, but to a heavenly community. We are presently in a state of exile from our true country. The natural world is little mentioned in the official prayers of the church, even though

149

the Psalms carry extensive references to the divine praise associated with the various natural phenomena. The Christian world is the world of the city. Its concerns are primarily supernatural. The rural world is the world of the pagan. The natural world is to be kept at a distance as a seductive mode of being.

In the Bible narrative, woman becomes the instrument for the entry of evil into the world and for the breakdown in human-divine relations. Only in a derivative sense, through their association with men, do women function in the public life of the sacred community. Later, in explanation of the lesser quality of female being, women are seen as biologically the consequence of some lack of vigor in the male component of the conception process, since in its full energy conception should produce a male child. In this context the whole of feminine existence becomes profoundly diminished as a mode of personal being.

The rulership of men in the church, by divine determination, assured the relegation of women to subordinate status in the religious community, the denial of integral participation in religious ritual, the identification of women with seduction and moral evil. Because women were considered so seductive, even in the sensuous quality of their voices, they were for centuries excluded not simply from the most essential ministries in the church, but even from participation in the official choir for church liturgies, except within their own convent enclosures.

A profound ambivalence can be observed in the Madonna figure of the medieval period. Undoubtedly the Madonna is the greatest cultural creation of the medieval period. This figure is so much the psychic center of the period that Henry Adams finds that the Virgin provides the period with its main archetypal identity. That this figure mitigated somewhat the patriarchal dimension of Western culture can be seen from events in the sixteenth century, when this feminine figure was rejected as a "pagan" intrusion into the Christian world.

And that is precisely the point. The divine Virgin can be considered as an effort to bring into the culture at least some remnant presence of the ancient Earth Mother. Indeed, the central church of Christendom, Chartres, was built over a shrine of the pre-Christian Mother Goddess. Even the Madonna figure worshiped in the cathedral of Chartres, until it was burned during the Revolution, was considered, at least in legend, to be itself a pre-Christian figure. That the Virgin was considered all powerful, even as a protection against God himself, indicates the divine power of the Virgin.

While all this is clear, however, the perpetual virginity of the Madonna figure was used as a symbol of the higher status of virginity over marriage, which involves sexual activity. Yet Saint Thomas Aquinas states quite clearly that maternity in itself is a superior status to virginity, which gets its high esteem from the absence of that state of passion in sexual activity that distances the mind from its sense of the divine and immerses human consciousness in the depths of matter—little appreciating, apparently, that this immersion into matter might also be considered as immersion into the divine.

Within cloistered life certain outstanding personalities could develop, although the greater numbers lived what now must be seen as suppressed and intimidated lives (one must be wary, however, when using today's values to judge other periods). With all of her confinements, Julian of Norwich in her anchorhold lived a remarkably expanded life. Dedicated religious life, in its origins, was a way of being liberated from the subjections and servitudes that existed in the marriage state in the late Roman period and that have continued to exist with some mitigations throughout the course of Western civilization. As the informal dedicated life became more formalized after the time of Saint Benedict and turned into the cloistered life, the discipline became more standardized. Even so, in this context some women, such as Hildegard of Bingen, Catherine of Siena, Julian of Norwich, and Teresa of Avila, could develop their personalities and play a considerable role in shaping the public consciousness of their times.

Throughout this period the deepest philosophical justification for male domination over human affairs was given in terms of matter and form as our primary way of understanding the physical universe. Matter is the passive element. Form is the active element. Matter receives both its existence and its determination from its associated form. When this is applied to gender, the feminine is seen as having a passive or subservient role in every aspect of the civilizational endeavor. The guiding function is the role of men.

The next patriarchal establishment that needs consideration is the nation-state. After the fifteenth century, a transition was made from the feudal states of the medieval period to the monarchies and city republics of the renaissance and the later period. This coincided with the growing power of the commercial classes, who demanded greater participation in government. The allegiance previously given to the universal ecclesiastical establishment and to the ideal of a universal Christian civilization was significantly diminished during the religious troubles of the sixteenth century. After this time religious and political allegiance were both given to the separate states that then dominated the European world. The new literacy, the merchant classes, the new technologies, shifted attention to the secular realm. The political philosophy of John Locke, the sense of personal freedom and free association—these led to a new political form in constitutional governments that were in theory the manifestation of the will of the people and the protection of their freedoms.

The new devotion was to the fatherland. National assemblies, national flags, national anthems, national histories, national educational programs, national economies, national currencies, came into being along with the entire range of infrastructures of modern industrial societies, transportation systems, postal systems, water and drainage systems, and public utilities of every kind.

This new devotion to the political community had about it something of a religious fervor. The birth of the nation, the date of the national revolution, became the most sacred day of the year. Revolutionary leaders became revered personalities. This was the moment of release from darkness and subjection to the world of daylight and freedom, the liberation moment. The ancient symbolism of the Exodus from Egypt to the Promised Land was experienced anew in this strangely different setting.

The civilizational enterprise was itself seen as being in the care of the political regime. European nations, especially England, saw themselves as saviors of the peoples of the earth in terms of their civilizing mission. This led to the colonial enterprise, the control of the peoples and lands and resources of the entire planet by the nation-states of the European world. This was all thought to be their sacred historical mission. Even the institution of slavery was brought into this process as a way of relating these other peoples to the higher purposes of the nations that were leading humanity toward its true fulfillment.

The nation-state might be considered the most powerful institution ever invented for organizing human societies. Above all, the concept of national sovereignty came into being. This concept might be considered a supreme expression of what we are here designating as patriarchy, the aggressive use of power in pursuit of the male values of conquest and dominion. In virtue of this concept, each nation declared itself an independent entity subject to no other power on earth. Any effort from without to influence the nation was seen as an infringement of sovereignty. No association of nations with one another that implied any diminishment of national sovereignty was acceptable. This sensitivity within was strangely associated with a compulsion of European nations to extend their power over the non-European world as if by some divine commission.

Because geographical determination of national boundaries and the allegiances of border peoples are seldom entirely clear, and also because historical resentments linger in their minds, the various Western peoples have consistently gone to war over the past few centuries in defense of national honor and in a vain effort at national security. This has led in turn to citizen armies, to universal conscription for military purposes. Such armies in modern times are an invention of the nation-state. In prior centuries the wars of Europe were fought by rulers with professional and mercenary armies hired for the purpose. The lives of the people were little affected when the rule of the territory passed from one regime to another. All of that changed with the calling to arms of the entire nation.

The concept of total war came into being. All the resources of the nation—the educational, scientific, and economic institutions, and the public media, especially—as well as military personnel were involved. Beyond the concept of total war is also the concept of world war. These wars have become so endemic, the instruments of warfare so destructive, and the financial cost of military activities so exhausting that we must wonder how long these conflicts and the threat of such conflicts can endure. They are driven obviously by the deepest of our civilizational pathologies, originating, as so many pathologies, in some distorted sense of the sacred.

Religion has always been recognized as having dangerous as well as divine aspects, since the demands of religion and the sense of the sacred are so absolute. When the ideal of the sacred becomes distorted, then all existence becomes endangered. This is precisely what has happened through the concept of the nation-state and its sovereignty. When protection of the nation and its glorification became the most sacred duty of the people, nuclear warfare became possible.

As with the ancient empires and the ecclesiastical establishment, so now with the nation-state; it was an affair carried out by men and for the ideals of men. Women were without power in the public realm, in its values, or in its functioning. Women functioned in areas withdrawn from the public life of the society: in the home, caring for children, serving men. This exclusion from public life became progressively less acceptable as women gained greater access to education and had more leisure time because of new technologies.

Women did not participate in the electoral process in the United States until 1920, in Great Britain until 1928. Even as late as 1987 there were only 2 women in the 100-member U.S. Senate, 24 in the 411-member House of Representatives. The first woman member of the Supreme Court was appointed in 1981. This type of imbalance was no longer acceptable to women, who comprise more than half the population. They were no longer willing to accept such control over their lives or over the public life of the society or over the integral functioning of the earth. The feminist movement became a pervasive influence throughout the society.

The modern corporation, whether industrial, financial, or commercial, can be identified as the fourth destructive manifestation of patriarchy, although it likes to project its image as the primary source of all those blessings that make for the well-being of the populace. Various corporate slogans are: "Progress is our most important product," "Better living through chemistry," "Fly the friendly skies," "The heartbeat of America."

Not only does the corporation provide life's most satisfying experiences, the corporation transforms the entire society in the basic modalities of its functioning. It provides jobs! By having jobs we make money, and with money we buy everything. We no longer grow our own food; we buy our food. We are no longer sustained in the ever-renewing cycle of nature; we live now within the cycle of industrial production and consumption. As a community we work at our jobs and produce the things that we buy with the money that we obtain from our jobs. The important thing is to have a job. To be jobless and without money is to be reduced to helplessness. Yet industrial society of its nature is so erratic in its functioning that it is unable to provide jobs consistently for the populace. Joblessness and its indignities are among the most unendurable afflictions imposed within our present industrial economy.

Regions without industrial or commercial establishments are seen as backward places, with neither present life nor future possibilities. Thus the competition among cities to attract corporations, the offering of tax abatements, the variations on land-use restrictions, the promise of additional infrastructures such as roads, public utilities, educational facilities, and a host of other enticements.

Whether industrial, financial, or commercial, the corporation is considered the primary instrument of "progress," although just what progress means is never clear. The supposition seems to be that the greater the devastation of the natural world through construction of highways, airports, development projects, shopping malls, supermarkets, and corporate headquarters, the closer we are to fulfilling the American Dream. It is precisely through this dream vision of a new humanly created wonderworld that the advertising industry brings about that level of heightened consumption upon which the corporation depends for its ever-increasing control over our society and its ever-increasing profits. Through advertising the corporation has gained control over the public media. Through the public media the corporation controls the deepest psychic as well as the most powerful physical forces of the planet.

Because the industrial-commercial corporation is so central to contempory existence, our educational programs have become subservient to its control. High school and college students must prepare themselves for jobs within this industrial-commercial setting. This industrial context of American life can be thought of as an all-enclosing bubble. Outside the bubble there is neither life nor joy nor any decent manner of human fulfillment. Within the bubble we can live and work and earn money and enjoy the ever-fascinating programs flowing across the television screen. In support of this process, our scientific research institutes—those in the universities and technical schools and those within industrial establishments— are constantly at work inventing a multitude of products that range from vast instruments of nuclear warfare to the frivolous products that have no purpose other than making a profit for some enterprising entrepreneur.

Since the 1880s this has been the age of the engineers, people of inventive genius joining scientific knowledge with technological skills, especially in the electronic and petrochemical industries. In the last two decades of the nineteenth century, the engineers took over the managerial role in shaping the original corporations that were formed at that time, corporations such as Westinghouse, General Electric, American Telephone and Telegraph, and a little later the automotive corporations. The engineers also advanced the chemical companies such as Du Pont and Dow and Allied Chemical. With this knowledge and these skills our engineers can build the great hydroelectric dams that destroy our rivers; drown our soil in chemical fertilizers, pesticides, and herbicides; throw satellites into space until the debris begins to clutter the heavens; and invent a million varieties of plastic objects that are scattered over both the land and the sea. They can do all that, but they seem to have not the slightest idea of how to establish a mutually enhancing mode of human presence upon the earth. They only make the human a deadly and intolerable presence on the planet.

The difficulty with our industrial wonderworld is that its products last for a brief period and then forever remain as a trashed and toxic world in which we and all future generations are condemned to live for an indefinite period. Like the illusion of a magician, we are presented with the blissful moment in the use of these inventions, with no indication of their abiding dark aspect. Human productions do not consistently renew themselves in the manner of natural forms.

The styrofoam cup used momentarily in some fast-food establishment must either remain forever in some ever-mounting trash deposit or else release its toxic components into the environment when it is destroyed. So with hospital equipment, so with plastic diapers. To label such products as "disposable" is to falsify the reality. In the natural world there is no such problem as that of disposing of some product. The waste product from one lifeform is the nourishment of another. We, on the other hand, are making a world of universal waste and maximal entropy. As noted by Elizabeth Dodson Gray, this inability to deal with waste matter is

157

a typical failure of the male in our society. Cleanup tasks have consistently been left for the women. As men have seldom shared in the cleanup tasks associated with their biological children, so they reveal their incompetence and lack of concern over the cleanup tasks associated with their industrial children. In this case, however, the consequences are a geological, biological, and, ultimately, human disaster.

Yet it all continues. In the United States our gross national product rose from $286 billion in 1950 to $4,200 billion in 1986. Corporate assets rose from $68 billion in 1970 to $260 billion in 1987. The advertising industry increased its expenditure from $12 billion in 1960 to $102 billion in 1986. In 1986 American Express had $99 billion in corporate assets, Citicorp had $196 billion, General Motors $72 billion.

This is power. The power of men. The power to profoundly disturb the most significant functioning of the earth. Women have had minimal presence, except as needed for service positions. In this regard, over the generations women have consistently been exploited by the various business processes. In the early days of the textile industry, women were employed as cheap labor that developed into the sweatshop system in the large cities of the East. In various business ventures women did the secretarial work. They were file clerks, typists, waitresses, cleanup persons. More-professional roles were found in nursing, social work, teaching, writing. Some women had brilliant careers in the performance arts: in music and song and dance and drama.

Yet these have not been the positions of power that are needed to alter the larger directions taken by our society. Those positions are still held by men, and for their own purposes. If mitigations have appeared, they have served only to make industrial processes more endurable. Thus the question of meliorism appears, the tendency to constantly modify an existing system without changing the basic pattern of its functioning. What is needed is a profound alteration of the pattern itself, not some modification of the pattern. To achieve this the basic principle of every significant revolution needs to be asserted: rejection of partial solutions. The tension of the existing situation must even be deliberately intensified so that the root cause of the destructive situation may become evident, for only when the cause becomes painfully clear will decisive change take place. The pain to be endured from the change must be experienced as a lesser pain to that of continuing the present course.

These four patriarchal establishments have made a world that carries within it a certain pathos. Assuredly there is grandeur in many of its achievements. Enormous energies have been expended in what has been thought to be beneficial to the larger human process. To realize suddenly that so much of this has been misdirected, alienating, and destructive beyond anything previously known in human history is a bitter moment indeed. It is good to know that critical moments are not unknown in our history. Until recently, however, it has been difficult to articulate the basic issues at their comprehensive level of significance. These issues go beyond the educational process and the lack of feminine participation in these establishments as they presently exist. Only now, in the late twentieth century, have the awesome dimensions of our cultural and institutional pathologies become clarified.

None of the other revolutionary movements in Western civilization has prepared us for what we must now confront. Quite naturally this demand for change, as with all such moments of radical confrontation, brings with it a heightened level of psychic intensity. Everything is at stake. This is something more than feminine resentment at personal neglect or oppression. It is possibly the most complete reversal of values that has taken place since the Neolithic period. The revelatory experience and the classical humanism on which our civilization has been founded—these are under challenge. Presently they are being severely criticized as manifestations of a biased mentality and as the context, if not the cause, of the universal devastation of the earth that is now taking place.

The ethical basis of our judgment concerning good and evil is itself being identified as antifeminist, antihuman, antiearth. Our legal system is seen as supportive of a patriarchal bias against the feminine dimension of the human and therefore as offensive to the human itself. The legal system is especially deficient in its radical inability to deal with questions of human-earth relationships. The medical profession has made some shocking mistakes in its inability to deal with the simplest aspects of the well-being of women and of children in their infant stage. Also it is revealing its inability to function effectively as a profession in the public arena in relation to the continuing toxification of the entire biosphere. When the breast milk of women becomes questionable nourishment for infants because of its contamination with toxins, something more in the form of public protest might be expected from the medical profession, as well as from the legal profession and the professional moralists.

The greatest support for the feminist, antipatriarchal movement can be found in the ecological movement. As regards the ecological integrity of the earth, the four establishments that we have mentioned all come under condemnation as leading to a nonviable mode of the human and even to a nonviable mode of the earth in its major life systems. As Norman Myers has indicated, we are bringing about an "extinction spasm" that is likely to produce "the greatest setback to the abundance and variety of life since the first flickering of life on earth some four billion years ago." That we should presently be killing off the rain forests at the rate of some fifty acres per minute is an irreversible tragedy. When we consider especially that these rain forests contain fully half the living species of life upon the earth and that they took some sixty-five million years to attain their present status, this is obviously a pathology beyond adequate description or comprehension.

The situation is further aggravated when we consider that none of the institutions that we have identified as the four basic patriarchal establishments has seriously protested the situation nor made serious efforts to stop its involvement in the process. They are indeed still fostering the industrial plundering of the planet as part of the progress myth from which the devastation took its beginning. What has become progressively clear is the association of the feminine issue with the ecological issue. This association has been given extensive consideration in two conferences that have been held on ecofeminism, and also in several books and essays written on the subject. Two books of special significance are those by Susan Griffin, *Woman and Nature* (1978), and Carolyn Merchant, *The Death of Nature* (1980). Also available is an impressive essay by Charlene Spretnak, "Ecofeminism: Our Roots and Flowering." To these must be added the superb study by Gerda Lerner, *The Creation of Patriarchy.*

These authors establish the basis not only for a new historical period, but also for a new interpretation of history itself. Every significant moment in Western cultural transformation requires for its psychic dynamism a new pattern of historical interpretation. This is precisely what is indicated by the use of the terms *prepatriarchy, patriarchy,* and *postpatriarchy* within the context of the feminist critique of our present situation. As indicated earlier, these terms equate with an earlier matricentric period, the patriarchal period, and the emerging ecological or ecofeminist period.

One of the main characteristics of the emerging ecological period is the move from a human-centered norm of reality and value to a nature-centered norm. We cannot expect life, the earth, or the universe to fit into our rational human designs of how life, the earth, or the universe should function. We must fit our thinking and our actions within the larger process. We must move from democracy to biocracy. We need a constitution for the North American continent, not simply a constitution for the humans occupying this continent. We need a United Species, not simply a United Nations.

We came into being within the life community through the billions of years that it took to shape a world into which humans could be born. It has been a creative maternal process throughout, with all the violence of the primordial fireball, the supernova explosions, and the volcanic eruptions from within the earth itself. However terrifying these transition moments, they have consistently been birth moments. We might hope that what we are now experiencing is another birth moment, yet the patriarchal period is too poignant in its past memories and its present realities for us to fully understand what is happening or what will emerge in the years to come. Too much of what we are doing is irreversible. What we can say is that the earth seems to be rising in defense of herself and her children after this long period of patriarchal dominion.

·12·

Bioregions:
The Context for
Reinhabiting the Earth

The universe expresses itself in the blazing radiance of the stars and in the vast reaches of the galactic systems. Its most intimate expression of itself, however, is in this tiny planet: a planet that could not exist in its present form except in a universe such as this one, in which it has emerged and from which it has received its life energies. The planet presents itself to us, not as a uniform global reality, but as a complex of highly differentiated regions caught up in the comprehensive unity of the planet itself. There are arctic and tropical, coastal and inland regions, mountains and plains, river valleys and deserts. Each of these regions has its distinctive geological formation, climatic conditions, and living forms. Together these constitute the wide variety of life communities that may be referred to as bioregions. Each is coherent within itself and intimately

163

related to the others. Together they express the wonder and splendor of this garden planet of the universe.

The human species has emerged within this complex of life communities; it has survived and developed through participation in the functioning of these communities at their most basic level. Out of this interaction have come our distinctive human cultures. But while at an early period we were aware of our dependence on the integral functioning of these surrounding communities, this awareness faded as we learned, through our scientific and technological skills, to manipulate the community functioning to our own advantage. This manipulation has brought about a disruption of the entire complex of life systems. The florescence that distinguished these communities in the past is now severely diminished. A degradation of the natural world has taken place.

Even though humans as well as the other species are in a stressful situation, few of us are aware of the order of magnitude of what is happening. Fewer still have any adequate understanding of its causes or the capacity to initiate any effective program for the revitalization of these life systems upon which everything depends. Disruption of the life process has led to a severe disruption of the human community itself. If social turmoil and international rivalries have evoked significant concern, the disruption of earth's life systems remains only a vague awareness in the human mind. This is strange indeed when we consider that the disruption of our bioregional communities is leading to a poisoning of the air we breathe, the water we drink, the soil and the seas that provide our food. We seek to remedy our social ills with industrial processes that lead only to further ecological devastation. Indeed our sensitivity to human conflict over the sharing of earth's resources has distracted us from the imperiled condition of these resources themselves, a peril associated with the loss of topsoil, the destruction of forests, the desertification of fruitful areas, the elimination of wetlands and spawning areas, the exhaustion of aquifers, the salinization of irrigated areas, the damaging of coral reefs.

The urgency of a remedy for this situation is such that all social groups and all nations are called upon to reassess the human-earth situation. As was indicated by Edward Schumacher, we must rethink our industrial approach to "development." This rethinking involves appropriate technologies, but also appropriate lifestyles, and, beyond those, appropriate human-earth relations.

The most difficult transition to make is from an anthropocentric to a biocentric norm of progress. If there is to be any true progress, then the entire life community must progress. Any progress of the human at the expense of the larger life community must ultimately lead to a diminishment of human life itself. A degraded habitat will produce degraded humans. An enhanced habitat supports an elevated mode of the human. This is evident not only in the economic order, but also throughout the entire range of human affairs. The splendor of earth is in the variety of its land and its seas, its life forms and its atmospheric phenomena; these constitute in color and sound and movement that great symphonic context which has inspired our sense of the divine, given us our emotional and imaginative powers, and evoked from us those entrancing insights that have governed our more sublime moments.

This context not only activates our interior faculties; it also provides our physical nourishment. The air and water and soil and seeds that provide our basic sustenance, the sunshine that pours its energies over the landscape—these are integral with the functioning of the fruitful earth. Physically and spiritually we are woven into this living process. As long as the integrity of the process is preserved, we have air to breathe and water to drink and nourishing food to eat.

The difficulty has come from our subversion of this integral life community, supposedly for our own advantage. In the process we have torn apart the life system itself. Our technologies do not function in harmony with earth technologies. With chemicals we force the soil to produce beyond its natural rhythms. Having lost our ability to invoke natural forces, we seek by violence to impose mechanistic patterns on life processes. In consequence of such actions, we now live in a world of declining fertility, a wasted world, a world in which its purity and life-giving qualities have been dissipated.

The solution is simply for us as humans to join the earth community as participating members, to foster the progress and prosperity of the bioregional communities to which we belong. A bioregion is an identifiable geographical area of interacting life systems that is relatively self-sustaining in the ever-renewing processes of nature. The full diversity of life functions is carried out, not as individuals or as species, or even as organic beings, but as a community that includes the physical as well as the organic components of the region. Such a bioregion is a self-propagating, self-nourishing, self-educating, self-governing, self-healing, and self-fulfilling community. Each of the component life systems must integrate its own functioning within this community to survive in any effective manner.

The first function, self-propagation, requires that we recognize the rights of each species to its habitat, to its migratory routes, to its place in the community. The bioregion is the domestic setting of the community just as the home is the domestic setting of the family. The community continues itself through successive generations precisely as a community. Both in terms of species and in terms of numbers, a certain balance must be maintained within the community. For humans to assume rights to occupy land by excluding other lifeforms from their needed habitat is to offend the community in its deepest structure. Further, it is even to declare a state of warfare, which humans cannot win since they themselves are ultimately dependent on those very lifeforms that they are destroying.

The second bioregional function, self-nourishment, requires that the members of the community sustain one another in the established patterns of the natural world for the well-being of the entire community and each of its members. Within this pattern the

166

expansion of each species is limited by opposed lifeforms or conditions so that no one lifeform or group of lifeforms should overwhelm the others. In this function of the community we include, for humans, the entire world of food gathering, of agriculture, of commerce, and of economics. The various bioregional communities of the natural world can be considered as commercial ventures as well as biological processes. Even in the natural world there is a constant interchange of values, the laying up of capital, the quest for more economic ways of doing things. The earth is our best model for any commercial venture. It carries out its operations with an economy and a productivity far beyond that of human institutions. It also runs its system with a minimum of entropy. There is in nature none of that sterile or toxic waste or nondecomposing litter such as is made by humans.

The third function of a bioregion is its self-education through physical, chemical, biological, and cultural patterning. Each of these requires the others for its existence and fulfillment. The entire evolutionary process can be considered as a most remarkable feat of self-education on the part of planet Earth and of its distinctive bioregional units. An important aspect of this self-educational process is the experiential mode of its procedures. The earth, and each of its bioregions, has performed unnumbered billions of experiments in designing the existing life system. Thus the self-educational processes observed in the natural world form a model for the human. There is presently no other way for humans to educate themselves for survival and fulfillment than through the instruction available through the natural world.

The fourth function of a bioregion is self-governance. An integral functional order exists within every regional life community. This order is not an extrinsic imposition, but an interior bonding of the community that enables each of its members to participate in the governance and to achieve that fullness of life expression that is proper to each. This governance is presided over in much of the world by the seasonal sequence of life expression. It provides the

167

order in which florescence and exuberant renewal of life takes place. Humans have traditionally inserted themselves into this community process through their ritual celebrations. These are not simply human activities, but expressions of the entire participating community. In human deliberations each of the various members of the community should be represented.

The fifth function of the bioregional community is self-healing. The community carries within itself not only the nourishing energies that are needed by each member of the community; it also contains within itself the special powers of regeneration. This takes place, for example, when forests are damaged by the great storms or when periods of drought wither the fields or when locusts swarm over a region and leave it desolate. In all these instances the life community adjusts itself, reaches deeper into its recuperative powers, and brings about a healing. The healing occurs whether the damage is to a single individual or to an entire area of the community. Humans, too, find that their healing takes place through submission to the discipline of the community and acceptance of its nourishing and healing powers.

The sixth function of the bioregional community is found in its self-fulfilling activities. The community is fulfilled in each of its components: in the flowering fields, in the great oak trees, in the flight of the sparrow, in the surfacing whale, and in any of the other expressions of the natural world. Also there are the seasonal modes of community fulfillment, such as the mysterious springtime renewal. In conscious celebration of the numinous mystery of the universe expressed in the unique qualities of each regional community, the human fulfills its own special role. This is expressed in religious liturgies, in market festivals, in the solemnities of political assembly, in all manner of play, in music and dance, in all the visual and performing arts. From these come the cultural identity of the bioregion.

The future of the human lies in acceptance and fulfillment of the human role in all six of these community functions. The change indicated is the change from an exploitive anthropocentrism to a participative biocentrism. The change requires something beyond environmentalism, which remains anthropocentric while trying to limit the deleterious effects of human presence on the environment.

We have limited our discussion so far to the inner functioning of the regional communities because these provide the most immediate basis of survival. If these communities do not fulfill their most essential functions, then the larger complex of bioregions cannot fulfill its role. Each of these bioregions is, as we have noted, *relatively* self-sustaining. None is fully self-sustaining since air and water flow across the entire planet, across all its regions. So it is with the animals. Some of them range widely from one end of a continent to the other. Birds cross multiple bioregional, and even continental, boundaries. Eventually all bioregions are interdependent. This interdependence is presently accentuated by the toxic waste poured into the environment by our industrial society. Such toxic materials are borne across entire continents and even across the entire planet by water and air. Such an extensive continental problem would not exist, of course, if each of the various bioregions functioned properly within its own context.

The larger functioning of bioregions leads to a consideration that the earth be viewed primarily as an interrelated system of bioregions, and only secondarily as a community of nations. The massive bureaucratic nations of the world have lost their inner vitality because they can no longer respond to the particular functioning of the various bioregions within their borders. A second difficulty within these large nations is the exploitation of some bioregions for the advantage of others. A third difficulty is the threatened devastation of the entire planet by the conflict between bureaucratic nations, with their weaponry capable of continental, and even planetary, devastation. To break these nations down into their appropriate bioregional communities could be a possible way to peace.

The bioregional mode of thinking and acting is presently one

169

of the most vigorous movements taking place on the North American continent. Its comprehensive concern is leading toward a reordering of all our existing establishments: political-legal, commercial-industrial, communications, educational, and religious. At present all of these establishments are involved in the devastating impact of industrial society on the natural world. The human arrogance they manifest toward the other natural members of the life communities remains only slightly affected by the foreboding concerning the future expressed by professional biologists and by others who have recognized that the imminent peril to the planet is not exactly the nuclear bomb, but the plundering processes that are extinguishing those very life systems on which we depend.

Yet the numbers of those speaking and acting and leading others in programs of reinhabiting the earth in a more benign relationship with the other members of these natural communities are growing constantly. This movement, often referred to as the Green movement, is fostering an ecological or bioregional context for every aspect of life, for education, economics, government, healing, and religion. So far, the movement remains a pervasive and growing mode of consciousness that is groping toward a more precise articulation of its own ideals, its institutional form, and its most effective programs of action.

Of primary importance in North America is identifying the various bioregions. To do that requires a sensitivity akin to that of the shamanic personality of tribal peoples. While bioregions have certain geographic boundaries, they also have certain mythic and historical modes of self-identification. This identification depends on ourselves as we participate in this process, which only now we begin to understand or appreciate.

·13·

The
Hudson River Valley:
A Bioregional Story

Tell me a story. How often we said that as children. Tell me a story. Story illumined the world for us in childhood. Even now we might make the request: tell me a story. Tell me the story of the river and the valley and the streams and woodlands and wetlands, of the shellfish and finfish. Tell me a story. A story of where we are and how we got here and the characters and roles that we play. Tell me a story, a story that will be my story as well as the story of everyone and everything about me, the story that brings us together in a valley community, a story that brings together the human community with every living being in the valley, a story that brings us together under the arc of the great blue sky in the day and the starry heavens at night, a story that will drench us with rain and dry us in the wind, a story told by humans to one another that will also be the story that the wood thrush sings in the thicket, the story that the river recites in its downward journey, the story that Storm King Mountain images forth in the fullness of its grandeur.

It's a long story, a story that begins with the fracture across the eastern borders of the North American continent resulting from the clashing and rifting of tectonic plates, and it includes the molten intrusion whereby the Palisades emerged to terminate in those massive cracked columns to the west. The story of the great hydrological cycle that has drawn up from the Gulf and across from the Pacific and down from the Arctic and in from the Atlantic entire oceans of water and has poured them down in unending sequence over this region to give to the valley its shape, its fertility, and made of it a meeting place as the northern extreme of southern lifeforms and the southern extreme of northern lifeforms.

The story of the valley is the story of the glaciation that came down from the frigid north as recently as fifty thousand years ago to cover this area with ice more than a thousand feet in height, driving southward the multitude of living beings for some thousands of years and then returning northward some fifteen thousand years ago, leaving this region to take on its present shape and luxuriance of life, its trees and grasses and flowers, its singing birds and ambling bears, its red foxes, pheasants, wild turkeys, and bobolinks.

The story of the valley is also the story of the Indians who originally dwelled in this region. Even now, in the names of the area, we recognize the ghosts of the indigenous peoples: the Mahicans, the Wappinger, the Hackensack and the Raritan, the Kitawonks, the Tappans across the river, the Sinsinks of the Ossining area. These names of earlier tribes carry a mysterious abiding quality. As Chief Seattle once said of us and our cities: "When the last Red Man shall have perished, and the memory of my tribe shall have become a myth among the White Men, these shores will swarm with the invisible dead of my tribe, and when your children's children think themselves alone in the field, the store, the shop, upon the highway, or in the silence of the pathless woods, they will not be alone." Chief Seattle then continues with a profound insight into the enduring trauma being shaped in the psychic depths of the white man: "At night, when the streets of your cities and villages are silent and you think them deserted, they will throng with the returning hosts that once filled them and still love this beautiful land. The White Man will never be alone."

These voices are there in the wind, in the unconscious depths of our minds. These voices are there not primarily to indict us for our cruelties, but to identify the distortions in our relations with the land and its inhabitants, and also to guide us toward a mutually enhancing human-earth relationship in this beautiful valley.

The valley was at the height of its grandeur when one day the mainmast of a strange sailing vessel broke over the horizon. The sails unfurled to their full expanse as the *Half Moon* came into full view and sailed across the bar at Sandy Hook and on through the Narrows into the channel and eventually up into the valley, past this region, to the shores of Albany.

Never was the region more brilliant in its color, in the exuberance of its life expression, in the grandeur of its tall white pines, in its beaver population, in the abundance of its oysters and clams, in its shad and tomcod and striped bass. Never were the woodlands more resonant with their songbirds, never were the skies more often witness to the peregrine falcon, the red-tailed hawks, and the bald eagles. Nor was the water ever more refreshing as it came down from the Adirondacks to meet the sea water around what later became Poughkeepsie.

We need to recall all this as we tell the story of the valley, for the valley required heavenly as well as earthly forces to bring it into being. It was a poignant moment then, when the sails from the east appeared over the horizon, for never again would the region have quite the mysterious brooding of the natural world in its pre-European phase, or that special mode of human presence to the natural world as was given by the indigenous peoples of this continent. When the sails appeared, the entire continent might have shuddered.

In 1907 there were numerous celebrations throughout the valley commemorating the arrival of our European ancestors in this region. Our settlements, our cultural and industrial achievements, were seen as high moments in the story of the valley. As we look back on these celebrations now, they appear to have had a certain naiveté, an exaggerated pride, even a certain arrogance, witnessing to our human tendencies toward self-glorification, oblivious of the larger consequences of our actions. These earlier celebrations honored the human at the expense of every other living being in the valley.

The distinguishing aspect of our more recent celebrations is that we now honor this region in and for itself, while trying to discover how our human presence to the region can be an enhancement rather than a diminishment. In this sense our celebrations are the opposite of those earlier celebrations. We have looked back over the centuries since the first European vessel sailed into the river and found that while they have been a period of glory and conquest for ourselves, what have they been from the standpoint of the valley in its natural forms.

What did it mean to the beaver that soon became extinct in much of the region? What did it mean to the millions of hemlock that were cut down simply for their bark for tanning hides? What did it mean for the great oyster beds and for the other shellfish that thrived so abundantly in the river? What did it mean to the organisms in the soil that later suffered from abusive agriculture? What did it forbode for the river that would receive the toxic runoff of chemical agriculture? What did it mean for the wetlands along the river that were filled in for trash heaps or to make way for railroads and highways? What did it mean for the river life when a nuclear generating station was set up at Indian Point? So we might ask ourselves those questions concerning the valley and the meaning of that moment when the mainmast of the *Half Moon* appeared above the Atlantic horizon.

As it came through the gap between Sandy Hook and the Rockaway Peninsula, through the Narrows into the upper bay, then into the river, the native peoples watching could have known nothing of their future or of the thoughts or intentions of the men in the great vessel. Nor could the men on the *Half Moon* have known fully their own minds nor the larger intentions of their political regimes nor the cultural ideals or economic forces that had brought them. Obscure forces were at work, driving an awesome transformation of this planet, ambivalent forces capable of both benign and deleterious consequences, forces with demonic intensity, forces ready to tear the North American continent to pieces in a stupendous effort to transcend the human condition in some serene millennial fulfillment.

We have all experienced these forces. A kind of possession seized us, and every being on this planet has felt its impact on a scale somewhat like those great geological upheavals or like the descent of a glacier. The valley and ourselves are both somewhat shattered. And yet the enormous creative forces deep in the reality of things are asserting themselves. Gratefully the valley before us has not been ruined so extensively as those valleys where a long sequence of dams has been built or where toxic wastes have completely ruined the aquatic life or where the water has been drained off into the fields for irrigation projects. We think of the Tennessee Valley, the Ohio, the Colorado, and the irreparable damage done to those and so many other regions over the years.

The Hudson River has not been dammed below the region of Troy. The abundant rainfall is sufficient for agricultural production. The river has, so far, been saved from exploitation of its fresh water because of the abundant water available from the Delaware Basin.

Even if the valley is more resilient than many other valleys of the North American continent and even if it has been saved from the devastation they have experienced, the river, the woodlands, and the soil have become seriously deteriorated over these past centuries, especially in this century, when the valley has been saturated with petrochemical residues in its air, its water and its soil. Every living species in the valley has experienced the deleterious influence of our human presence. Even now the increased occupation of the land for shopping malls, parking lots, roadways, corporate headquarters, industrial sites, and development projects is progressively eliminating habitat needed by various bird and animal as well as insect and plant species. Even now our chemical agriculture is damaging the soil and poisoning the streams; industrial waste products and city sewage are pouring through the valley. Realizing all this, we must ask what has happened?

It would appear that we could not possibly have done all this or presently be doing this, for we see now that it is all self-destructive. We must have been in a trance state—caught up in our illusory world of wires and wheels and concrete and steel and roadways— where we race back and forth in unending frenzy.

The world of life, of spontaneity, the world of dawn and sunset and starlight, the world of soil and sunshine, of meadow and woodland, of hickory and oak and maple and hemlock and pineland forests, of wildlife dwelling around us, of the river and its well-being—all of this some of us are discovering for the first time as the integral community in which we live. Here we experience the reality and the values that evoke in us our deepest moments of reflection, our revelatory experience of the ultimate mystery of things. Here, in this intimate presence to the valley in all its vitality, we receive those larger intuitions that lead us to dance and sing, intuitions that activate our imaginative powers in their most creative functions. This, too, is what inspires our weddings, our home life, and our joy in our children. Even our deepest human sensitivities emerge from our region, our place, our specific habitat, for the earth does not give itself to us in a global sameness. It gives itself to us in arctic and tropical regions, in seashore and desert, in prairie-lands and woodlands, in mountains and valleys. Out of each a unique shaping of life takes place, a community, an integral community of all the geological as well as the biological and the human

176

components. Each region is a single community so intimately related that any benefit or any injury is immediately experienced throughout the entire community.

So it is also with ourselves. We who live here in the Hudson River Valley constitute a single organic community with the river and the lowlands and the surrounding hills, with the sunlight and the rain, with the grasses and the trees and all the living creatures about us. We are all in some manner needed by one another. We may disdain the insects and the lowly plankton in the river, we may resent the heat of summer or the ice of winter, we may try to impose our mechanistic patterns on the biological rhythms of the region, but as soon as any one of these natural functions is disturbed in its proper expression, we are in trouble, and there is no further support to which we can appeal.

The natural world has produced its present variety, its abundance, and the creative interaction of all its components through billions of experiments. To shatter all this in the belief that we can gain by thwarting nature in its basic spontaneities is a brash and foolish thing, as is amply demonstrated by many of our past activities. If we do not alter our attitude and our activities, our children and grandchildren will live not only amid the ruins of the industrial world, but also amid the ruins of the natural world itself. That this will not happen, that the valley will be healed where it is damaged, preserved in its present integrity and renewed in its creative possibilities, is the hope that is before us.

Just now we are, as it were, returning to the valley, finding our place once again after a long period of alienation. At such a moment in our own history, as well as in the history of the region, we need first of all an extreme sensitivity to the needs of all the various components of the valley community—the needs of the river, the soil, the air; the needs of the various living forms that inhabit the valley; and the special needs of the human community dwelling here in the valley. We need to know how these relate

177

to one another. Prior to our coming from abroad, all of these components of the region had worked out a mutually enhancing relationship. The valley was flourishing.

When we arrived we brought with us an attitude that the region was here for our exploitation. Even though we broke our treaties with the Indian tribes, we did recognize their rights and made treaties with them. It never entered our minds that we should also have made treaties with the river and with the land and with the region as a whole. In this we failed to do what even God did after the flood: "I set my rainbow in the cloud and it shall be a sign of the covenant between me and the earth. When I bring clouds over the earth and the rainbow is seen in the clouds, I will remember my covenant which is between me and you and every living creature of all flesh; and the waters shall never again become a flood to destroy all flesh."

Such a treaty, or some such spiritual bond, between ourselves and the natural world, is needed, a bonding based on the principle of mutual enhancement. The river and its valley are neither our enemy to be conquered, nor our servant to be controlled, nor our mistress to be seduced. The river is a pervasive presence beyond all these. It is the ultimate psychic as well as the physical context out of which we emerge into being and by which we are nourished, guided, healed, and fulfilled. As the gulls soaring above the river in its estuary region, as the blossoms along its banks, the fish within its waters, so, too, the river is a celebration of existence, of life lived in intimate association with the sky, the winds from every direction, the sunlight. The river is the binding presence throughout the valley community. We do not live primarily in Poughkeepsie or Peekskill, Newburgh or Yonkers. We live primarily along the river or in the valley. We are river people and valley people. That fact determines more than anything else the way we live, the foods we eat, the clothes we wear, how we travel. It also provides the content and context for celebrating life in its most sublime meaning.

We celebrate the valley not in some generalized planetary context, but in the specific setting that we have indicated. It is a celebration of our place, but our place as story, for we need only look about us to appreciate the grandeur of these surroundings. The grandeur of the valley is expressed most fully in its story.

The story, as we have seen, is a poignant one, a story with its glory, but not without its tragedy. Now the story begins to express the greatest change in the valley since the modern story of the valley began in 1609. This is the moment of change from a sense of the valley as subservient to human exploitation to a sense of the valley as an integral natural community which is itself the basic reality and the basic value, and of the human as having its true glory as a functioning member, rather than as a conquering invader, of this community. Our role is to be the instrument whereby the valley celebrates itself. The valley is both the object and the subject of the celebration. It is our high privilege to articulate this celebration in the stories we tell and in the songs we sing.

·14·

The Historical
Role of the
American Indian

The Indian peoples of this hemisphere will soon be ending their first five centuries of contact with the European peoples who have been occupying this region of the world since the early sixteenth century. While there was a certain historical inevitability in this meeting, no adequate interpretation of this event is yet available. It remains, however, one of the most significant events in the total history of the earth. At first glance it was pure tragedy on one side, unmeasured gain on the other, but this is too simple a view. The final evaluation has not yet been made. Just now there is a deeply tragic aspect on the human level for all concerned.

The effects of this meeting have varied in South America, in Mexico and Central America, in the United States, in Canada. The Spanish, Portuguese, French, English, and Dutch were the earliest to occupy the North American continent. Other peoples of Europe came later. Peoples from Africa were brought here. Then, more recently, peoples of Asia arrived. Among all these newcomers the Indian peoples maintain their unique status as the original dwellers in this region of the world. They have this position of honor not merely by their temporal priority, but also by their mystical understanding and communion with the continent.

The continent itself and the living beings upon it were safe and the Indian secure until the invasion took place. Since then, the continent, with its rivers and valleys, its mountains and plains, has been exploited with all the violence that modern science and technology could summon. The Indian tribes have suffered to hold onto at least some of their territory and to maintain some semblance of their way of life. From having been one of the freest peoples who ever lived, they have become one of the most confined, culturally as well as physically.

Even so, there have been renewals within the Indian traditions. Within this century, after a decline in the nineteenth century, new strengths have developed, numbers have increased, cultural expression has expanded, political competence has grown. Yet the aggression of the Euroamericans against the Indians and their territory continues, directly and in more subtle ways. Extensive efforts to improve the situation remain ineffective because there is still too exclusive a commitment to the white man's values, his lifestyle, and his sense of superiority. The very structure of our technological civilization prevents us from communicating in depth with the native peoples.

There does exist, however, a widespread awareness that the Indians on this continent have a significant place in the historical and cultural development of the human community. Survival and development within their own cultural traditions concerns not only the Indians; it concerns the other peoples of this continent, as well as the human community itself.

If we assume that the Indian peoples have such significance, it

181

is all the more important that the other peoples of this continent develop attitudes that will make the next five centuries a creative period for the Indians. It is especially important that the Euroamericans develop confidence in the extensive human resources that are available to these original inhabitants of this continent. If we have broken their rhythm of development, it is important that we assist in the recovery of the rhythm. Only if we recognize and appreciate this rhythm will we be able to step aside to let the deeper qualities of the tradition develop from within.

Our first duty is to see that the Indians dwelling here have the land, the resources, and the independence they needed to be themselves. This involves radical abandonment of the policy of assimilation. To do this requires much of us because of our compulsive savior instincts. We take up the burden of saving others even when in fact we destroy them. Religious personalities from the European culture have been especially limited in their ability to see the profoundly religious and spiritual qualities of the Indian traditions. European-derived peoples have consistently had difficulty communicating with others within a shared human context. We have tended to confer salvation—whether political, social, economic, or religious—and have resisted incorporating the resources offered by others into our own process of becoming.

However we like to think of our presence here as righteous, benign, elevated in its intentions, and justified by our civilizational mission, the consequences have been disastrous to the extreme. Yet there will be little mention here of the violent forces that have been at work. We recognize all the destructive events of Indian-White relationships that have taken place during these centuries: the dispossession of Indians from the land; the rapaciousness of settlers; the communication of disease that wiped out many tribes and critically weakened others; the destruction of Indian food supply; the corruption and mismanagement of government administrations; the exploitation of natural resources; the pollution of air, water, and earth; the denial of basic Indian rights; and the betrayal of solemn treaties. Repeated mention of these events has its uses, but also its limitations.

For both ourselves and the native peoples it is also useful to reflect on the interior sources of renewal that are available to the Indian. These are our hope for the future. Activation of these inner responses of the Indian could assist in shaping the future of all the peoples of this continent. Even more, it could assist in the survival of the continent itself as a viable habitat for all those living beings that presently inhabit this region of the earth.

One resource from which American tribal peoples draw strength for cultural survival and renewal is their awareness of having won a moral victory of unique dimensions during the past five centuries. Many peoples have been besieged in the course of history, many have disappeared from the earth, many have survived over long periods to rise in renewed vigor. It would, however, be difficult to find a people who over such a long period have undergone such destructive influences, yet who have survived and preserved their identity so firmly as the American Indian.

We have won our battles with the Indian in the military-political order, in the possession of property, in the power to control the exterior destinies of the native peoples; but we have lost in the moral sphere to such a degree that we are ourselves amazed to discover the depth and violence of our destructive instincts, and this not just as a speculative truth, but as the lived reality of our own existence. That our deeds were sometimes done for "sacred" purposes and with the highest cultural intentions is an irony that baffles any human effort of understanding.

Even with such recognition by the white man, no immediate cessation of our aggressive deeds can be expected. The economic and political realities of our lives have set us on a course that apparently will continue into the indefinite future. On occasion this aggression can be mitigated, but it can no longer assume the position of righteousness that it once did. In principle a counteraction has been initiated that in time must have its effects. The Indians,

strengthened by a new consciousness of themselves and their resources, are now able to resist more effectively. Whatever the situation, however, it is important that they have not retreated simply
into a negative or merely antagonistic position. They have established a creative response rooted in their ability to sustain life in
its moment of high tragedy and to continue their human development in its most distinctive aspects. This attitude has been adopted
on a wide scale. Awareness of their moral victory has always existed, but it has now led to an increasing confidence and is beginning to function more effectively. The peoples of this continent
have a genius that cannot forever be denied its expression.

A second support for the native peoples of this continent is the
awareness that they give to the human mode of being a unique
expression that belongs among the great spiritual traditions of mankind. It is an observed fact in history that high religious traditions
are often carried by peoples who are not as numerous, as powerful, or as advanced in science and technology as other peoples.
Just as other traditions have their specific glories—as India has its
awareness of divine transcendence, China its mystical humanism,
and Europe its sense of a historical divine savior—so the Indian
peoples of America have their own special form of nature mysticism.
Awareness of a numinous presence throughout the entire cosmic
order establishes among these peoples one of the most integral
forms of spirituality known to us. The cosmic, human, and divine
are present to one another in a way that is unique. It is difficult
to find a word or expression for such a mode of experience. It
might simply be called a nature mysticism. This is precisely the
mystique that is of utmost necessity at the present time to reorient
the consciousness of the present occupants of the North American
continent toward a reverence for the earth, so urgent if the biosystems of the continent are to survive.

This numinous mode of consciousness has significance for the
entire human community. Indeed, one of the primary instincts of
the human community is to protect and foster such primordial ex-

184

periences. These experiences, which generally present themselves as divine revelations, are irreplaceable. They provide the foundations upon which the cultural systems of the various peoples are established. They also determine the distinctive psychic structure of individual personalities within the culture. Together these revelations form the ultimate psychic support for the human venture itself.

The Indian peoples have become increasingly aware that they carry a primordial tradition of great significance for the entire human community. Because of their hurt in association with the dominant political powers of the continent, the Indians might well conceal the inner mysteries of their spiritual traditions lest they be trivialized by a secular society that destroys the inner meaning of everything it touches. But the reality is there; it is widely recognized. Its inner resplendence is finding its fitting modern expression and the wide influence it deserves.

A third resource that the native peoples possess is the instinctive awareness of their own qualities of endurance. Those historians acquainted with the larger range of human cultural development witness that frequently the peoples of the earth, the dispossessed peoples, those lowest in the social hierarchy, have greater survival value than those with higher status, with ruling power, or even with higher intellectual achievements. This happened in Europe: with the assertion of the tribal languages over the Latin imposition, with Gothic architecture, with English common law over Roman legal codes, with Protestant revolt against Roman Catholicism in the sixteenth century. It occurred in India when peoples of a higher civilization invaded the region in the middle of the second millennium B.C. During the first centuries of occupation, the incoming group established itself in a dominant position in various areas of life, but almost immediately the peoples who were closer to the earth, the peoples without the more sophisticated culture, the peoples with less political or social prestige, began to make their presence felt in every sphere of life, from the simplest elements of lifestyle to the highest spiritual insights. A process of transformation from below was initiated and continues even to the present. The history of India may accurately be interpreted as the acculturation from below of a dominant social order, external in its origins, massive in its power, and extensive in its intellectual sophistication.

A similar process can be observed in those Latin American countries that still have significant Indian populations. It may not take place to such a degree in North America because of the limited numbers of native peoples that survive in this region. Still, the influence of the indigenous peoples on the incoming Europeans has been more extensive than is commonly realized. Further modifications can be expected in the future.

Another great strength of the Indian peoples lies in their interior communion with the archetypal world of the collective unconscious. This is manifested in their extensive capacity for the use of symbolism, by their visionary experience, by their dream power, and by their use of language. To renew their ancient symbolisms is to renew their ancient techniques of power. Just how these will function in modern times is less clear than we might wish, yet the Indian capacity to reach deep into the realms of numinous power remains evident in their life, art, literature, and ritual observances. The various tribes are renewing their vision quest. The sweatlodge ceremonies are being performed once again, even in prisons, where there is special need for this renewal experience. The Plains Indians are again performing the sun dance, with all its cosmic renewal symbolism. The number of those working in the various arts is increasing. Writers such as Scott Momaday and Paula Gunn Allen and a long list of others are producing a new literature. Vine Deloria has enabled the Indians to establish a legal defense of their own rights. Scholars in every branch of study, but especially in anthropology, have begun to appear. Alfonso Ortiz is a principal editor and writer in the eighteen-volume *Handbook on the North American Indian* being published by the Smithsonian Institution. A helpful interpretation of these renewal activities can be found in the work of Jamake Highwater, *The Primal Mind.*

186

This intimate communion with the depths of their own psychic structure is one of the main differences between the psychic functioning of the Indian and the psychic functioning of the Euroamerican in modern times. We have so developed our rational processes, our phenomenal ego, that we have lost much of the earlier communion we had with the archetypal world of our own unconscious. The American Indian, on the other hand, is the living exemplification of recent understanding of the collective unconscious. All the symbolisms are there—the journey symbol, the heroic personality, the symbolism of the center, the mandala symbolism of the self, the various transformation symbols. Of special importance is the Earth Mother archetype. While this is found universally among the various tribes, it has had a special development with the Navajo in their approach to the earth as Corn Mother or as Spider Woman. When a child is born, an ear of corn is placed beside it as a way of acknowledging the role of a mothering principle with powers beyond that of the human mother.

Other symbols have found expression in the creation myths, the initiation ceremonies, the sacred pipe, the healing rituals, the sun dance, the vision quest. They are also evident in the literature. Some of the oral literature is passing into a written literature. The hope must be that more of this oral literature will be committed to writing, not only in the tribal languages, but also in English—the most available transtribal language for the Indian peoples. This is important since literature must always be one of the main sources of guidance as well as a main source of psychic energy for the task of renewal.

In the new literature of writers such as Scott Momaday, the interior dynamics of Indian renewal find their finest expression, although this expression can be discovered throughout the various forms of artistic creation that are once again emerging. In such periods the first step is the recovery and renewal of esteem for the ancient arts and literature. Then come the new art and the new literature, which bring the ancient cultural dynamics into present expression. In the future we can expect the Indian traditions of dance and song to emerge in a new creative context.

The arts of the Indians in these past five centuries indicate their capacity to absorb outside influences and to reshape them in accord with their own genius. So with the beadwork of the Indians. There was beadwork prior to the arrival of the European, but it flourished with new vigor once modern beads were available. Beads were then able to express visions they had never expressed previously. They became a resplendent display of the interior grandeur of the human. This capacity for absorption and re-creation in the cultural order could be illustrated in almost every phase of Indian life. Powerful cultural forces were already at work in the depths of the Indian mode of consciousness, forces that enabled the Indian to interact with the white man's traditions, even in such things as the ghost dance and in establishing the peyote cult. Earlier it can be observed in the religious movement begun by Handsome Lake among the Seneca.

This is, of course, only one aspect of the interplay of cultural forces that has taken place between these two peoples. The other aspect is the influence exerted by the native peoples on the incoming European. One of the most fundamental is the influence of the Indian on the development of modern dance and its relations to the rhythms of the earth. Isadora Duncan, originator of interpretative dance in America, was, in her early years, influenced by the dance rhythms and movements of the Indian peoples.

In other realms of life, the Euroamerican has also been deeply influenced, so much so that C. G. Jung claimed that often in his dealings with Americans in psychotherapy he found an American Indian component in the psyche. The basic ideals of freedom found in the American peoples have been as profoundly influenced by the Indian ideals of personal freedom as by those traditions derived from their European ancestry. In the development of the U.S. Constitution, there was early reference to the Iroquois confederacy as a model. These examples are only a few of the areas of life that have been influenced by the Indian. One area, however, that has not been influenced by the Indian, or even modified, is our sense of private property, but that, too, may change in the future.

A fifth source of strength for the native peoples of this continent is their appreciation of human relations with the earth. Even those desolate regions assigned to the Indian tribes by the white peoples seem to become sources of strength. This has become true particularly for the Navajo. After having been removed from their original land and placed in starving conditions for years, the Navajo were given back a desolate part of their former territory. Despite their displacement, they survived in communion with this territory to become the most populous of all the tribal peoples of the continent. What is profoundly impressive is the subjective communion that takes place between the Indian and the North American continent.

This communion with the natural world, understood with a certain instinctive awareness by tribal peoples, is something that we, with all our science and technology, seem unable to appreciate, even when our very existence is imperiled. As Europeans on this continent, we have had a certain sense of ourselves as above all other living forms, as the lordly rulers of the continent. We see the North American continent as divinely presented to us to do with as we please. We were the bearers of that mystical something that we call "civilization." The continent was simply there as an abiding reality that would by some inevitable law not only provide our basic needs, but also endure whatever affliction we might lay upon it. It would sustain any amount of damage as an inexhaustible store of nourishment and of energy for carrying out our divine mission. With supreme shock we discover that our historic mission is not what we thought it was. Beyond that we discover that this continent is a delicate balance of life systems, that the fuels for our machines are limited, that defacing the earth defiles ourselves and destroys the divine voice that speaks so powerfully through every phase of cosmic activity.

The Indian now offers to the Euroamerican a mystical sense

189

of the place of the human and other living beings. This is a difficult teaching for us since we long ago lost our capacity for being present to the earth and its living forms in a mutually enhancing manner. This art of communion with the earth we can relearn from the Indian. Thus a reverse dependence is established. Survival in the future will likely depend more on our learning from the Indian than the Indian's learning from us. In some ultimate sense we need their mythic capacity for relating to this continent more than they need our capacity for mechanistic exploitation of the continent.

A sixth source of strength for the Indian is the traditional heroic ideal. The Indians have never accepted human life as ordinary, as something that can be managed in a controlled or painless manner. They realize that life tests the deepest qualities within the human personality, qualities that emerge in heroic combat not merely with others, but also with oneself and with the powers of the universe. The sacred function of enemies was to assist one another to the heroic life by challenge, even by the challenge of death. For this to be effective, however, it was necessary that there be a certain equality between the protagonists.

The Indians and ourselves will long be at war. It has never ceased and possibly will not cease in the foreseeable future. What must be hoped for is not exactly "peace," but a creative tension. Peace does not create heroic achievement. There must be challenge that forces the best that is in us to emerge into its proper expression, challenge that brings about dimensions in human achievement that would not otherwise be attained. Just now, however, the disproportion in size and power seems to remove all possibility of truly creative relationships that would be neither destructive nor paternalistic. Yet in the dialectic of human affairs, size and power eventually become self-destructive; the inequalities may eventually be leveled and the ancient fruitful combat relationships revived in a new setting.

What can be said is that the heroic life attitude is available and even demanded in the line of the Indian development itself. The great chiefs of the past have attained an immortal place in the annals of the human community. They are not simply tribal personalities, nor are they simply personalities of the American continent; they are personalities alongside the greatest leaders known to us. They have exhibited strength, spiritual insight, and compassion, as well as an aptitude for public affairs and a capacity for leadership in periods of unspeakable tragedy. A people who can hearken back to such leaders as Tecumseh, Little Turtle, Handsome Lake, Black Kettle, Geronimo, Seattle, Red Cloud, Crazy Horse, Chief Joseph, and Black Elk are necessarily a people capable of amazing human achievement. These men of the past talked with the nations of the world on a plane of equality. They spoke as equals with the highest officials in the land, including presidents in Washington. They stood in their regalia before the world, representing something beyond what the white man could understand at the time. They stood as numinous figures in a world that had lost its numinous qualities in favor of the practical qualities of exploitation and oppression.

This tradition of leadership has not been lost, even amid the physical and cultural disintegration that has taken place in many situations. Even in our modern cities Indians live in their own psychic world that seems an indestructible reality. This not so much in a role of antagonism, but simply as another mode of consciousness, expressing itself in a language that is not only foreign, but also mysterious. Translation is less a matter of linguistic skill than of feeling insight.

Among the resources we have least understood is the powerful intellectual tradition of the pre-Columbian Indian, shown by the Indian's capacity to interact creatively with the environment. Such emphasis is placed on Indian spiritual and aesthetic traditions that there is a tendency to downgrade Indian achievement in the social, scientific, and technological orders. Here we must attend to the wider range of Indian accomplishments throughout the Western hemisphere and see the Indian within the region of the United States as a border group, who, in contrast to the more elaborate Indian societies of Central and South America, remained by choice committed to the more free and diversified mode of tribal existence.

The greatest single achievement of the Indian was, of course, the occupation of this hemisphere, an event of vast significance, but one dimly appreciated by historians. After occupation of the hemisphere in a period some ten thousand years before the earliest Neolithic villages of the Near East, the sequence of civilizational development in the Indian world took place at a different pace than in some other parts of the Eurasian world. The New World civilizations were lacking in many of the achievements of the Eurasian world, but achieved much that did not or could not take place in the earlier phases of the Eurasian world.

Many parallel social structures developed in both hemispheres. Monumental religious centers were erected. Writing was developed. Astronomical calculations of extreme refinement were made. Mathematics of a high order appeared. The zero was discovered, probably at a time prior to the discovery of the zero in India. More animals were domesticated in Europe, but the New World domesticated more plants. It is estimated that Indian-derived plants now provide close to half the world's foods. Principal among these are corn and the potato. Then there are the pumpkin, squash, peanut, and several kinds of beans, among a much longer list that could be drawn up. Corn is the third largest grain crop in the world, after wheat and rice. Domestication of corn is considered a much more difficult achievement than that of either wheat or rice.

If we consider that an early Neolithic village mode of living, with domesticated plants, was achieved in the New World around 3400 B.C., we can see that this was not far behind the earliest village life of the Eurasian life. The higher civilizations in the New World, dating from around 700 B.C., were not much later in developing than the Chinese, the latest of the Eurasian civilizations. Without compiling more-extensive data on the subject, it is clear that the civilizational achievements were fully comparable in their human quality and in an equivalent order of magnitude to the civilizational achievements of the Eurasian world.

If not all of this was spread evenly throughout the North American continent, some of these achievements—especially the domestication of plants, mound building, and the capacity for erecting complex shelters—were widespread. Few Indian groups lacked corn. Indeed, the basic human capacities were found everywhere in a high stage of development. This was quickly recognized by European settlers and was one reason the Indian was so feared and assaulted, a rival who had reached a similar level of human achievement and certainly on occasion a higher moral and spiritual level.

The rhythm of Indian cultural development has been broken, but it has not been destroyed. The wilderness is largely gone and will never again be what it once was. Yet the psychic structure of the Indian, however shattered in recent centuries, retains an amazing integrity with itself; and these memories of the past demonstrate that the capacities claimed for the Indian are not a romantic conception of what might have been, but a reality that has been and even now remains an abiding influence on this continent. Neither the Indian nor ourselves have yet shown any adequate understanding of total Indian presence in this hemisphere and its meaning for the future. This will almost certainly, however, be one of the next stages in the development of Indian consciousness, as well as in our understanding of the Indian presence to our own European-derived culture.

These resources of the original peoples of this continent are also the basic resources that emerge from the depths of the earth process itself. The destinies of the Indian are inseparable from the destinies of the American earth. As we deal with one, so will we deal with the other—and in the end so will we deal with ourselves. The fate of the continent, the fate of the Indian, and our own fate are finally identical. None can be saved except in and through the others.

·15·

The Dream of the Earth: Our Way into the Future

In this late twentieth century we are somewhat confused about our human situation. We need guidance. Our immediate tendency is to seek guidance from our cultural traditions, from what might be designated as our cultural coding. Yet in this case our need seems to be for guidance that is beyond what our cultural traditions are able to give. Our cultural traditions, it seems, are themselves a major source of our difficulty. It appears necessary that we go beyond our cultural coding, to our genetic coding, to ask for guidance.

We seldom consider going to our genetic coding for guidance in our cultural development because we are generally unaware that our genetic coding provides the basic psychic and physical structure of our being. Our genetic coding determines not only our identity at birth; its guidance continues also in every cell of our bodies

194

throughout the entire course of our existence, a guidance manifested through the spontaneities within us. We need only to listen to what we are being told through the very structure and functioning of our being. We do invent our cultural coding, but the power to do so is itself consequent on the imperatives of our genetic coding.

Beyond our genetic coding, we need to go to the earth, as the source whence we came, and ask for its guidance, for the earth carries the psychic structure as well as the physical form of every living being upon the planet. Our confusion is not only within ourselves; it concerns also our role in the planetary community. Even beyond the earth, we need to go to the universe and inquire concerning the basic issues of reality and value, for, even more than the earth, the universe carries the deep mysteries of our existence within itself.

We cannot discover ourselves without first discovering the universe, the earth, and the imperatives of our own being. Each of these has a creative power and a vision far beyond any rational thought or cultural creation of which we are capable. Nor should we think of these as isolated from our own individual being or from the human community. We have no existence except within the earth and within the universe.

The human is less a being on the earth or in the universe than a dimension of the earth and indeed of the universe itself. The shaping of our human mode of being depends on the support and guidance of this comprehensive order of things. We are an immediate concern of every other being in the universe. Ultimately our guidance on any significant issue must emerge from this comprehensive source.

Nor is this source distant from us. The universe is so immediate to us, is such an intimate presence, that it escapes our notice, yet whatever authenticity exists in our cultural creations is derived from these spontaneities within us, spontaneities that come from an abyss of energy and a capacity for intelligible order of which we have only the faintest glimmer in our conscious awareness.

195

Our bonding with the larger dimensions of the universe comes about primarily through our genetic coding. It is the determining factor. It provides constant guidance in the organic functioning that takes place in all our sense functions; in our capacity for transforming food into energy; in our thought, imaginative, and emotional life. In a particular manner the genetic coding brings about a healing whenever we sustain any physical injury. Our genetic coding enables us to experience joy and sorrow on appropriate occasions. It provides the ability to speak and think and create. It establishes the context of our relation with the divine. All this is carried out by the spontaneities within us.

Although we must respond critically with these spontaneities to assure their authentic expression, we have ultimately no other source of guidance that possesses such inherent authenticity or which can function so effectively as a norm of reference in our actions. In earlier times these spontaneities were considered as revealing the natural law, the ultimate inner norm of guidance for human conduct, since they are the human phase of those instincts that enable a bird to build its nest, find its food, and discover its migratory route. Ultimately these instincts come from that mysterious source from where the universe itself came into being as articulated entities acting together in some ordered context.

Saint John tells us that in the beginning all things took on their shape through the word. The word was seen as psychic and personal. This was the numinous reality through which all things were made and without which was made nothing that has been made. The word, the self-spoken word, by its own spontaneities brought forth the universe and established itself as the ultimate norm of reality and of value. This is in accord with Lao Tzu, the Chinese sage, who tells us that the human models itself on the earth, earth models itself on heaven, heaven models itself on tao, tao models itself on its own spontaneity.

This spontaneity as the guiding force of the universe can be thought of as the mysterious impulse whereby the primordial fireball flared forth in its enormous energy, a fireball that contained in itself all that would ever emerge into being, a fireball that was the present in its primordial form, as the present is the fireball in its explicated form. What enabled the formless energies to emerge into such a fantastic variety of expression in shape, color, scent, feeling, thought, and imagination?

As with any aesthetic work, we attribute it especially to the imaginative capacities of the artist, for only out of imaginative power does any grand creative work take shape. Since imagination functions most freely in dream vision, we tend to associate creativity also with dream experience. The dream comes about precisely through the uninhibited spontaneities of which we are speaking. In this context we might say: In the beginning was the dream. Through the dream all things were made, and without the dream nothing was made that has been made.

While all things share in this dream, as humans we share in this dream in a special manner. This is the entrancement, the magic of the world about us, its mystery, its ineffable quality. What primordial source could, with no model for guidance, imagine such a fantastic world as that in which we live—the shape of the orchid, the coloring of the fish in the sea, the winds and the rain, the variety of sounds that flow over the earth, the resonant croaking of the bullfrogs, the songs of the crickets, and the pure joy of the predawn singing of the mockingbird?

Experience of such a resplendent world activated the creative imagination of Mozart in *The Magic Flute,* of Dante in his *Divine Comedy,* and gave to Shakespeare that range of sensitivity, understanding, and emotion that found expression in his plays. All of these derive from the visionary power that is experienced most profoundly when we are immersed in the depths of our own being and of the cosmic order itself in the dreamworld that unfolds within us in our sleep, or in those visionary moments that seize upon us in our waking hours. There we discover the Platonic forms, the dreams of Brahman, the Hermetic mysteries, the divine ideas

197

of Thomas Aquinas, the infinite worlds of Giordano Bruno, the world soul of the Cambridge Platonists, the self-organizing universe of Ilya Prigogine, the archetypal world of C. G. Jung.

Each of these is enormously attractive, having a certain inner coherence and revealing some aspect of the universe and of the planet Earth that is fascinating to the human mind. They can be understood as facets of a mystery too vast for human comprehension, a mystery with such power that even a fragment of its grandeur can evoke the great cultural enterprises that humans have undertaken. In this context we have shaped our languages and lifestyles, our poetry and music, our religious scriptures, our political ideals, our humanistic literature, our life-sustaining economies. Of special importance is the grand sequence of rituals whereby we insert ourselves into the ever-renewing sequence of springtime renewals in nature.

The excitement of life and the sustaining of psychic vigor are evoked by our participation in this magnificent process. Even before we give expression to any intellectual statement about the natural world, we stand in awe at the stars splashed in such prodigal display across the heavens, at the earth in its shaping of the seas and the continents, at the great hydrological cycles that lift such vast quantities of water up from the seas and rain them down over the land to nourish the meadows and the forests and to refresh the animals as the waters flow down through the valleys and back again to the seas. We marvel, too, at the millionfold sequence of living forms, from the plankton in the sea and the bacteria in the soil to the larger lifeforms that swim through the oceans and grow up from the soil and move over the land.

Much could be said, too, about the human as that being in whom this grand diversity of the universe celebrates itself in conscious self-awareness. While we emerge into being from within the earth process and enable the universe to come to itself in a special mode of psychic intimacy, it is evident that we have also a special power over the universe in its earthly expression. Therein lies the dramatic issue that is being played out in these centuries of human time that succeed to the ages of geological and biological time.

From our vantage point we can sketch out the great story of the universe from its beginning until now. We can recognize the earth as a privileged planet and see the whole as evolving out of some cosmic imaginative process. Any significant thought or speech about the universe finds its expression through such imaginative powers. Even our scientific terms have a highly mythic content—such words as *energy, life, matter, form, universe, gravitation, evolution.* Even such terms as *atom, nucleus, electron, molecule, cell, organism.* Each of these terms spills over into metaphor and mystery as soon as it is taken seriously.

As regards the origin and shaping forces in the universe, the geneticist Theodosius Dobzhansky considers that the universe in its emergence is neither determined nor random, but creative. This word *creative* is among the most mysterious words in any language. As with our words generally, this term, too, has been trivialized. Its numinous and its magic qualities have been diminished, also its visionary quality. We have substituted our real world of facts and figures for our visionary world.

We must reflect, however, on what we have gained in this substitution and what we have lost. We have lost our principal means of entering into the primordial directive and sustaining forces of the universe. We have in a very special manner lost our presence to the life-sustaining forces of the earth. Whatever our gains in terms of scientific advances or in our industrial economy, neither of these is very helpful in establishing an integral presence to the more profound depths of our own being or into the more powerful forces shaping both the universe and the planet on which we live.

Inherent in the human situation is the problem of keeping our cultural expression integrally related to our genetic endowment. Through our genetic endowment we maintain our intimate presence to the functioning of the earth community and to the emergent processes of the universe itself. This problem of properly relating cultural coding to the imperatives of our genetic coding is the central, the immediate, problem, a problem that does not exist, or exists in a minimal degree, with other species.

The human, we must understand, is genetically coded toward a further transgenetic cultural coding whereby we invent ourselves in the human expression of our being. While this capacity for self-formation is a high privilege, it is also a significant responsibility, since the powers we possess also give us extensive control over a wide range of earthly affairs. This cultural coding, once it is articulated as the functioning norm of a human community, is handed on by educational processes through parental care from the moment of birth. After birth a long educational process takes place that requires not only a family context, but also the assistance of a larger human community.

Because this cultural coding is freely determined, it finds expression in a wide diversity of forms throughout the human community. Once established as the normative reference of reality and value within the community, this cultural coding is carried on and expressed in the language and in the symbols that are learned quite early in life. The relation between our cultural coding and our genetic coding is evident in our use of language. We are genetically coded to speak; the specific manner of our speech, however, is our own invention. So, too, with the genetic imperative that we live in society. Just how we shape our social functioning is again our own invention. So it is with the rituals whereby we insert ourselves into the ever-renewing processes of the natural world and establish our world of meaning, our sense of reality and value.

All these are means whereby we articulate our special mode of being and fulfill our role in the universal order of things, all in response to the spontaneities that emerge from our genetic coding; ultimately, of course, they emerge from the larger community of life, from the integral functioning of the planet Earth, from the comprehensive functioning of the universal order of things, and from that numinous source from which all things receive their being, their energy, and their inherent grandeur.

We need to remember that this process whereby we invent ourselves in these cultural modes is guided by visionary experiences that come to us in some transrational process from the inner shaping tendencies that we carry within us, often in revelatory dream experience. Such dream experiences are so universal and so important in the psychic life of the individual and of the community that techniques of dreaming are taught in some societies.

In some societies, also, the early-morning gatherings are used for interpretation of the dream experiences of the previous night. This was the case with the Algonquin peoples of this continent when they were first observed by European missionaries. In some of the early reports, dreams were seen as so important that the religion of the Indians was identified as a religion of dreams.

Dreams were the main instrument of guidance in their daily activities as well as in the larger interpretation of life, for if our daytime experience is needed for awakening to the phenomenal world, our nighttime experience is needed for communion with those numinous powers from which the daylight forms themselves come into being. The great phases of cultural development are consistently attributed to such experiences.

Over the centuries this cultural coding of human communities has been articulated in its early Paleolithic tribal phase, in its Neolithic village phase, then in its classical civilizational phase, when the more populous centers arose with their more spacious architecture, their written literatures, their more elaborate religious, political, and economic establishments.

These achievements, which are sometimes designated as the full realization of the human mode of being, have a certain tendency to disintegrate in the manner that we are presently experiencing. Giambattista Vico, the eighteenth-century Neapolitan interpreter of human history, considered that the eighteenth century was the period when a second barbarism, a barbarism of refinement, erupted in the civilizational enterprise. A new descent into a more primitive state must then come about, a reimmersion in the natural forces out of which our cultural achievements came about originally. The forces of primitive imagination once again were required to renew the cultural integrity. A new contact with genetic coding was mandated.

Even while we indicate the role that is played by the dream vision in the cultural development of the human, we must also realize that the dream vision can be destructive as well as creative. It is a dangerous process if we are not fully sensitized to what our genetic coding is telling us. It has become especially dangerous in Western civilization when our cultural coding has set itself deliberately against our genetic coding and the instinctive tendencies of our genetic endowment are systematically negated. Such is the origin of our present situation.

Our secular, rational, industrial society, with its amazing scientific insight and technological skills, has established the first radically anthropocentric society and has thereby broken the primary law of the universe, the law of the integrity of the universe, the law that every component member of the universe should be integral with every other member of the universe and that the primary norm of reality and of value is the universe community itself in its various forms of expression, especially as realized on the planet Earth.

This new industrial coding, which arose first in Western society, has now been spread throughout the entire earth. Few peoples anywhere have escaped its influence. The relation of the human community to its genetic coding and to the entire functioning of the natural world is decisively altered. A profound shift in meaning is given to the entire evolutionary process.

The immediate advantages of this new way of life for its prime beneficiaries have been evident throughout these past two centuries. But, now, suddenly we begin to experience disaster on a scale never before thought possible. For a long while we looked back at prior times and the mythic accounts of how the world came into being, the sequence of transformations and the role of the human in the larger processes of nature; we looked back at these stories, at the revelatory dreams of these earlier peoples, at their sense of numi-

nous energies governing the phenomenal world, at their efforts
to establish contact with these powers through strange shamanic
performances or through more-programmed initiatory and sacrificial
rituals; we looked back at all this with a certain disdain for these
dark ages, although with a restrained envy of the visions recorded
in their sacred literature, of their heroic experiences, and often of
an artistic grandeur that we could not match.

We were the sane, the rational, the dreamless people, the chosen
people of destiny. We had found the opening to a more just society,
a more reasoning intellectual life. Above all we had the power to re-
engineer the planet with our energy systems, our dams and irrigation
projects, our great cities. We could clear the forests, drain the
marshes, construct our railways and highways, all to the detriment of
the other living forms of earth, to the elimination of needed habitat,
to the obstruction of migration paths, to the cutting off of access to
waterways. We could subdue the wilderness, domesticate the planet.
We were finally free from the tyranny of nature. Nature was now our
servant, delivering up to us its energies, altering its biological rhythms
in accord with our mechanical contrivances.

The human condition could be overcome by our entrepreneurial
skills. Nuclear energy would give us limitless power. Through
genetic engineering we could turn chickens into ever more effective egg-laying machines, cows into milk-making machines, steers
into meat-making contrivances, all according to human preference,
not according to the inner spontaneities of these living beings as
determined by their genetic coding, a coding shaped through some
billions of years of experiment and natural selection.

Ever-heightened consumption was the way to ultimate human
fulfillment. Every earthly being was reduced from its status as a
sacred reality to that of being a "natural resource," available for
human use for whatever trivial purposes humans might invent. It
would take a while to describe what has been happening in all our
professions and institutions in this period of assumed cultural
progress.

This magical word *progress!* Although long ago discredited as an illusory belief, we still hear the word spoken with a kind of religious reverence, even as a final norm of reference in any consideration of reality and value. Loren Eiseley has written a description of our present relationship with nature: "We have reentered nature, not like a Greek shepherd on a hillside hearing joyfully the returning pipes of Pan, but rather as an evil and precocious animal who slinks home in the night with a few stolen powers. The serenity of the gods is not disturbed. They know on whose head the final lightning will fall."

Suddenly we awaken to the devastation that has resulted from the entire modern process. A thousand pages would be needed to recount what has happened. It can best be summarized by the title of Rachel Carson's book, *Silent Spring,* a title taken from Keats: "The sedge is withered from the lake/and no birds sing." The book itself is dedicated to Albert Schweitzer, who tells us: "Man has lost the capacity to foresee and to forestall. He will end by destroying the earth."

This is a bitter moment, not simply for the human, but for the earth itself. The biblical slaughter of the innocents is only a faint foreshadowing of the slaughter of the innocents taking place in these times, when the innocents are not simply individuals capable of replacement within their species, but the slaughter of species themselves, irreversibly, eternally.

It is a bitter moment especially because our hopes were so high, our arrogance unrestrained even by simple modesty. It is a bitter moment, also, because the origins of our actions go so deep into our spiritual and cultural traditions, fostering a sense that we are the measure of all things. Our sense of endless progress emerges from the millennial expectations of our scriptures. From the prophetic period onward our scriptures speak to us of a period when the human condition would be surmounted, when justice would reign, when the fruits of the earth would be available in lavish abundance. All this fostered a profound resentment against our human condition.

We somehow did not belong to the community of earth. We were not an integral component of the natural world. Our destiny was not here. We deserved a better world, although we had not even begun to appreciate the beauty and grandeur of this world or the full measure of its entrancing qualities.

What we seem unwilling or unable to recognize is that our entire modern world is itself inspired not by any rational process, but by a distorted dream experience, perhaps by the most powerful dream that has ever taken possession of human imagination. Our sense of progress, our entire technological society, however rational in its functioning, is a pure dream vision in its origin and in its objectives. This dream vision of the coming Day of the Lord, as mentioned by the prophets, was taken up by Daniel in his interpretation of the apocalyptic dream of Nebuchadnezzar. Although this entrancing vision of the universe was originally presented as the spiritual triumph of the divine kingdom, it was later described by John the Evangelist as a blissful period beyond the human condition, to be experienced within the historical order prior to the ultimate transference of the kingdom to its celestial setting.

The story of this dream vision and the manner of its transformation into the vision of progress has become the central story of the human community, even of the earth process itself. René Dubos caught the significance of our more recent commitment to progress in the title of his book *The Dreams of Reason*. That very rational process that we exalt as the only true way to understanding is by a certain irony discovered to be itself a mythic, imaginative dream experience.

The difficulty of our times is our inability to awaken out of this cultural pathology. Thousands of articles have been written and a long list of books could be compiled concerning this commitment to progress and to the sense of unlimited growth that it evokes. Yet its control over the human venture remains more vigorous than ever. Whatever the validity of the original vision of an unfolding spiritual progress, this vision has proved too much for humans to manage in any disciplined way.

The difficulty is that this dream of a millennial transformation to be achieved by science and technology under the direction of the modern corporation is thought of as the singular reality controlling all things and giving meaning to the whole of history. This vision alone makes life worthwhile. That is why the millennial vision is so important to the advertising industry, with its projection of a paradise that can be obtained through product consumption, any product.

When the absurdity of progress through exponential growth was indicated a few years ago in a work entitled *The Limits to Growth,* a general outcry could be heard across the country. That outcry was more than a justified criticism of the specific data or the time scale of future events. It was resentment against the indication that the dynamism of our consumer society was the supreme pathology of all history.

Use of the term *supreme pathology* can be justified by the observation that the change that is taking place in the present is not simply another historical transition or another cultural transformation. Its order of magnitude is immensely more significant in its nature and in its consequences. We are indeed closing down the major life systems of the planet.

We are acting on a geological and biological order of magnitude. We are changing the chemistry of the planet. We are altering the great hydrological cycles. We are weakening the ozone layer that shields us from cosmic rays. We are saturating the air, the water, and the soil with toxic substances so that we can never bring them back to their original purity. We are upsetting the entire earth system that has, over some billions of years and through an endless sequence of experiments, produced such a magnificent array of living forms, forms capable of seasonal self-renewal over an indefinite period of time.

That the changes taking place are of this order of magnitude can be supported by reference to a conference held in September 1986 in Washington, D.C., a conference on the future of living species sponsored by the National Academy of Sciences and the Smithsonian Institution. There our foremost biologists expressed their forebodings concerning the future.

E. O. Wilson from Harvard indicated that we are losing ten thousand species each year and that this rate of loss is increasing. Norman Myers, a specialist in the rain forests and vegetation of the world, said that the "impending extinction spasm" is likely to produce the "greatest single setback to life's abundance and diversity since the first flickerings of life almost four billion years ago." Other speakers agreed that our present extinction of living forms is, in its order of magnitude, paralleled only by the great geological and climatic upheavals that changed the earth in the distant past.

Paul Ehrlich, who has studied the questions of extinction for more than twenty years, made some of the most startling statements. He observed that "humanity will bring upon itself consequences depressingly similar to those expected from a nuclear winter," and he expects them to be accompanied by the famine and epidemic disease generally associated with the concept of nuclear winter.

Both Wilson and Ehrlich were concerned with questions of human conduct in dealing with such a devastating situation. Wilson proposed that in the end "I suspect it will all come down to a decision of ethics, how we value the natural world in which we have evolved and now—increasingly—how we regard our situation as individuals." Ehrlich considers that to look to technology for a solution "would be a lethal mistake." His final suggestion was that "scientific analysis points, curiously, toward the need for a quasi-religious transformation of contemporary cultures."

My own suggestion is that we must go far beyond any transformation of contemporary culture. We must go back to the genetic imperative from which human cultures emerge originally and from which they can never be separated without losing their integrity and their survival capacity. None of our existing cultures can deal with this situation out of its own resources. We must invent, or reinvent, a sustainable human culture by a descent into our prerational, our instinctive, resources. Our cultural resources have lost their integrity. They cannot be trusted. What is needed is not transcendence but "inscendence," not the brain but the gene.

The assumption about traditional cultural codings is that they will foster rather than suppress or extinguish those more profound imperatives that govern the universe in its physical structures, its chemical composition, and its biological forms, as well as in its human expression. Indeed the species coding of the human carries within itself all those deeper spontaneities that guide the authentic developments of our cultural codings.

The genetic coding that gives to the human its species identity is integral with this larger complex of codings whereby the universe exists, whereby the earth system remains coherent within itself and capable of continuing the evolutionary process. To remain viable a species must establish a niche for itself that is beneficial both for itself and for the surrounding community. The difficulty generally with this proposal is that our genetic endowment is considered to be a mere physical determination of our being, not also our richest psychic endowment, our guiding and inspiring force, especially when the cultural process has entered into a destructive pathology.

This pathology is manifest in the arrogance with which we reject our role as an integral member of the earth community in favor of a radical anthropocentric life attitude. The critical moment of rejection of our role as an integral member of the earth community was reached in the work of Thomas Huxley in his famous Romanes lecture, "Evolution and Ethics," given in 1893. Human social progress he considered as "a checking of the cosmic process at every step and the substitution for it of another, which may be called the ethical process. . . . "

Sigmund Freud wrote even more strongly to this effect in his essay "Civilization and Its Discontents": "Against the dreaded external world one can only defend oneself by some kind of turning away from it, if one intends to solve the task by oneself. There is, indeed, another and better path: that of becoming a member of the human community, and, with the help of a technique guided by science, going over to the attack against nature and subjecting her to the human will.''

Both Huxley and Freud saw the human as essentially alien to the larger community of creatures. The basic need was to subject the natural world to the human lest the human become subjected to and possibly destroyed by the natural world. In this context it is easy to understand the attitude that other earthly beings are instruments to be used or resources to be exploited for human benefit. We are too good for the natural world. In ourselves the natural world goes beyond itself into a new and more sublime form of grandeur. Neither Huxley nor Freud had any idea of the disastrous consequences of such an attitude on the integral functioning of the earth or on our human destiny.

These consequences are now becoming manifest. The day of reckoning has come. In this disintegrating phase of our industrial society, we now see ourselves not as the splendor of creation, but as the most pernicious mode of earthly being. We are the termination, not the fulfillment of the earth process. If there were a parliament of creatures, its first decision might well be to vote the humans out of the community, too deadly a presence to tolerate any further. We are the affliction of the world, its demonic presence. We are the violation of earth's most sacred aspects.

The anthropocentrism from which this violation proceeds is ultimately not an invention of the nineteenth century. Nor is it due simply to the secular scholars of this period. It is enshrined both in our humanistic learning and in our religious and spiritual teachings. As indicated earlier, the present situation is so extreme that we need to get beyond our existing cultural formation, back to the primary tendencies of our nature itself, as expressed in the spontaneities of our being.

Yet it is not easy for us to move beyond those basic humanistic ideals that have directed our cultural traditions over the past millennia. These anthropocentric traditions have determined our language, our intellectual insights, our educational programs, our spiritual ideals, our imaginative power, our emotional sensitivities. All these can now be seen not only as inadequate, but also as distorted and as the origin of the deteriorating influence that we have on the life systems of the earth.

Our traditional languages express most clearly the anthropocentrism from which our difficulties have emerged. Our imagination is filled with images that sustain the present direction of our culture. Our spiritual values are disorientating with their insistence on the flawed nature of the existing order of things and the need for relief by escape from the earth rather than on a greater intimacy with the earth. Constantly we assert the value of the human over the merely resource values of the natural world. Our legal system fosters a sense of the human as having rights over the rights of natural beings. Our commerce, industry, and economics are based on the devastation of the earth. Disengagement from such basic life commitments requires a certain daring.

In order to get a sense of just how difficult it is to change basic commitments, we might recall the story of the *Titanic* on her maiden voyage. Abundant evidence indicated that icebergs were ahead. Nevertheless, the course was set, and no one wished to alter the direction. Confidence in the survival capacities of the ship was unbounded, and there were already a multitude of other concerns related to carrying out the simply normal routine of the voyage. I relate the story of the *Titanic* here as a kind of parable, since even in dire situations we often do not have the energy required to alter our way of acting on the scale that is required. For us there is still time to change course, to move away from our plundering economy to a more sustainable ecological economy.

We cannot obliterate the continuities of history. Nor can we move into the future without guidance from the more valid elements of our existing cultural forms, yet we must reach far back into the genetic foundations of our cultural formation for a healing and a restructuring at the most basic level. This is particularly true now, since the anthropogenic shock that is overwhelming the earth is of an order of magnitude beyond anything previously known in human historical or cultural development. As we have indicated, only those geological and biological changes of the past that have taken hundreds of millions of years for their accomplishment can be referred to as having any comparable order of magnitude.

The new cultural coding that we need must emerge from the source of all such codings, from revelatory vision that comes to us in those special psychic moments, or conditions, that we describe as "dream." We are, of course, using this term not only as regards the psychic processes that take place when we are physically asleep, but also as a way of indicating an intuitive, nonrational process that occurs when we awaken to the numinous powers ever present in the phenomenal world about us, powers that possess us in our high creative moments. Poets and artists continually invoke these spirit powers, which function less through words than through symbolic forms.

In moments of confusion such as the present, we are not left simply to our own rational contrivances. We are supported by the ultimate powers of the universe as they make themselves present to us through the spontaneities within our own beings. We need only become sensitized to these spontaneities, not with a naive simplicity, but with critical appreciation. This intimacy with our genetic endowment, and through this endowment with the larger cosmic process, is not primarily the role of the philosopher, priest, prophet, or professor. It is the role of the shamanic personality, a type that is emerging once again in our society.

More than any other of the human types concerned with the sacred, the shamanic personality journeys into the far regions of the cosmic mystery and brings back the vision and the power needed by the human community at the most elementary level. The shamanic personality speaks and best understands the language of the various creatures of the earth. Not only is the shamanic type emerging in our society, but also the shamanic dimension of the psyche itself. In periods of significant cultural creativity, this aspect of the psyche takes on a pervasive role throughout the society and shows up in all the basic institutions and professions. The great scientists do their best work through this dimension of the psyche.

This shamanic insight is especially important just now when history is being made not primarily within nations or between nations, but between humans and the earth, with all its living creatures. In this context all our professions and institutions must be judged primarily by the extent to which they foster this mutually enhancing human-earth relationship.

If the supreme disaster in the comprehensive story of the earth is our present closing down of the major life systems of the planet, then the supreme need of our times is to bring about a healing of the earth through this mutually enhancing human presence to the earth community. To achieve this mode of pressure, a new type of sensitivity is needed, a sensitivity that is something more than romantic attachment to some of the more brilliant manifestations of the natural world, a sensitivity that comprehends the larger patterns of nature, its severe demands as well as its delightful aspects, and is willing to see the human diminish so that other lifeforms might flourish.

These sensitivities are beginning to emerge throughout the human community in the multitude of activities that can generally be indicated under the general title of ecological movements. Ecology can rightly be considered the supreme subversive science. In responding to the external situation and to the imperatives of our own nature, these ecological movements are threatening all those cultural commitments that have brought about the present devastation of the earth. This rising conflict is beginning to dominate every aspect of the human process.

The ecology movement is answering the countergenetic process that was inaugurated through the industrial revolution. Even deeper than the industrial process, this ecological expression of the genetic imperative is demanding a reorientation of the entire religious-cultural order. Only recently, however, have the religious, cultural, and educational programs taken the ecological movement seriously. The first and most powerful impact of the ecology movement is felt in a rising resentment toward the economic and industrial processes that are the immediate causes of the difficulty.

Three basic aspects of the ecology movement can be observed: the confrontational, transformational, and creative aspects. Such movements as Greenpeace and Earth First! have a powerful confrontational aspect. The arrogance of the industrial order requires an opposed force of somewhat equal order of commitment. The industrial order is locked into our present cultural coding as well as into our economic institutions. Any radical adjustment appears as a threat to the very existence of the society.

The power of the industrial system is in the pervasive feeling throughout the society that there is no truly human survival or fulfillment except in opposition to the genetic codings of the natural world. Nothing must be left in its natural state. Everything must be sacralized by human use, even though this is momentary and the consequence is an irreversible degradation of the planet.

To the ecologist, survival is possible only within the earth system itself, in the integrity of the earth's functioning within the genetic codings of the biosphere, the physical codings of earth process, and within those comprehensive vast codings that enable the universe to continue as an emergent creative reality. The ultimate coding is expressed in the curvature of the emergent universe. This curve is sufficiently closed to hold all things within an ordered pattern, while it is sufficiently open to enable the creative process itself to continue.

These are the two radical positions—the industrial and the ecological—that confront each other, with survival at stake: survival of the human at an acceptable level of fulfillment on a planet capable of providing the psychic as well as the physical nourishment that is needed. No prior struggle in the course of human affairs ever

213

involved issues at this order of magnitude. If some degree of reconciliation has taken place, it remains minimal in relation to the
changes that are needed to restore a viable mode of human presence
to the earth.

Yet beginnings are being made. A multitude of institutional
changes are being effected. The World Bank is reassessing its activities of the past years: older, destructive programs are being abandoned; new, ecologically viable programs are being introduced.
Healing of damaged ecosystems is in process. The Nature Conser-
vancy is managing a large number of natural sites as habitat for a
variety of species. The Natural Resources Defense Council is forc-
ing governmental powers to carry out programs to prevent further damage to the earth. A multitude of other organizations are
actively engaged in preservation projects.

Foundations are funding projects with a new sense of the urgency,
both cultural and economic, of maintaining the integral functioning of the earth. One of the most helpful projects funded in recent
years is the World Resources Institute, which is providing an amazing amount of information on what is happening to the planet. The
Worldwatch Institute also is providing a much-needed assessment
of our present situation. These are relatively new institutes that must
be added to the much older organizations that remain the dominant forces in leading the human community toward a more benign
presence upon the earth.

It would take too long to enumerate even the most significant
of these movements on a local, national, and international scale.
Merely to enumerate the various aspects of our present society that
are now actively involved in this renewal of the earth would be
difficult. We would have to include the political, legal, economic,
and educational activities, the religious and cultural activities, as
well as the communications media.

In addition to the confrontational and transformational movements that are presently functioning, we find those even more
significant movements that are creating the vision and the func-

214

tional processes about which the new cultural, economic, social, and legal structures can be developed. Of special mention here might be the bioregional movements. They represent the context for human presence within the natural life communities into which the earth is divided. In the summer of 1987, a North American Green Movement in politics took further shape on a national scale. In the same summer a beginning was made in developing a concern for the future of the earth within the Christian religious traditions.

What I am proposing here is that these prior archetypal forms that guided the course of human affairs are no longer sufficient. Our genetic coding, through the ecological movement and through the bioregional vision, is providing us with a new archetypal world. The universe is revealing itself to us in a special manner just now. Also the planet Earth and the life communities of the earth are speaking to us through the deepest elements of our nature, through our genetic coding.

In relation to the earth, we have been autistic for centuries. Only now have we begun to listen with some attention and with a willingness to respond to the earth's demands that we cease our industrial assault, that we abandon our inner rage against the conditions of our earthly existence, that we renew our human participation in the grand liturgy of the universe.

·16·

The Cosmology
of Peace

The universe, earth, life, and consciousness are all violent processes. The basic terms in cosmology, geology, biology, and anthropology all carry a heavy charge of tension and violence. Neither the universe as a whole nor any part of the universe is especially peaceful. As Heraclitus noted, Conflict is the father of all things.

The elements are born in supernovas. The sun is lit by gravitational pressures. The air we breathe and the water we drink come from the volcanic eruptions of gases from within the earth. The mountains are formed by the clash of the great continental and oceanic segments of the earth's crust.

Life emerges and advances by the struggle of species for more complete life expression. Humans have made their way amid the harshness of the natural world and have imposed their violence

216

on the natural world. Among themselves humans have experienced unending conflict. An enormous psychic effort has been required to articulate the human mode of being in its full imaginative, emotional, and intellectual qualities, a psychic effort that emerges from and gives expression to that dramatic confrontation of forces that shape the universe. This confrontation may give rise to "the tears of things," as described by Virgil, but its creative function would be difficult to ignore.

Thus while we reflect on the turmoil of the universe in its emergent process, we must also understand the splendor that finds expression amid this sequence of catastrophic events, a splendor that set the context for the emerging human age. This period of the human in its modern form that began perhaps sixty thousand years ago, after some two million years of transitional human types, roughly coincides with the last glacial advance and recession. The recession period is especially important since it was also the Neolithic period of permanent villages, horticulture, and weaving. Humans began establishing patterns of life controlled by intelligence and human decision, which impinged with progressive destructiveness on the patterns of the natural world.

A new violence was released over the planet. But if in prior ages the violence of the natural world was essentially creative in the larger arc of its unfolding, the violence associated with human presence on the planet remains ambivalent in its ultimate consequences. From Heraclitus to Augustine, to Nicholas of Cusa, Hegel, and Marx, to Jung, Teilhard, and Prigogine, creativity has been associated with a disequilibrium, a tension of forces, whether this be in a physical, biological, or consciousness context.

If these tensions often result in destructive moments in the planetary process, these moments have ultimately been transformed in some creative context. As human power over the total process has increased, however, and the spontaneities of nature have been suppressed or extinguished, the proper functioning of the planet has become increasingly dependent on human wisdom and human

217

decision. This dependence began with human intrusion into the natural functioning of the land, that is, with agriculture and the control of water through irrigation. Since then a conquest mentality has been generated coextensive with the civilizational process. The conquest of the earth and its functioning was extended to the conquest of peoples and their lands. The sectioning of the earth and its human inhabitants is a dominant theme in the story of the planet over these many years, until now more than 160 nation-states have established their identity.

These nations exist in an abiding sequence of conflicts that have grown especially virulent in more recent years as our scientific and technological skills have given us increasing control over the enormous powers contained in the physical structures of the earth. The destructive power now available is such that a change of perspective in every phase of earthly existence is required to understand what is happening on the planet and what is happening to the planet. For the first time the planet has become capable of self-destruction in many of its major life systems through human agency, or at least it has become capable of causing a violent and irreversible alteration of its chemical and biological constitution such as has not taken place since the original shaping of the earth occurred.

In our present context, failure in creativity would be an absolute failure. A present failure at this order of magnitude cannot be remedied later by a larger success. In this context a completely new type of creativity is needed. This creativity must have as its primary concern the survival of the earth in its functional integrity. Concern for the well-being of the planet is the one concern that, it is hoped, will bring the nations of the world into an international community. Since the earth functions as an absolute unity, any dysfunctioning of the planet imperils every nation on the planet.

After this concern for the integrity of the earth, the next concern is to see the human itself as an integral member of the earth community, not as some lordly being free to plunder the earth for human utility. The issue of interhuman tensions is secondary to earth-human tensions. If humans will not become functional members of the earth community, how can humans establish functional relationships among themselves? It is not exactly the question of whether the nations can survive each other, nor is it even the question of whether intelligent beings can survive the natural forces of the planet; it is whether the planet can survive the intelligence that it has itself brought forth.

My proposal is that the cosmology of peace is presently the basic issue. The human must be seen in its cosmological role just as the cosmos needs to be seen in its human manifestation. This cosmological context has never been more clear than it is now, when everything depends on a *creative resolution of our present antagonisms.* I refer to a *creative resolution of antagonism* rather than to *peace* in deference to the violent aspects of the cosmological process. Phenomenal existence itself seems to be a violent mode of being. Also, there is a general feeling of fullness bordering on decay that is easily associated with *peace.* Neither *violence* nor *peace* in this sense is in accord with the creative transformations through which the more splendid achievements of the universe have taken place. As the distinguished anthropologist A. L. Kroeber once indicated: The ideal situation for any individual or any culture is not exactly "bovine placidity." It is, rather, "the highest state of tension that the organism can bear creatively."

In this perspective the present question becomes not the question of conflict or peace, but how we can deal creatively with these enormous tensions that presently afflict our planet. As Teilhard suggests, we must go beyond the human into the universe itself and its mode of functioning. Until the human is understood as a dimension of the earth, we have no secure basis for understanding any aspect of the human. We can understand the human only through the earth. Beyond the earth, of course, is the universe and the curvature of space. This curve is reflected in the curvature of the earth and finally in that psychic curve whereby the entire universe reflects back on itself in human intelligence.

This binding curve that draws all things together simultaneously produces with the inner forces of matter that expansive tension whereby the universe and the earth continue on their creative course. Thus the curve is sufficiently closed to hold all things together while it is sufficiently open to continue its creative emergence into the future. This tenuous balance between collapse and explosion contains the larger mystery of that functional cosmology which provides our most profound understanding of our human situation, even if it does not bring it within reach of our rational processes.

In this context our discussion of peace might well be understood primarily in terms of the Peace of Earth. This is not simply *Pax Romana* or *Pax Humana,* but *Pax Gaia,* the Peace of Earth, from the ancient mythic name for the planet.

We can understand this Peace of Earth, however, only if we understand that the earth is a single community composed of all its geological, biological, and human components. The Peace of Earth is indivisible. In this context the nations have a referent outside themselves for resolving their difficulties. The earth fulfills this role of mediator in several ways. First, the earth is a single organic reality that must survive in its integrity if it is to support any nation on the earth. To save the earth is a necessity for every nation. No part of the earth in its essential functioning can be the exclusive possession or concern of any nation. The air cannot be nationalized or privatized; it must circulate everywhere on the planet to fulfill its life-giving function anywhere on the planet. It must be available for the nonhuman as well as for the human lifeforms if it is to sustain human life. So it is with the waters on the earth. They must circulate throughout the planet if they are to benefit any of the lifeforms on the planet.

Second, we must understand that the Peace of Earth is not some fixed condition, but a creative process activated by polarity tensions requiring a high level of endurance. This creative process is not a clearly seen or predetermined pattern of action; it is rather a groping toward an ever more complete expression of the numinous mystery that is being revealed in this process. Groping implies a disquiet, an incompleteness; it also has the excitement of discovery, ecstatic transformation, and the advance toward new levels of integration.

This Peace of Earth is never quite the same from one period to another. In its prehuman period it is different from its expression in its human period. In its tribal period, too, this Peace of Earth is expressed in the ritual and poetry and patterns of living that are integral with the natural phenomena. The Peace of Earth in the classical civilizational period is articulated in a more elaborate human-earth and interhuman relationship. In the period of the great industrial empires, the Peace of Earth was massively disturbed in the plundering of the earth and the more deadly weaponry of war. At that time an effort was made to build a new world, functioning not by the ever-renewing spontaneities of nature, but by the use of nonrenewable resources. An effort was made to substitute a peace of human contrivance for the peace of an integral human presence to the earth community in its organic functioning. Now, in the early phases of the post-industrial period, the outlines of an integral ecological community appear.

A third aspect of the Peace of Earth is its progressive dependence on human decision. Presently this human decision is being made dominantly by the industrialized nations in both economics and politics. The severe tensions existing among the great powers are of a planetary order of magnitude because the resolution of these tensions is leading to a supreme achievement: the global unity toward which all earthly developments were implicitly directed from the beginning. This unity would be a final expression of the curvature of space: the return of the earth to itself in conscious reflection on itself.

A fourth aspect of this Peace of Earth is its hopefulness. Evidence for this hopefulness is found in the sequence of crisis moments through which the universe and, especially, the planet Earth have passed from the beginning until now. At each state of its development, when it seems that an impasse has been reached, most improbable solutions have emerged that enabled the Earth to continue its development. At the very beginning of the universe, the rate of expansion had to be at an infinitesimally precise rate so that the universe would neither explode nor collapse. So it was at the moment of passage out of the radiation stage: only a fragment of matter escaped antimatter annihilation, but out of that fragment has come the galactic systems and the universe entire. So at the shaping of the solar system: if the Earth were a little closer to the sun, it would be too hot; if slightly more distant, it would be too cold. If closer to the moon, the tides would overwhelm the continents; if more distant, the seas would be stagnant and life development could not have taken place. So with the radius of the Earth: if it were a little greater, the Earth would be more gaseous, like Jupiter; if a little less, the Earth would be more solid, like Mars. In neither case could life have evolved in its present form.

After the appearance of cellular life, when the original nutrients were consumed, the impasse was averted by invention of photosynthesis, upon which all future life development has depended. So it has been with the great story of life in its groping toward unlimited variety of expression; the mysteries of life multiply, but the overall success of the planet became increasingly evident, until the Neolithic phase of the human.

This story of the past provides our most secure basis of hope that the earth will so guide us through the peril of the present that we may provide a fitting context for the next phase of the emergent mystery of earthly existence. That the guidance is available we cannot doubt. The difficulty is in the order of magnitude of change that is required of us. We have become so acclimated to an industrial world that we can hardly imagine any other context of survival, even when we recognize that the industrial bubble is dissolving and will soon leave us in the chill of a plundered landscape.

None of our former revelatory experiences, none of our renewal or rebirth rituals, none of our apocalyptic descriptions are quite adequate for this moment. Their mythic power remains in a context far removed from the power that is abroad in our world. But even as we glance over the grimy world before us, the sun shines radiantly over the earth, the aspen leaves shimmer in the evening breeze, the coo of the mourning dove and the swelling chorus of the insects fill the land, while down in the hollows the mist deepens the fragrance of the honeysuckle. Soon the late summer moon will give a light sheen to the landscape. Something of a dream experience. Perhaps on occasion we participate in the original dream of the earth. Perhaps there are times when this primordial design becomes visible, as in a palimpsest, when we remove the later imposition. The dream of the earth. Where else can we go for the guidance needed for the task that is before us.

The Dream of the Earth

Bibliography
and Selected Readings

Abbey, Edward. *Desert Solitaire*. New York: McGraw-Hill, 1968.

_____. *The Journey Home*. New York: Dutton, 1977.

_____. *Down the River*. New York: Dutton, 1982. Edward Abbey has written extensively of his personal experiences in western mountain and desert regions. The Earth First! movement was influenced in its origins by the challenging position he takes in some of his writings.

Adams, Henry. *Mont-Saint-Michel and Chartres*. Boston: Houghton Mifflin, 1905. This first professional American medieval scholar immediately perceived the dominant role of the madonna figure in the shaping of medieval civilization.

Augros, Robert M., and George N. Stanciu. *The New Story of Science*. Chicago: Regnery Gateway, 1984. A useful introduction to recent scientific awareness of the psychic dimension of the universe.

Beckett, Samuel. *Endgame. A Play in One Act*. New York: Grove, 1958. A stark presentation of existentialist perception of an absurd universe.

Bennis, Warren, and Burt Nanus. *Leaders: The Strategies for Taking Charge*. New York: Harper & Row, 1985. Guidance for taking organizational control of commercial-industrial establishments.

Berg, Peter, ed. *Reinhabiting a Separate Country: A Bioregional Anthology of Northern California*. San Francisco: Planet Drum Foundation, 1978. An introduction and first publication in a bioregional series.

Bibliography and Selected Readings

Berger, John J. *Restoring the Earth: How Americans Are Working to Renew Our Damaged Environment.* New York: Anchor/Doubleday, 1987. Impressive accounts of what individuals with insight and initiative have done to reconstitute natural environments.

Berry, Wendell. *The Unsettling of America: Culture and Agriculture.* New York: Avon/Sierra Club Books, 1978. A classic. Superb presentation of the interdependence of humans and the land.

Bertell, Rosalie. *No Immediate Danger? Prognosis for a Radioactive Earth.* Toronto: Women's Educational Press, 1985. Extensive data, well researched and documented, on the larger consequences involved in our use of radioactive materials.

Bookchin, Murray. *The Ecology of Freedom: The Emergence and Dissolution of Hierarchy.* Palo Alto, Calif.: Cheshire Books, 1982. A fundamental statement on social ecology by the most distinguished American writer on this subject, from the standpoint of a radical socialist scholar and activist.

Brown, Joseph Epes, ed. *The Sacred Pipe: Black Elk's Account of the Seven Rites of the Oglala Sioux.* Baltimore: Penguin, 1971. An important source for information on the spiritual orientation of the Plains Indians.

Brown, Lester R., et al. *State of the World, 1988: A Worldwatch Institute Report on Progress Toward a Sustainable Society.* New York: Norton, 1988. Annual publication since 1984. One of the best sources for reliable information on the present condition of the basic life systems of the earth.

Calder, Nigel. *Timescale: An Atlas of the Fourth Dimension.* London: Hogarth Press, 1984. Extremely useful as a reference in identifying the time sequence of the evolution of the universe.

Capra, Fritjof, and Charlene Spretnak. *Green Politics.* New York: Dutton, 1984. The first complete study and evaluation of the Green movement in its political expression.

Carson, Rachel. *Silent Spring.* Cambridge, Mass.: Riverside Press, 1962. The first startling presentation of the chemical poisoning of the land and its consequences. A book with enduring historical significance.

Coates, Gary. *Resettling America: Energy, Ecology, and Community.* Andover, Mass.: Brick House Pub., 1981. An account of group efforts to establish sustainable human relations with the earth.

Commoner, Barry. *The Closing Circle: Nature, Man, and Technology.* New York: Alfred A. Knopf, 1971. Our best-known urban ecologist. A standard work.

Conable, Barber B. Address to World Resources Institute, May 1987. Unpublished paper. Important announcement of the World Bank's new ecological orientation in its allocation of funds by the president of the bank, one of the most significant world financial institutions.

Cooper, James Fenimore. *The Pioneers: Or, The Sources of the Susquehanna.* New York: New American Library, 1964. Original edition, 1823. One of the earliest discussions of the devastation the settlers were already inflicting on this continent.

Crèvecoeur, J. Hector Saint John. *Letters from an American Farmer.* New York: Dutton, 1957. Original edition, 1782. An eighteenth-century statement of the ideals and practices for creating the new American personality. He often notes the mistreatment of the land by the settlers.

Daly, Herman E., ed. *Toward a Steady-State Economy.* San Francisco: Freeman, 1973. An economist with a program for integrating our economic activities with the ever-renewing resources of the earth. An antigrowth statement.

Dawson, Christopher. *The Dynamics of World History.* New York: Sheed and Ward, 1956. A historian of cultures who combines comprehensive erudition with exceptional powers of interpretation. His central thesis is that religion is the most powerful determinant in cultural formation.

Deloria, Vine, Jr. *God Is Red.* New York: Dell, 1983. A knowledgeable native American writer, with both theological and legal training. Here he contrasts the spiritual vision of Indians with that of Christians.

Devall, Bill, and George Sessions. *Deep Ecology: Living as If Nature Mattered.* Salt Lake City: Peregrine Smith Books, 1985. A study that contrasts the biocentric orientation of the ecologists with the anthropocentric orientation of environmentalists, stating that we can deal with our problems effectively only through a biocentric norm in our sense of reality and value.

Dillard, Annie. *Pilgrim at Tinker Creek.* New York: Harper & Row, 1974.

_____. *Teaching a Stone to Talk: Expeditions and Encounters.* New York: Harper & Row, 1983. A naturalist writer, poet, and essayist with extraordinary depth of interpretation.

Dobzhansky, Theodosius. *Mankind Evolving: The Evolution of the Human Species.* New Haven: Yale University Press, 1962.

_____. *The Biology of Ultimate Concern.* New York: Meridian, 1969. A distinguished geneticist with a comprehensive appreciation of the evolutionary process and the role of the human.

Drucker, Peter F. *Innovation and Entrepreneurship: Practice and Principles.* New York: Harper & Row, 1985. The dean of American writers on management, extremely influential in developing graduate courses leading to the master's degree in business administration. Presently, in his view, we are moving from a managerial to a dominant entrepreneurial economy.

Dubos, René. *Mirage of Health: Utopias, Progress, and Biological Change.* New York: Doubleday, 1959.

_____. *The Dreams of Reason: Science and Utopias.* New York: Columbia University Press, 1961.

_____. *Celebrations of Life.* New York: McGraw-Hill, 1981. A research scientist who worked in microbiology at Rockefeller University, with extensive concern for the larger human issues involved in our technological society. A superb writer.

Dyson, Freeman. *Disturbing the Universe.* New York: Harper & Row, 1979. A physicist and cosmologist concerned with the meaning of science and with the larger questions of human destiny. One of the many contemporary scientists with great skill in interpreting their work in an accomplished writing style.

Ehrenfeld, David. *The Arrogance of Humanism.* New York: Oxford University Press, 1981. An incisive critique of the entire range of Western humanist tradition. A basic reference in any depth evaluation of Western civilization.

Ehrlich, Paul R., and Anne H. Ehrlich. *Extinction: The Causes and Consequences of the Disappearance of Species.* New York: Random House, 1981. A well-researched, well-documented study of the endangerment of the human through the extinction of other species.

Ehrlich, Paul R., Anne H. Ehrlich, and John P. Holdren. *Ecoscience: Population, Resources, Environment.* San Francisco: Freeman, 1977. One of the first comprehensive surveys of the entire range of issues related to human survival. A reference work of enduring value.

Eiseley. Loren. *The Firmament of Time.* New York: Atheneum, 1960.

_____. *The Immense Journey*. New York: Random House, 1960.

_____. *The Unexpected Universe*. New York: Harcourt Brace Jovanovich, 1972.

_____. *The Star Thrower*. New York: Times Books, 1978. An anthropologist and naturalist, one of our most impressive thinkers on the human situation within the rhythms and the mystique of the earth. Also one of the finest writers in the American literary tradition.

Elliott, David K. *Dynamics of Extinction*. New York: John Wiley & Sons, 1986. A strictly scientific study of how species develop and how they become extinct in both earlier and recent times.

Ellul, Jacques. *The Technological Society*. New York: Vintage/Random House, 1964. Original French edition, 1954. One of the earliest and still one of the most profound critiques of the effects of technology on the quality of human life.

Emerson, Ralph Waldo. *Nature: A Facsimile of the First Edition with an Introduction by Jaroslav Pelikan*. Boston: Beacon Press, 1985. Original edition, 1836. The first book published by Emerson. A basic statement of the spiritual rapport between the human and the natural, with special reference to the American scene.

Erdoes, Richard, and Alfonso Ortiz. *American Indian Myths and Legends*. New York: Pantheon, 1984. A valuable collection for appreciating the interplay of humans with all the other members of the earth community.

Ferguson, Marilyn. *The Aquarian Conspiracy: Personal and Social Transformation in the 1980s*. Los Angeles: Tarcher, 1980. An extensive listing of new-age writers who are moving away from merely rational to more intuitive modes of perception, in all areas of human thought and activity.

Forrester, Jay W. *World Dynamics*. 2d edition. Cambridge: MIT Press, 1973. A leading proponent of systems theory and its application to social issues in America.

Fossey, Dian. *Gorillas in the Mist: A Remarkable Woman's Thirteen-Year Adventure in Remote African Rain Forests with the Greatest of the Great Apes*. Boston: Houghton Mifflin, 1983. A rare instance of a human becoming intimately present within a society of anthropoids.

Frieden, Bernard J. *The Environmental Protection Hustle.* Cambridge: Joint Center for Urban Studies/MIT Press, 1979. Accusation that environmentalists are an elitist group out to protect their own advantage against the benefit of others.

Fukuoka, Masanobu. *One-Straw Revolution: An Introduction to Natural Farming.* New York: Bantam, 1985. Account of extraordinary success in horticulture by following the inherent processes of nature.

Georgescu-Roegen, Nicholas. *The Entropy Law and the Economic Process.* Cambridge: Harvard University Press, 1971. The basic study of economics that includes consideration of our resource base in the economics of nature.

Gimbutas, Marija. *The Gods and Goddesses of Old Europe, 7000 to 3500 B.C.: Myths, Legends, and Cult Images.* London: Thames & Hudson, 1974; Berkeley: University of California Press, 1974. A well-documented study of Old Europe as a matricentric culture that existed from around 6500 B.C. until it was overwhelmed by the incoming Aryan peoples around 3500 B.C.

Gray, Elizabeth Dodson. *Green Paradise Lost.* Wellesley, Mass.: Roundtable Press, 1979. A well-presented feminist critique of Western civilization, especially in its modern phase.

Griffin, Susan. *Woman and Nature: The Roaring Inside Her.* New York: Harper & Row, 1978. A powerful statement of the feminine in its integral relations with the natural world.

Heilbroner, Robert. *An Inquiry into the Human Prospect.* Revised ed. New York: Norton, 1980.

_____. *The Making of Economic Society.* 7th ed. Englewood Cliffs, N.J.: Prentice-Hall, 1985. One of our more thoughtful writers on the economic-social order of our times.

Highwater, Jamake. *The Primal Mind: Vision and Reality in Indian America.* New York: Harper & Row, 1981. A gifted writer and critical thinker in the American Indian tradition.

Hughes, J. Donald. *Ecology in Ancient Civilizations.* Albuquerque: University of New Mexico Press, 1975. Survey of the consistent failure of the last five thousand years of civilizational endeavor to establish viable relationships with the natural world.

Huxley, Anthony. *Plant and Planet*. Revised ed. New York: Pelican Press, 1978. Exceptional insight into the inner "psychic" life of plants. A fascinating work.

Huxley, Thomas H. *Collected Essays*. Vol. 9. New York: Appleton, 1902. This collection contains his most famous essay, "Evolution and Ethics."

Hyams, Edward. *Soil and Civilization*. New York: Harper Torchbooks, 1976. Original edition, 1952. Well-written survey, including clear indications of the decline of civilizations with the impoverishment of their soils.

Illich, Ivan. *Medical Nemesis: The Expropriation of Health*. New York: Bantam, 1977.

———. *Deschooling Society*. New York: Harper & Row, 1983. In these and in his other writings Ivan Illich has shown himself to be one of the most severe critics of contemporary institutions and professions because they are consistently so counterproductive.

The International Permaculture Seed Yearbook, 1986. Dan Hemenway, ed. Orange, Mass.: Yankee Publications, 1985. Annual publication dedicated to promoting the use and availability of useful plants, particularly those suited to cultivation in areas that experience frozen ground.

International Union for Conservation of Nature and Natural Resources (IUCN) with the United Nations Environment Programme (UNEP) and the World Wildlife Fund (WWF). *World Conservation Strategy: Living Resource Conservation for Sustainable Development*. Gland, Switzerland: IUCN, 1980. A program worked out by more than seven hundred scientists from more than one hundred different countries, with special concern for the future of the developing world.

Jackson, Wes. *New Roots for Agriculture*. Lincoln: University of Nebraska Press, 1985. First edition, 1980. Founder-director of the Land Institute of Salina, Kansas, he does extensive research and teaching concerning the renewal of prairie grasses, permaculture, and effective human rapport with the land.

Jackson, Wes, Wendell Berry, and Bruce Colman. *Meeting the Expectations of the Land: Essays in Sustainable Agriculture and Stewardship*. San Francisco: North Point Press, 1984. A valuable collection of essays by Gary Snyder, John Todd, Donald Worster, Wendell Berry, and Wes Jackson, among others.

Jantsch, Erich. *The Self-Organizing Universe: Scientific and Human Implications of the Emerging Paradigm of Evolution.* New York: Pergamon, 1980. A superb presentation of the inner dynamism of the universe from its origin through the appearance and development of the human. Based on the work of Ilya Prigogine.

Kastner, Joseph. *A Species of Eternity.* New York: Dutton, 1978. An account of the early naturalists in America from Cadwallader Colden and Alexander Garden in the colonial period to John James Audubon and Thomas Nutthall in the mid-nineteenth century.

Kohr, Leopold. *The Overdeveloped Nations: The Diseconomies of Scale.* New York: Schocken Books, 1978. Original edition, 1962, in Spanish and German. The earliest reasoned challenge to the growth mystique. Kohr was a significant influence on the work of E. F. Schumacher.

Krutch, Joseph Wood. *The Voice of the Desert: A Naturalist's Interpretation.* New York: William Morrow, 1955.

_____. *The Great Chain of Life.* Boston: Houghton Mifflin, 1956. A literary critic turned naturalist, with special interest in the desert.

Lappé, Frances Moore, and Joseph Collins. *Food First: Beyond the Myth of Scarcity.* New York: Ballantine, 1979. A documented study indicating that the peoples of the developing world can grow their own food if they have possession of their land, keep their traditional skills in agriculture, and adopt the best of recently developed organic farming methods.

Leopold, Aldo. *A Sand County Almanac.* New York: Oxford University Press, 1949. A central personality in developing the ecological movement in America. The essay "A Land Ethic" in this book is still the most succinct statement of the ethical principles governing human-earth relationships.

Lerner, Gerda. *The Creation of Patriarchy.* New York: Oxford University Press, 1985. A thorough and convincing study of the historical phases in the development of patriarchy in the Western world. For women to know the historical context of their present situation is essential if they are to understand and fulfill their contemporary role in relation to themselves and in relation to the social structures of the present.

Lilly, John C. *Lilly on Dolphins.* Garden City, N.Y.: Anchor/Doubleday, 1975. Contains revised editions of *Man and Dolphin, The Mind of the Dolphin,* "The Dolphin in History," and scientific papers.

————. *Communication Between Man and Dolphin: The Possibility of Talking with Other Species.* New York: Crown, 1978. A fascinating account of experiments in human communication with nonhuman species.

Lopez, Barry Holstun. *Of Wolves and Men.* New York: Scribner's, 1978.

————. *Arctic Dreams.* New York: Scribner's, 1986. In these and in his other writings Barry Lopez is most impressive for his depth of insight and his sensitivity as well as for the brilliance of his description of natural phenomena and of the living beings that inhabit the earth.

Lovell, Bernard. *In the Center of Immensities.* New York: Harper & Row, 1978. A British cosmologist presents the origin and development of the universe with exceptional clarity.

Lovelock, J. E. *Gaia: A New Look at Life on Earth.* New York: Oxford University Press, 1979. The first thorough presentation of the biological evidence for considering the earth as an organism capable of reacting to outer stimuli and inner processes in a unified, self-adjusting manner.

Lovins, Amory B. *Soft-Energy Paths: Toward a Durable Peace.* New York: Harper Colophon Books, 1979. The basic book on the need and possibility of using more benign or soft-energy processes rather than the plundering and toxic processes now in use.

Lovins, Amory, and L. Hunter Lovins. *Brittle Power.* Andover, Mass.: Brick House Pub., 1982. A later study of the energy issue and its relation to the social process.

McHarg, Ian L. *Design with Nature.* Garden City, N.Y.: Natural History Press/Doubleday, 1971. One of the finest presentations of architectural design that gives proper consideration to the integration of our human structures with their natural surroundings.

Margulis, Lynn, and Karlene V. Schwartz. *Five Kingdoms: An Illustrated Guide to the Phyla of Life on Earth.* San Francisco: Freeman, 1982. A remarkably clear presentation of this subject.

Matthiessen, Peter. *The Snow Leopard.* New York: Viking Press, 1978. One of our most versatile writers in the natural history tradition.

Meadows, Donella H., Denis L. Meadows, Jorgen Randers, and William W. Behrens III. *The Limits to Growth: A Report for the Club Of Rome's Project on the Predicament of Mankind.* New York: Universe Books, 1972. The first comprehensive survey of the earth, its resources, and its rate of use by humans within the context of systems theory. Its somewhat pessimistic predictions based on exponential rates of increase in the use of natural resources came as a shock to most readers. It initiated extensive controversy.

Merchant, Carolyn. *The Death of Nature: Women, Ecology, and the Scientific Revolution.* New York: Harper & Row, 1980. A study based on extensive research, depth of insight, and poise of judgment. One of the finest works of scholarship concerned with women and nature.

Milbrath, Lester W. *Environmentalists: Vanguard for a New Society.* A sociological study of the environmental movement as a revolutionary change in cultural pattern. Valuable for both its data and its interpretation.

Miller, Lawrence. *American Spirit: Visions of a New Corporate Culture.* New York: Warner Books, 1984. One of many books in recent years seeking to bring the powers of mythic symbolism and even humanist and spiritual qualities into the service of the new entrepreneurial economy.

Mollison, Bill. *Permaculture Two: Practical Design for Town and Country in Permanent Agriculture.* Stanley, Tasmania, Australia: Tagari Books, 1979. A new agricultural process that avoids disturbing the land by annual plowing.

Mollison, Bill, and David Holmgren. *Permaculture One: A Perennial Agriculture for Human Settlements.* Winters, Calif.: Tagari Books/International Tree Crops Institute, 1981.

Momaday, N. Scott. *The Way to Rainy Mountain.* Albuquerque: University of New Mexico Press, 1976. An esteemed and even revered native American writer in the second half of the twentieth century. His essays, his novel, and his poetry all carry a special intimacy with the North American continent and with the traditional sensitivities of the Indian peoples.

Mowat, Farley. *Never Cry Wolf.* Boston: Atlantic Monthly Press/Little, Brown, 1963.

_____. *The Great Betrayal: Arctic Canada Now.* Boston: Little, Brown, 1976. A Canadian naturalist who writes mostly of the northern regions of the earth.

Muir, John. *The Yosemite.* New York: Century, 1912.

_____. *My First Summer in the Sierra.* Boston: Houghton Mifflin, 1917. Reprinted 1979.

_____. *The Mountains of California.* Berkeley: Ten Speed Press, 1977. Original edition, 1894. A unique person who gives us sublime accounts of the California mountains and valleys and their luxuriant vegetation before so much of them were spoiled by settlers. Founder of the Sierra Club.

Mumford, Lewis. *The City in History: Its Origins, Its Transformations, and Its Prospects.* New York: Harcourt, Brace, and World, 1961. The dean of American historians of cultures, with a strong sense of the need for human habitat to be in accord with its natural setting.

Myers, Norman. *The Primary Source: Tropical Forests and Their Destruction.* New York: Norton, 1984. A knowledgeable and experienced scholar on all that concerns the rain forests of the world and the consequences of their destruction.

Myers, Norman, and Gaia Ltd. staff. *Gaia: An Atlas of Planet Management.* Garden City, N.Y.: Anchor/Doubleday, 1984. An indispensable reference work on the condition of the planet in the late twentieth century. Exceptionally well illustrated. A book that everyone should have available.

Naisbitt, John. *Megatrends: Ten New Directions Transforming Our Lives.* New York: Warner Books, 1984. A journalistic survey of the economic situation in the closing decades of the century. Almost jubilant over the marvelous prospects of what might be accomplished if we take advantage of the new possibilities for economic progress in the capitalist tradition. Consequently a "best-seller."

Nash, Roderick. *Wilderness and the American Mind.* Revised ed. New Haven: Yale University Press, 1973. One of the basic books to be read as background for the entire range of ecological issues.

Neihardt, John G. *Black Elk Speaks: Being the Life Story of a Holy Man of the Oglala Sioux.* New York: Washington Square Press, 1972. Original edition, 1932. The story of one of the most remarkable spiritual personalities of the late-nineteenth and early-twentieth centuries.

· Bibliography and Selected Readings ·

Noble, David F. *America by Design: Science, Technology, and the Rise of Corporate Capitalism.* New York: Oxford University Press, 1977. A most important presentation of the development of the modern corporation from the period when scientific technologies first came into being in the last two decades of the nineteenth century with the electronic and chemical industries.

Ortiz, Alfonso, et al., eds. *Handbook of North American Indian Series.* Vol. 9, *Southwest.* Washington: Smithsonian Institution, 1979. Eighteen volumes projected. This handbook series, when completed, will become the basic reference work in the study of the Indian peoples of the North American continent.

Parkman, Francis. *The Oregon Trail.* New York: New American Library, 1950. Original edition, 1849. A valuable account of the journey made in 1846 by one of the earliest American historians through the territories of the Sioux Indians just before the Indian-white antagonism became so intensified that such a journey with Indian tribes became impossible.

Peters, Thomas J., and Robert Waterman. *In Search of Excellence; Lessons from America's Best-Run Companies.* New York: Harper & Row, 1982. The most popular account of the new entrepreneurial mystique with its emphasis on the humanistic, visionary, and creative sources of large-scale economic success.

Prigogine, Ilya, and Isabelle Stengers. *Order out of Chaos: Man's New Dialogue with Nature.* New York: Bantam, 1984. This Nobel Prize winner, a Russian chemist working in Belgium, explains his theory of the self-organizing processes of the natural world.

Prucha, Francis Paul, ed. *Americanizing the American Indians: Writings by the "Friends of the Indian," 1880–1900.* Cambridge: Harvard University Press, 1973. A collection of basic documents from the late nineteenth century of considerable importance in understanding the Euro-American efforts to draw the indigenous peoples of the North American continent into the civilizational lifestyle of European peoples and their religious and humanistic values.

Raven, Peter. "We Are Killing the Earth." Unpublished address to the Society for the Advancement of Science, Spring 1987. A succinct presentation of the specific data concerning the consequences of our present industrial plundering of the planet.

Register, Richard. *Ecocity Berkeley: Building Cities for a Healthy Future.* Berkeley: North Atlantic Books, 1987. A well-designed program for restoring the original ecosystems of the city through a sequence of transformation stages.

Rifkin, Jeremy, with Nicanor Perlas. *Algeny.* New York: Viking, 1983. The first, and so far the best-known, critical evaluation of the consequences that can be expected from the unregulated human intrusion into the realms of biological engineering.

Rodale, Robert. *Our Next Frontier: A Personal Guide for Tomorrow's Lifestyle.* Carol Stoner, ed. Emmaus, Pa.: Rodale Press, 1981. This author can be considered one of the most effective persons in our times in recalling our society to more integral lifestyles and telling us how they can be achieved, especially in all that concerns food production and its distribution.

Rodale, Robert, ed. *The Basic Book of Organic Gardening.* New York: Ballantine, 1981.

Roszak, Theodore. *The Making of a Counter-Culture.* New York: Anchor Books, 1969.

_____. *Person/Planet: The Creative Disintegration of Industrial Society.* Garden City, N.Y.: Doubleday, 1978. One of our most effective writers in his critique of the cultural impasse of the contemporary industrial society. He is also quite clear in giving directions for a more creative, more satisfying, and more sustainable order in human affairs.

Sale, Kirkpatrick. *Human Scale.* New York: Coward McCann & Geohegan, 1980. A book written in the tradition of Leopold Kohr and E. F. Schumacher and applying their principles in a more extensive way to contemporary society.

_____. *Dwellers in the Land: The Bioregional Vision.* San Francisco: Sierra Club Books, 1985. A knowledgeable and clear writer. He has given us the first book-length study of the bioregional perspective and its status as of the year of its publication.

Schumacher, E. F. *Small Is Beautiful.* New York: Perennial/Harper & Row, 1975. A brief book, amazing in its efficacy in showing the deleterious consequences of the growth obsession that has dominated our industrial economy. The critique is effective because an alternative is given: scale down the monstrous size of our economic establishments and our technologies!

Simon, Julian L. *The Ultimate Resource.* Princeton: Princeton University Press, 1982. An unbelievable defense of the industrial plundering of the planet, along with an attack on every aspect of the ecological movement.

Simon, Julian L., and Herman Kahn, eds. *The Resourceful Earth: A Response to Global 2000.* New York: Basil Blackwell, 1984. A negative critique by a group of economic and social scholars of a basic document that was not entirely correct in some of its predictions, but which was absolutely correct in identifying the disaster of exponential rates of increase in industrial use of earth's resources.

Skolimowski, Henryk. *Eco-Philosophy: Designing New Tactics for Living.* Boston: Marion Boyars, 1981. Brief presentation of a philosophical vision suited to the emerging ecological age.

Snyder, Gary. *Earth House Hold.* New York: New Directions, 1969.

———. *Turtle Island.* New York: New Directions, 1974.

———. *Good. Wild. Sacred.* Hereford, U.K.: Five Seasons Press, 1984. In this and in many other publications of his poetry and essays, Gary Snyder has provided insight and inspiration to the present generation in our return to the basic realities and values of our human mode of being within the functioning of the natural world.

Spretnak, Charlene. *Lost Goddesses of Early Greece: A Collection of Pre-Hellenic Myths.* Berkeley: Moon Books, 1978; Boston: Beacon Press, 1984. A small collection giving the myths of the feminine deities in the pre-Aryan period of early Greece. Told with the special grace and clarity found in the writings of this author.

———. *The Spiritual Dimension of Green Politics.* Santa Fe, N.M.: Bear & Co., 1986. An essential book for appreciating the deeper sense of reality and value involved in the ecology movement. A spirituality is essential to Green Politics if the movement is not to be trivialized.

Spretnak, Charlene, ed. *The Politics of Women's Spirituality: Essays on the Rise of Spiritual Power Within the Feminist Movement.* Garden City, N.Y.: Anchor/Doubleday, 1982. An excellent anthology, with essays from many of the best women writers on feminine issues.

Swimme, Brian. *The Universe Is a Green Dragon: A Cosmic Creation Story.* Santa Fe, N.M.: Bear & Co., 1984. A fascinating little book by a scientist with a gift of imagery and, at times, lyric phrasing in presenting the interplay between the universe and the human mind.

Taylor, Paul W. *Respect for Nature. A Theory of Environmental Ethics.* Princeton: Princeton University Press, 1986. A somewhat pedantic presentation of all those questions that arise in developing an environmental ethic that is rationally based. A superior presentation in a thoroughly reasoned form, yet a typical case of where our reasoning processes are unequal to the majesty and the fascination of their subject matter.

Teilhard de Chardin, Pierre. *The Phenomenon of Man.* New York: Harper, 1959. This presentation of the story of the universe, completed in its first version in 1940, was the earliest scientific account of the universe as a psychic-spiritual as well as a physical-material process, written by a professional geologist and paleontologist. As an interpretative work it goes beyond the norms of strictly scientific demonstration, especially in its later sections concerning the future. It still remains a valuable work, with many insights that have been validated through later scientific developments. An irreplaceable work.

Thibodeau, Francis R., and Hermann H. Field, eds. *Sustaining Tomorrow: A Strategy for World Conservation and Development.* Hanover, N.H.: Tufts/University Press of New England, 1984. An impressive collection of papers concerned with the most significant issues related to the survival of the earth in its life-giving functioning.

Thirgood, J. V. *Man and the Mediterranean Forest: A History of Resource Depletion.* New York: Academic Press, 1981. That the classical Mediterranean world, with all its humanism, was so incompetent in taking care of its forests reveals how much stress civilization has placed on the natural world.

Thompson, William Irwin. *Passages About Earth.* New York: Harper & Row, 1974. An original thinker and impressive writer about our human situation in this late twentieth century.

Thoreau, Henry David. *The Selected Journals of Henry David Thoreau.* Carl Bode, ed. New York: Signet/New American Library, 1967.

_____. *The Natural History Essays.* Layton, Utah: Gibbs M. Smith, 1980. Henry David Thoreau, along with John Muir, has become an archetypal figure in establishing an intimate rapport between the human community and the natural world on the North American continent. These two figures are without precise parallel in other countries.

Todd, John, and Nancy Jack Todd. *The Village as Solar Ecology*. East Falmouth, Mass.: The New Alchemy Institute, 1980.

_____. *Bioshelters, Ocean Arks, City Farming*. San Francisco: Sierra Club Books, 1984. John and Nancy Todd have for more than two decades fostered human technologies that function in intimate accord with the physical and biological technologies of the natural world.

Todd, John, and George Tukel. *Reinhabiting Cities and Towns: Designing for Sustainability*. San Francisco: Planet Drum Foundation, 1981.

Toffler, Alvin. *The Third Wave*. New York: Bantam, 1981. A survey of Western civilization periods, leading to an appreciation of the present as a period of pervasive turmoil, but for that very reason a vastly creative period in economics and human well-being as well as in the expansion of our knowledge of the universe and of our control over the forces of the earth. Exaggerated expectations.

Tucker, William. *Progress and Privilege: America in the Age of Environmentalism*. Garden City, N.Y.: Anchor/Doubleday, 1982. A negative critique of the environmental movement as the effort of a privileged group firmly established in the present and unwilling to accept further progress because it would disturb the existing situation.

Turner, Frederick. *Beyond Geography: The Western Spirit Against the Wilderness*. New York: Viking Press, 1980. A remarkable account of Western civilization and its pervasive antagonism toward the natural world. Written in a splendid prose style.

_____. *Rediscovering America: John Muir in His Time and Ours*. San Francisco: Sierra Club Books, 1985. New insight into the career of John Muir and the special qualities of his thinking.

Vico, Giambattista. *The New Science of Giambattista Vico*. Unabridged ed. Thomas G. Bergin and Max H. Fisch trans. from Italian. Ithaca, N.Y.: Cornell University Press, 1984. The first of the modern philosophers of history. An Italian who published his first version of this work in 1725, Vico had a vivid sense of the need for periodic renewal of cultures through a return to earlier phases of mythic consciousness.

Wallace, David Rains. *Life in the Balance.* New York: Harcourt Brace Jovanovich, 1987. One of the most fascinating of our nature writers. This book gives a superb description of the topography of the earth as a setting for the expansion of life: the skies, forests, grasslands, mountains, deserts and polar regions, rivers and wetlands—all these and other phases of earth's topography are presented. Delightful reading and wonderfully informative.

White, Gilbert. *The Natural History of Selborne.* New York: Penguin, 1977. Original edition, 1788–1789. Sometimes considered the first presentation of the ecological interdependence of lifeforms. Written as personal journals. A strong influence on Thoreau.

White, Lynn, Jr. "The Historical Roots of Our Ecological Crisis." *Science* 155(3767), 10 March 1967. A famous essay proposing that Christianity bears an "immense" amount of guilt for the Western mistreatment of the natural world. Many papers have been written in response to this essay.

Wilson, Edward O., *Biophilia.* Cambridge: Harvard University Press, 1984.

Wilson, Edward O., ed. *Biodiversity.* Proceedings of the National Forum held by the National Academy of Sciences and the Smithsonian Institution, 21–24 Sept. 1986. Washington: National Academy Press, 1988. One of the most competent contemporary biologists. Also an excellent writer in presenting the role of the human in the community of life.

Wittfogel, Karl A. *Oriental Despotism: A Comparative Study of Total Power.* New York: Random House, 1981. One of the most competent of Western scholars in dealing with the social formation and functioning of China. His main concern is to make clear the Western sense of personal freedom as contrasted with the "despotism" of the Asian world.

World Charter for Nature. United Nations General Assembly. New York: United Nations, A/RES/37/7, 9 Nov. 1982. One of the most impressive documents of the twentieth century. It deserves much more attention than it has received.

The World Commission on Environment and Development. *Our Common Future.* New York: Oxford University Press, 1987. Thousands of people from all over the world were involved in working out this statement, intended as a guide toward human survival at an acceptable level of human fulfillment. The commission was constituted by the United Nations Assembly to carry out this study and to submit this report, which was three years in the making.

Index